The Immortal
BEAVER

THE WORLD'S GREATEST BUSH PLANE

SEAN ROSSITER

D1073087

Douglas & McIntyre
VANCOUVER / TORONTO / BERKELEY

Douglas & McIntyre
2323 Quebec Street, Suite 201
Vancouver, British Columbia
Canada V5T 4S7
www.douglas-mcintyre.com

Editing by Robin Brass
Cover & text design by Peter Cocking
Front cover photo by Graham Osborne
Airplane diagrams by Rhonda Ganz & Peter Cocking
Printed and bound in Canada by Friesens
Printed on acid-free paper
Distributed in the U.S. by Publishers Group West

The publisher gratefully acknowledges the assistance of the
Canada Council for the Arts and of the British Columbia
Arts Council. The publisher also acknowledges the financial
support of the Government of Canada through the Book
Publishing Industry Development Program.

Canadian Cataloguing in Publication Data
Rossiter, Sean, 1946–
    The immortal Beaver
    ISBN 1-55054-724-0
    1. Beaver (Transport planes). I. Title.
TL686.D4R67 1996   387'.73343   C96-910459-6

Contents

Acknowledgements

Τhis project originated with the photographer Alex Waterhouse-Hayward, who caught me in a moment of weakness—leaving a downtown Vancouver bar, where he had been drinking soda water and I beer—and asked me to write a magazine article about the de Havilland Beaver. He wanted to photograph the aircraft and needed someone to write an article for him to illustrate. I said sure. This is one of the few promises made in bars that I have kept.

The article, headlined "The Beaver Then and Now," appeared in the *Georgia Straight*. It explained the Beaver's importance as today's sole means of transport to many outposts along the British Columbia coast and was a finalist for a 1995 Western Magazine Award. *Straight* editor Charles Campbell deserves credit for buying an arcane idea, and the final result reflected careful editing and fact-checking by Martin Dunphy and Naomi Pauls. Scott McIntyre read that article and suggested this book.

In a coincidence that is unprecedented in my twenty-three years of freelance writing, *Western Living* magazine's Sue Fisher asked me to write a Canadian Classics column on the Beaver at the same time. Editor-in-chief Paula Brook gracefully confirmed the assignment anyway, and that piece focused on the engineering decisions that resulted in the Beaver's distinctive silhouette.

Aside from Dick Hiscocks, who has been available to me over more than two years for several formal interviews and numberless editorial chores, a number of survivors from the impressive de Havilland Canada team that conceived, designed and built the Beaver were generous with their time, memories and materials. First among these is Russ Bannock, the Beaver's first test pilot and later president of the company during the difficult period of its ownership by the federal government. George Neal followed Bannock into the left-hand seat of CF-FHB, the prototype Beaver, certified it for float operation, and gave me an account of his occasionally-dangerous test flights. Neal is, like Bannock, a member of Canada's Aviation Hall of Fame.

CF-FHB was registered in honour of Fred H. Buller, its chief design engineer and the man who more than any other was responsible for DHC's successful postwar line of Short Takeoff and Landing (STOL) aircraft. His widow, Betty, and son, Christopher, offered personal insights into the wide-ranging mind and creative engineering approach of their husband and father. Chris, a heart surgeon, met Ernest Krahulec after performing a quadruple-bypass on his father's wartime colleague, who filled me in on Fred's pre-DHC contribution to the war effort and Krahulec's own years working on FHB.

Others from the DHC team who offered unique perspectives were Bill Burlison, whose experimental shop constructed FHB, and Charlie Smith, who worked all night in the stores department in case the technicians who were readying FHB for its first flight needed any parts. John Garratt, son of then-DHC president Phil Garratt, who conceived the Beaver, provided valuable recollections of his father and the Beaver project. I relied heavily upon Fred Hotson's accounts of the Beaver design process in *The de Havilland Canada Story*.

Steve Todd of Campbell River, British Columbia, a lifelong student of Beaver history, contributed many anecdotes from his extensive collection of Beaver lore. Among the West Coast pilots who told me their adventure stories covering fifty years of flying the Beaver were Tom Baxter, proprietor of Baxter Air of Nanaimo, B.C.; Lee Frankham of Campbell River; Larry Langford of Vancouver Island Air, Campbell River; Maurie Mercer of Finning Tractor, Vancouver; Bill Pennings, chief pilot of Harbour Air, Vancouver; Jack Schofield of Victoria, editor of *West Coast Aviator* and founder of Orca Air; and Gary Richards of Tofino Air Lines.

Special thanks to Paul Stenner, an Air Canada pilot who twice demonstrated his Beaver for me. Former flying-doctor pilot Joe Harvey of Perth, Australia, and the staff of the Royal New Zealand Air Force Museum at Wigram (especially Sgt. Cath Rowland) led me to accounts of the Beaver's career Down Under.

Colin Fisher and Anita Paalanen of the de Havilland Regional Aircraft Division of Bombardier have been supportive from this project's beginnings. And no writer about airplanes could have a better friend and mentor than Peter M. Bowers, who made his usual contribution to both the visual and written sides of this book.

Russ Bannock, Fred Hotson and Dick Hiscocks read the manuscript and eliminated countless mistakes. Robin Brass, who has edited many important works of Canadian aviation history, brought his unique insights and care to this project. Those errors of fact and judgement that remain despite the best efforts of these gentlemen are my responsibility alone.   —SEAN ROSSITER

Preface

Beavers return to Dick Hiscocks's watery backyard

Our young American pilot stepped out of the freshly restored, pristine white Lake Union Air de Havilland Beaver onto the dock behind the Bayshore Hotel on Vancouver's Coal Harbour waterfront. He could not have been more than twenty-five. It was all too obvious that he would have been very young in 1967, when the last Beaver was assembled. You like your pilot to be older than the aircraft if at all possible.

"Gotta treat this airplane with respect," he said, reaching up to steady himself by grabbing the wing bracing strut. "It's at least ten years older than I am."

Respect it? He worshipped it. He was still briefing me after the half-hour flight as he helped me and the three other passengers out onto the dock at the company terminal on Lake Union in downtown Seattle. What an honour it was to fly a de Havilland Beaver, the greatest bush plane ever, he said. Did I know that the Beaver was named the year before as one of the ten outstanding Canadian engineering achievements of the past century?

Well, no. I didn't.

He went on. Did I know we were just past the fortieth anniversary of the Beaver's first flight on August 16, 1947? And that it is powered by an engine, the Pratt & Whitney Wasp Junior, that could become the first aero engine still in scheduled use a hundred years after it was designed?

We took off that summer day in 1988 with a lot of noise but no fuss of any other kind. Floatplanes are known for taking forever to get off the water, which is not the airplane's natural element. Mounties who flew the Norseman, Canada's first purpose-built bush plane, used to say its takeoff on floats was obscured by the curvature of the earth.

The impression that remains from our takeoff in the Beaver is of being in some cartoon airplane that stuck its nose up, gathered itself by collapsing back on its tail and floats, straightened itself out and leaped into the air.

If the takeoff was not sufficiently spectacular, the landing certainly was. The Beaver practically stopped in the air as it crossed over the Aurora Bridge, one of the stratospheric iron-age engineering wonders that connect Seattle's seven hills high above intervening bodies of water. The airbrake effect of the flaps as our floats barely cleared the bridge's streetlights was palpable and caused a faint ripple of alarm among the four passengers. We exchanged brief glances. But the Beaver was fully under control. This kid and his old airplane could fly. We alighted on Lake Union like some mallard skidding, straight-legged and leaning back, along the surface of a pond. Only images from animation describe the Beaver's takeoff and landing performance.

So it was that, as so often happens with noteworthy Canadian achievements, it took an American to describe and showcase the Beaver to someone who ought to have known about it all along. Canada is such a strange place, so eager to dwell on its failures. There are, by my count, six books on the Avro CF-105 fighter-interceptor, of which six prototypes were made. One of these books is actually entitled *Shutting Down the National Dream.*

And yet this is the first lengthy account of the most successful Canadian airplane design ever, a design the merits of which Americans were among the first to recognize. The American armed forces bought more than one-half of the 1,631 Wasp Junior-powered Beavers built, and their requirements resulted in significant improvements in the basic airplane. It was the first foreign aircraft ever ordered in peacetime by both the U.S. Air Force *and* Army.

The de Havilland team had wondered whether to begin Beaver production three years before the Americans ordered it, when the market was still glutted with war-surplus planes. Instead, de Havilland Canada managing director Phil Garratt put aside the Beaver design studies to produce a military training aircraft, the DHC-1 Chipmunk.

Building the first twenty Beavers was considered a "million-dollar gamble," as the company advertised it. They were right about that. The Royal Canadian Air Force bought none. Eventually, though, Beavers were sold to sixty-five countries, making this tough, hard-working little airplane one of Canada's greatest export successes after lumber. Half-a-dozen land features in Antarctica are named for the Beaver, from which they were first spotted.

Only now that many of those Beavers sold abroad are returning to Canada, often as corroded hulks, and mostly in the region where they have yet to be replaced as reliable everyday transportation—along the rugged Washington–British Columbia–Alaska coastline—is the Beaver beginning to be fully appreciated as the engineering masterpiece it has been for nearly fifty years. As these hulks are returned to airworthiness, certified to carry twice the load they were originally designed to handle, we can see the Beaver's unique place in the annals of aviation. No other aircraft in history was flying in greater numbers as it approached its fiftieth birthday than were flying ten years before, when I flew from Vancouver to Lake Union and back. The Beaver has simply never been replaced. Only a Beaver can replace a Beaver.

Aside from my own revelation about the de Havilland Beaver from a young American whose name I had not the wit to ask, that same weekend happened to be fraught with weighty Canadian–American implications. I returned to Vancouver to see newspapers headlining the fact that the highest scorer in National Hockey League history, Wayne Gretzky, then the country's greatest sporting treasure, had been sold to the Los Angeles Kings, setting off one of those paroxysms of self-examination that make up so much of Canada's national discourse.

Issued October 5, 1982, this Canadian stamp honours the Beaver prototype, CF-FHB. It is one of four stamps issued by Canada Post to commemorate aircraft that opened up the nation's vast northern regions. The others pictured were the Fairchild FC-2W1, Noorduyn Norseman, and Fokker Super Universal. The artist is Robert Bradford. CANADA POST

R.D. "Dick" Hiscocks, the aerodynamicist who shaped the Beaver, happens to live on the other side of Vancouver's Stanley Park from the Bayshore. From his apartment he often hears Beavers revving up for takeoff. They can be distinguished from other piston-engined aircraft by the unbelievably loud *Rrrr-aapp* sound made by the Wasp Junior's two-blade propeller, whose tips at full power approach the speed of sound.

The story of the Beaver's origins is one of the early successes of niche marketing. Hiscocks is the first to say that the Beaver was a team effort. The renaissance man who would become de Havilland Canada's greatest design engineer, Fred Buller, was responsible for most of what went underneath Hiscocks's blunt-nosed shape. Garratt, the managing director, had been thinking about a bush plane even before the Downsview factory's huge wartime contracts were cancelled in 1945, leaving the company with a superior design and production staff and the facilities to mass-produce advanced aircraft. Garratt envisioned an all-metal bush plane and had a preliminary design drawn by his chief design engineer, W. J. Jakimiuk, even before the war ended. Jakimiuk, a war refugee from Poland, happened to be a pioneer of European all-metal aircraft construction. Buller and Hiscocks, young engineers with rich wartime experience, reworked Jakimiuk's ideas. As the design took shape over the next two years, Canada's bush-flying community was intensively consulted—especially the pilots of the Ontario Provincial Air Service. Asked for his opinion, the dean of western Canadian bush flying, Punch Dickins, endorsed the design by agreeing to sell it.

The Beaver's success was no accident. Extraordinary talent, capably directed from above and guided by the ideas of the people who would fly it, made the Beaver a milestone of aircraft engineering.

As we flew low over the San Juan Islands in the Lake Union Air Beaver—low enough to see people washing cars—I wondered whether our youthful pilot, knowledgeable as he was, fully understood the ancient design origins of the machine he was flying. The Beaver looks older than it is, an artful mix of sheer utility and conscious flair. Its ancestry extends back to the first fighters to engage the Luftwaffe at the dawn of World War II. It has the gracefully S-shaped trademark de Havilland fin that adorned the company's wartime Tiger Moth trainer and Mosquito bomber. The Beaver's throttle, propeller and fuel mixture levers move vertically in grooves in the middle of a "Streamline Moderne" dashboard—more of a dashboard than an instrument panel. The Pratt & Whitney Wasp Junior powerplant is, by today's standards, colossally noisy. And it is very close at hand.

"You hear big pilots say, 'Why did you have to put the engine so close?'" Hiscocks chuckles. "Well, the plane wouldn't balance any other way."

Radials also run rough, so everything vibrates. Other aircraft have been described as 10,000 parts flying in close formation, but very few of the others are still in the air.

The Beaver survives because it has enough thoughtful features to have been a reinvention of the bush plane. Four doors instead of the more usual one, the rear ones wide enough to roll an oil drum through. Most aircraft have their gas tanks in the wings, feeding the engine by gravity, but that means pumps, hoses and rickety ladders for refuelling. The Beaver's tanks are under the floor, with fillers low on the fuselage. The fuel-drain stops are oversized so they can be unscrewed with mitts on. Engine oil can be thinned within the engine for easier cold-weather starts. Oil can be added *in flight*, although the process can be messy, from a filler spout located near the base of the control column.

Chief pilot Bill Pennings of Vancouver's Harbour Air, who has logged a remarkable 10,000 hours on the company's fourteen Beavers, says he has flown snowmobiles in them, a useful capability in the north, by removing the cargo doors on each side and letting the ski-doo's front and back hang out. He has a 1991 Bush Pilots calendar in which the September photo shows a float-equipped Beaver towing a loaded barge. *Heh-heh-heh....*

Nearly a thousand of the Beavers built, by Hiscocks's estimate, are still busy, an amazing number considering that they are used in the most forbidding parts of the world and are veterans of two wars. Half of those survivors are in Canada. They are worth about ten times the factory price, about $250,000, still a bargain compared with, say, the single-engine Cessna Caravan at $1.5 million. Dozens of little improvements have made it a better airplane. Today's Beaver is cleared to carry more weight than when it came out of the factory at Downsview.

Dick Hiscocks talks about the immortal Beaver much as Leopold Mozart must have talked about his son Wolfgang. Likewise, the Beaver is a thing unto itself, an immediate success that is still irreplaceable along British Columbia's convoluted coastline, darting through mountain passes into small bays and coves, alighting on the water and getting out again where few other aircraft venture.

By definition, of course, a classic comes close to perfection. Its essentials cannot be improved upon. Twice de Havilland attempted to increase the Beaver's performance by installing yet more powerful engines. Neither time did the new model catch on—although the Turbo Beaver was the victim of a decision by new owners of the company to close the production line. An old aviation saying, often applied to the wartime de Havilland Mosquito, is that if it looks right, it will fly right.

Dick Hiscocks lives in one of the most admirably sited apartment buildings anywhere: the one closest to Stanley Park's southeastern edge. He overlooks an urban wilderness, where bush pilots fly executives to downtown office towers. He can see a continual parade of Beavers on final approach for landings in Burrard Inlet. They take off with a sound that reverberates around the grain elevators that line Burrard Inlet. One by one, the Beavers are returning to Dick Hiscocks's saltwater backyard pond.

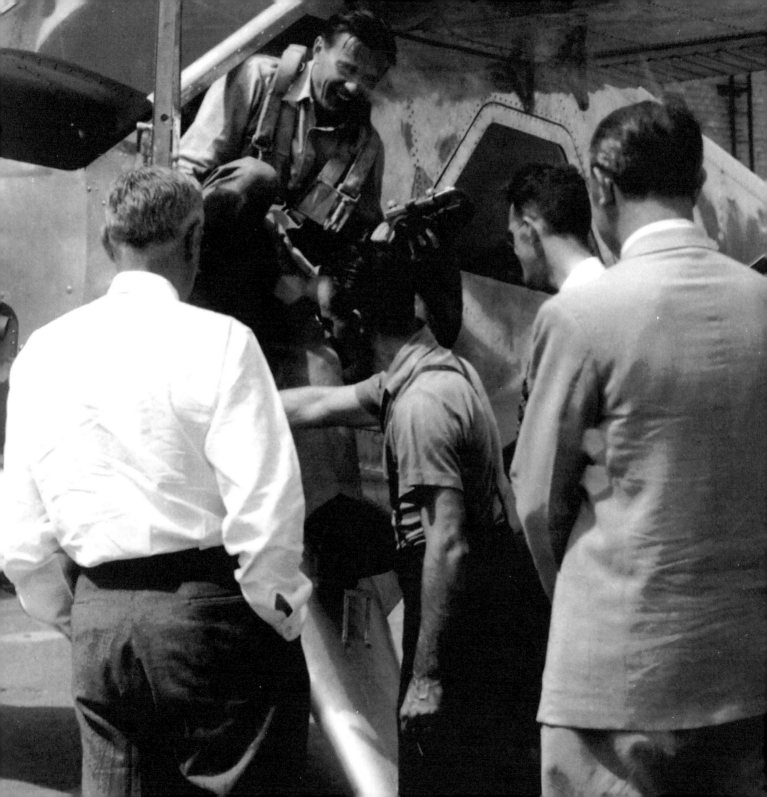

Chapter One

The Beaver takes off

n o matter how much metalworking finesse goes into the construction of a prototype airplane, there is a roughness around the edges, a dimpled aluminum skin and a general lack of finish that is the mark of a handbuilt machine. Details come later. The esthetics can wait. No need for a racy paint job yet. Let's see if this thing will fly.

Still, the de Havilland Canada DHC-2 Beaver prototype that Wing Commander Russ Bannock climbed into shortly before 10 A.M. on August 16, 1947, was a handsome airplane in its own way: a sturdy-looking, squared-off, pug-nosed fuselage, fronted with a big, flat, no-nonsense radial engine, with its bulk set on thick landing-gear struts that gave it the look of a heads-up bulldog ready to leap off the ground.

To the eyes of the engineers who had designed and built it, though, this first Beaver looked distinctly odd on wheels. The Beaver had been intended from the beginning to operate from water, a more demanding medium to leave and return to than concrete or grass. It looked better on floats. Still does.

In fact this prototype had, until a few weeks before, been mounted on floats in Bill Burlison's experimental shop. Its reserve of power in operating from water would be the Beaver's competitive advantage over other single-engine bush planes, including the one that looked to be the Beaver's main competition in the postwar market, the Fairchild Husky (which had flown for the first time more than a year before near Montreal). The Husky was a bigger plane powered by the same engine, giving the Beaver a performance edge.

It is part of the lore of the Beaver that only during those last few weeks before its first flight did it occur to someone in the shop that the de Havilland Aircraft of Canada (DHC) factory at Downsview is totally landlocked. The city of Toronto lay between the factory and the Lake Ontario waterfront. The Beaver was on floats.

"In our preoccupation with the floatplane the design and construction of a wheeled undercarriage had been postponed," the Beaver's aerodynamicist, Dick Hiscocks, dryly recalls.[1] By July the Beaver was photographed with a wheel landing gear while undergoing its fuselage stress tests.

Its landing gear was not the Beaver's only improvised feature, but it was one of the most successful. In a matter of hours "a block of rubber in a sort of nutcracker arrangement," as Hiscocks characterizes it, "was pressed into service."[2] With more time, a more conventional oleo, or combined air-and-oil type of shock strut arrangement, might have been used. No doubt such a mechanism would have given trouble in the north, where oleo seals froze solid and then leaked.[3] In fact, the use of rubber as a shock-absorbing device was an old engineering ploy of the English de Havilland company of Hatfield. It was used, in a different way, on the company's wartime Mosquito fighter-bomber.

Nevertheless, from that time on, a Beaver on wheels has always looked odd and somehow incomplete, like Ginger Rogers in a wheelchair. Ernest Krahulec, who would be the Beaver prototype's mechanic when it went into service with Russ Baker's Central British Columbia Airways and later Pacific Western Airlines, always took care to save that particular set of wheeled landing gear for that unique aircraft. Only that set of landing gear would fit that airplane.

The first Beaver was singular in other ways. The valleys and wrinkles on the aluminum fuselage skin, where hand-formed panels were riveted to the interior structure, were emphasized by seemingly random reflections off the polished metal on the sunny morning of its first flight. A crew in the experimental shop had stayed up all night polishing the Beaver, while Charlie Smith manned the stores-department desk in case they needed any last-minute parts. A matte black anti-glare panel in front of the windshield was the only paint on the Beaver's gleaming fuselage.

Most of the markings an aircraft carries are meant to identify it. If anyone from outside the DHC plant—or most of the workers inside it, for that matter—wondered what the strange, angular airplane was, no clue was offered by the white lettering on a horizontal black stripe running across the prototype's vertical tail: CF-FHB-X. CF made it a Canadian-registered airplane, which revealed very little. The letters FHB said a lot to anyone who knew what they stood for.

Those letters were a tribute to the Beaver's chief design engineer, a low-key, can-do, problem-solving wizard named Frederick Howard Buller. The x was for Experimental.

There was almost nothing experimental or tentative about the Beaver that morning, aside from the fact that it had not yet flown. All successful aircraft are designed with specific missions in mind, but few have succeeded so spectacularly and for so long in such demanding circumstances as the Beaver. In conditions where arrival and departure involve dangerous terrain or capricious weather, there is no substitute for a Beaver. Unlike most fixed-wing aircraft, the Beaver can get out of pretty much any

CF-FHB-X, the handbuilt and polished Beaver prototype, undergoing engine runups and control surface tests shortly before its two-part first flight the morning of August 16, 1947.
DHC VIA PETER M. BOWERS

situation it can get itself into. The demand for Beavers is such that they are being rebuilt better than new. More Beavers are flying today than ten years ago—not just as millionaires' restorations, but as hard-working commercial aircraft flying in the most unpredictable weather conditions in the world along the foggy and mountainous North Pacific coast from Portland to Anchorage.

Histories of flight are usually organized to show the advances in speed, ceiling, range and payload—the categories in which aviation records are set. But it is also possible to see the history of aviation as a quest for the most important goal, safety aloft, with the Beaver as its outcome. As early as 1929, with the Guggenheim safe aircraft competition that offered $150,000, a lot of money in the twenties, the search had begun for an aircraft that could meet such stringent conditions as a requirement that it be controllable in flight at only 35 mph.[4]

Hiscocks, who formulated the Beaver's wing and its high-lift devices, makes his own claim for the Beaver when he calls it "the first serious short takeoff and landing (STOL) airplane."[5] By this he means that, while there were STOL aircraft, such as the Guggenheim competitors and Germany's wartime Fieseler Storch, that offered short-field performance even better than the Beaver's, not until the Beaver appeared did such an aircraft carry useful commercial payloads. And, while some subsequent turboprop STOL aircraft (including the Turbo Beaver) exceed the Wasp Junior-powered Beaver's takeoff and landing performance because of their greater power, the turboprop engine is not at its best in the kind of short-haul, low-level, island-hopping work that is the Beaver's forte.

Following the Beaver's success came a line of de Havilland Canada aircraft that continued to embody the single most critical element of flight safety: the ability to fly slowly and under control, and thereby take off and land in as short a distance as possible.

The Fairchild F-11 Husky first flew more than a year before the Beaver, and was its competition for a 25-30-plane order from the Ontario Provincial Air Service. The Beaver's performance edge won it the OPAS contract. About a dozen Huskies were built. PETER BOWERS

Russ Bannock was hired as much for his organizational abilities as for his talent as a pilot. He was taken on by DHC managing director Phil Garratt, firstly as operations manager and second as chief test pilot. Bannock eventually became president of the company during the mid-1970s—a difficult period in the company's history when spiralling developmental costs on the Dash-7 commuter airliner series led to a government takeover.

As a test pilot, Bannock had more in common with the future breed of scientific evaluators than the daredevils of the past who had flown the wings off new types in terminal-velocity dives. He had made it his business to be present when most of the important engineering decisions about the Beaver were made. The prototype was no stranger to him when it was rolled out of Bill Burlison's experimental shop that August 16 morning.

Although Bannock was no engineer, he had worked closely with the engineering department to resolve the difficult issue of what engine should power the Beaver. Once that was decided, Bannock stayed in touch with the changes mandated by the new engine, changes that extended from nose to tail. His preparation for the first flight would be to work out and review "a test program to develop handling characteristics, performance criteria, and all the data required to take the aircraft up to certification by the Department of Transport."[6]

Inside the cockpit of this outwardly spartan prototype, there were touches of something close to the exotic. Four doors on a small airplane! Having doors for both pilot and co-pilot verged on the luxurious, but was pure practicality for an airplane expected to be so fully loaded the rear doors would be blocked, an airplane that would normally park on one side or another of a dock. In time, two more hatches, in the roof and floor, would be added.

The instrument panel was as streamlined as anything else on the aircraft. It curved back and down from the base of the windshield with its three vertical slots down the upper middle for the throttle, propeller pitch and fuel mixture levers—equally accessible to pilot and co-pilot—and was neatly finished at the bottom of the slots with a chrome strip on which black paint outlined the shiny capital letters DE HAVILLAND. There were no seats in the prototype except for the pilot's.

That morning Bannock looked like the fighter ace he was, in the same Royal Canadian Air Force sunglasses and blue-grey flight suit he had worn on Mosquito operations. Not a hair was out of place. His flight suit, besides fitting well, had plenty of pockets for the pencils, pens, notebooks, maps and calculated data he would carry on the flight. The trousers, rather short to give him freedom in operating the rudder and brake pedals, were crisply ironed. Thick, off-white parachute straps converged from his shoulders and crotch at a quick-release latch on his lower midriff.

Although most test pilots would say that flying a wide variety of aircraft is the best preparation for test flying, very few could claim to have flown every type in the RCAF wartime inventory, with the British Commonwealth Air Training Plan and then overseas, or that their logbooks had recorded recent post-overhaul test flights in PBY Canso and Catalina flying-boats, DC-3 transports "and even Lancasters"—four-engine wartime bombers converted by DHC for peacetime mapping survey and maritime patrol missions.

For the finishing touch to his preparations, Bannock had recently flown with George Phillips, chief pilot of the Ontario Department of Lands and Forests, in one of the government's Stinson Reliants, which had the Beaver's high-wing layout, a less powerful engine than the Beaver's Wasp Junior, and was also mounted on floats. Bannock was killing two birds with one stone by getting to know Phillips. Lands and Forests, on behalf of the Ontario Provincial Air Service, was dangling an order for twenty-five airplanes to replace the prewar Stinsons, one of which had shed its wing in flight, before the eager design teams at Fairchild in Montreal and DHC in Downsview. Lands and Forests was a major influence on the Beaver's preliminary design, encouraging DHC's engineering director, Doug Hunter, a wartime expatriate from the English parent company, to give it a design load factor of 5.25—that is, the Beaver is theoretically capable of carrying five times its gross weight.

The first flight of a new airplane in 1947 was a much less complicated affair than it is today. No special instrumentation was carried in the Beaver, and no computer-generated schedule governed Bannock's actions in the air. He was pretty much on his own. He recalls his first-flight agenda for the Beaver. It was simplicity itself.

Plans for the first flight included the following:
Ground handling checks, including taxi tests.
High-speed taxi tests on the main runway to check directional control and rudder forces.
High-speed taxi tests to liftoff with and without flaps to check all control forces.
Takeoff and climb to approximately 3,000 feet and carry out general handling and engine performance [tests] and obtain a general impression of speeds at different power settings.

One strong memory Bannock retains after fifty years is the group of people whose labours had produced the creation he would now subject to a thorough investigation. They were bunched together on the concrete apron outside the experimental shop at the north end of Runway 33.

"I recall seeing Philip Garratt, managing director; Doug Hunter, engineering director; Jaki Jakimiuk, chief designer; Fred Buller, chief design engineer; Dick Hiscocks, chief aerodynamicist, and Jim Houston, power plant engineer."

All six were wearing white shirts, in the formal style of their wartime generation of professionals, four of them with ties. The Beaver's design team, the next day's *Globe and Mail* photo caption stated, "consists of three young Canadians and an expert from Poland and England."

Among the five men most responsible for the Beaver that morning, only their supervisor, the aristocratic Pole known to his colleagues as Jaki Jakimiuk, continued to wear his suit under the hot mid-morning August sun. It was heavily wrinkled at the elbows and knees. None of them wore sunglasses. Sunglasses were for pilots.

Garratt, also in shirtsleeves, was photographed later that day with a distinguished group that included Punch Dickins and Frank MacDougall, Ontario's Deputy Minister of Lands and Forests. MacDougall would soon effectively decide, with his initial twenty-five-aircraft order, whether the Beaver or the Husky would be the bush plane to go into production.

"With full fuel (79 Imperial gallons) and a single pilot," Bannock recalls, "we were well within the calculated centre-of-gravity range, so there was no ballast on-board.

"It was a lovely summer day, with a slight northwest wind, so I taxied out onto Runway 33 at approximately 10 A.M. and commenced the high-speed taxi tests, a series of skip-hops, checking brakes, checking rudder control—directional control.

The Beaver prototype during flight tests later in 1947, after it had earned the nose-to-tail speed line that characterized most civil production Beavers. DHC

"At the south end of Runway 33 (which gave me 6,000 feet of paved runway), I went through the takeoff checks that we had established. Runway 33 faces northwest, into the prevailing wind. I was hoping there would be no crosswinds.

"I commenced a series of high-speed taxi tests doing a short liftoff for the last two or three. I remember thinking I didn't have enough brake-pedal travel for directional control on the ground. Later we installed pads on the brake pedals, which gave me greater leverage on the brakes. The next time I would taxi back and open up and just get airborne at the end of the run. I probably did that four or five times, checking longitudinal control, lateral control, just general handling, before deciding to take off.

"Using about 10 degrees of flap I opened up the engine to takeoff power (36 MP at 2,300 rpm) and was surprised how quickly the aircraft became airborne [in 15 seconds, according to the *Globe and Mail*'s story[7]]. A climbing speed of 74 mph was established with power reduced to 30 MP [manifold pressure, a measure of power derived from the amount of air being pumped into the engine] at 2,000 rpm. I levelled out at about 3,000 feet, staying within gliding distance of the field in case I had any powerplant problems. Cruise power was set at 28 MP at 1,800 rpm.

"After doing some gentle turns, climbs and descents, my first reaction was how pleasant the Beaver was to fly. It had good pilot visibility, good aileron response, and I had the feeling of lots of power up front."

It was at just this moment, with Bannock warmed by the midsummer sun shining through a windshield that, on the prototype alone, was faired back overhead and into the wing's leading edge, and the satisfaction of knowing the Beaver could fly and fly well, that the crisis struck.

For most of the flight so far, barely more than ten minutes, Bannock had been preoccupied with the flight controls. He now paused to look out over the farmland that is now North York and Richmond Hill. Thornhill was a separate village,

Experimental shop and engineering staff peer at the pool of engine oil dripping from FHB's powerplant after the abbreviated first flight. Access panels to the engine's equipment bay are open. DHC

surrounded by fields. Dufferin Street was still a rural two-lane road which, during the war, had been interrupted by a liftgate at the end of Runway 27 whenever a newly built Mosquito fighter-bomber was being flight-tested.

Bannock, reassured by the big Wasp Junior's steady throb on the climbout and the upward spiral he had maintained to stay over the airfield in case of trouble, had glanced at the engine instruments only a couple of times, and then very quickly. Now he looked again.

The oil-pressure gauge on the prototype was located on a three-in-one dial near the middle of the instrument panel. The all-important cylinder-head temperature gauge took up the top half, with the oil- and fuel-pressure gauges side-by-side below.

When Bannock glanced at it, the oil pressure was reading 35 pounds per square inch. The ideal figure is 60 psi. That concerned him, but his first reaction was to assume there was some problem with the instrument rather than the engine, which sounded normal. If the engine was losing oil, he knew, that oil would be streaming along the underside of the fuselage, out of sight.

That small, inconspicuous instrument now had Bannock's full attention. His eyes returned to it in a matter of seconds. It read 10 psi.

It no longer mattered whether the problem was with the engine or the gauge. Damaging the engine would put the Beaver program that much further behind Fairchild's Husky.

Bannock reached up toward the centre of the instrument panel and pulled the throttle lever back to the bottom of its slot, leaving the engine to idle. He trimmed the Beaver's nose down, noting that the response from the elevators was not quite what he would have liked.

As he began a gliding circuit to the left with the engine barely ticking over, he could hear the fuselage skin popping in and out in the slipstream. The Beaver's thick wing had been formulated to provide the maximum possible lift with the less-powerful engine it was originally designed around, so it was all the more effective when the Wasp Junior was adopted. This wing also made the Beaver a pretty good glider. So much so, in fact, that Bannock regards his dead-stick, or power-off, landing as no more than "reasonable."

To the knots of white-shirted men who anxiously watched Bannock approach in near-silence, flying an airplane whose engine tests had been characterized by an unholy racket, this landing was impressive airmanship. Happy to see it on the ground and in one piece, they gathered around the Beaver, asking questions of Bannock as his door opened, then crouched down as the propeller ceased its desultory windmilling and, duckwalking underneath, looked up.

Ugly streaks of oil defiled the carefully-polished aluminum underside of the Beaver. Some of it began to drip on the concrete apron.

Facing page: This PZL P-11 was an immediate forerunner of the P-11c fighters flown by Capt. Mieczyslaw Medwecki and his wingman, Lt. Wladyslaw Gnys, when they took off at first light September 1, 1939, after hearing bombs explode in the distance. A development of the P-7, the P-11 was an early product of Wsiewolod Jakimiuk, who supervised the team that designed the Beaver. A.U. SCHMIDT, VIA PETER M. BOWERS

Chapter Two

First to fight:
Jaki Jakimiuk and the PZL fighters

Impressive as test pilot Russ Bannock's wartime career as an eleven-victory night-fighter ace was, it was not that much more distinguished than the careers of other members of the team that developed the Beaver. In fact, the chief engineer of the Beaver design team, Wsiewolod Jakimiuk, was part of aviation history long before the Beaver appeared. He was responsible for the first fighters to engage the Luftwaffe at the dawn of the Second World War.

There is something Canadian in the Beaver having design origins so far from its Downsview birthplace—in a suburb of Warsaw, Poland, where the most advanced fighter planes of their time appeared in 1929. It is likely that no combat aircraft so advanced at its conception was as obsolete when called upon to fight as the PZL P-11c Jedenastka (Eleventh) was in the minutes before first light, September 1, 1939, when the German pilots had been at work over western Poland for less than an hour.

The PZL's superannuation makes its gallant record in the defence of Poland all the more noteworthy. The 1,941 warplanes allocated Nazi Germany's Luftwaffe for Operation *Ostmarkflug*, the invasion of Poland, were much more modern.

The Luftwaffe outnumbered Poland's air force ten-to-one in aircraft and three-to-one in fighters.

The many reconnaissance flights that presaged the invasion showed that even Germany's Dornier Do 17 bomber had a 20-km/hr speed advantage over the PZL. The Messerschmitt Bf 109 fighter had a 150-km/hr edge and 2,000-metre higher ceiling, giving its pilot the oft-decisive advantage of initiating and breaking off combat at will.

At 05:30 hours, less than sixty minutes into the war, an open-cockpit gull-winged P-11C piloted by Lieutenant Wladyslaw Gnys of 121 *Eskadra*, the "Winged Arrows," shot down the first of 285 aerial raiders that Polish Military Aviation, the *Lotnictwo Wojskowe*, would destroy during the brief but intense resistance by the first of Hitler's victims to fight back.

In his little P-11C, Gnys—old for a fighter pilot at one week past his 29th birthday—had scarcely more firepower at his disposal than his World War I forebears. In fact, his mount was conceptually similar and nearly identical in layout to the Fokker D.VIII, the epitome of combat aircraft development in 1918. Through such advances as all-metal construction, structural detail development and the use of up-to-date licence-built engines developed in England, the PZL series established "new standards of aerodynamic cleanliness"[1] when the PZL P-1 prototype first flew on September 25, 1929. (PZL stands for *Panstwowe Zaklady Lotnicze*, or State Aircraft Factory, which still exists.)

So rapid was combat aircraft development in the previous few years that, although Lieutenant Gnys's P-11C may have been built less than four years before, it was at least a generation behind Germany's Messerschmitt Bf 109E and Britain's Spitfire I, which were conceived in 1935 and had been continuously developed ever since—the Messerschmitt spurred by its operational testing during the Spanish Civil War. Nevertheless, the 175 P-11C fighters of the *Lotnictwo Wojskowe* claimed the vast majority of the fighter force's 126 confirmed victories during the sixteen-day invasion. This figure is thought to be only half the number of Luftwaffe aircraft the PZLs actually shot down.[2]

The opportunity for a leap forward in fighter design occurred, as it often does, because of the recent availability of advanced engines. Poland's Skoda works had begun licence-building the Bristol Aeroplane Company's Mercury radial engine in 1930.

Radials, so named because their cylinders radiate out from a central crankcase, are air-cooled engines. Their advantages include dispensing with the weight of liquid-cooling plumbing and the coolant itself, thus increasing payload. As fighter powerplants, radials are less susceptible to battle damage; a stray bullet through a radiator could disable a liquid-cooled fighter's engine in seconds. The radial's drawback was its need to be open to the air, causing drag. At that time, suitable methods of smoothing the airflow around a radial's cylinders were only just being developed, so the liquid-cooled engine, which allows a nearly pointed nose profile, still held the aerodynamic advantage.

The Mercury was a de-stroked development of Bristol's well-proven Pegasus radial; its shorter cylinders formed a smaller-diameter, if still blunt, nose.

On the airframe side, PZL, an expansion of the previous Central Aviation Workshops, was founded with a specific purpose in mind: to undertake the next step forward in aircraft structures by taking advantage of the lightness and strength of all-metal construction.

The series forerunner, the P-1, was designed under the leadership of Dipl.-Ing. Zygmunt Pulawski, who appears to have been a talented designer. He had produced a glider while at Warsaw Technical University, had won an apprenticeship at France's Breguet plant by designing the third-place finisher in Poland's 1924 contest for a combat aircraft design, and had learned to fly when the PZL organization was founded by Poland's government the first day of 1928. But Pulawski, not yet thirty, died in an airplane crash March 31, 1931.[3]

With Pulawski's death, the PZL fighter's development was taken over at an early stage by his assistant, a big, cultured and worldly engineer named Wsiewolod J. Jakimiuk (pronounced Jaki-mook). Jaki, as he became known much later at Downsview, was a natural team leader. Physically imposing at over six feet and 200 pounds, with fine engineering credentials of his own, multilingual and an opera buff, Jakimiuk had easy social graces and was married to a talented French-English wife, Mary.

In 1931 the P-1 was the most advanced fighter plane in a world that would continue building its possible rivals out of wood, wire and linen for years to come. The first prototype had a neatly-streamlined, water-cooled Hispano-Suiza V-12 engine, and its high-set gull wing met the upper fuselage at the aerodynamically-optimum 90-degree angle before extending horizontally outward to its gracefully rounded tips. The engine's in-line cylinder heads formed the same angle as that of the wing roots behind them, producing a forward view for the pilot over this shallow V wing centre-section and engine that was outstanding. The P-1 won a fighter competition in Bucharest in 1931 over such contemporaries as the British Bristol Bulldog and the French Dewoitine D.27, and was extensively showcased for a year, appearing, among other places, at the 1932 National Air Races at Cleveland.

The P-1's wing, covered with finely corrugated duralumin alloy grooved front-to-back, was imitated by at least seven European aircraft types.[4] Pulawski took the basic P-1 design through a number of beautifully-streamlined V-12-powered developments until, at the Polish military's insistence, the P-6 was fitted with the more readily available licence-built Bristol radial near the time of his death.[5] The 500-hp Jupiter radial (which also powered the Bulldog) was an important advance in powerplant technology in its day, but it altered some of the more desirable features of Pulawski's original conception, such as the uninterrupted vision forward.

The Beaver would go more successfully through a similar design evolution from a more-streamlined but less-powerful in-line powerplant installation to a more-easily-available air-cooled radial, making it, like the PZL, more of a blunt object—louder, tougher, brawnier, more muscular. Moreover, the absence of liquid coolant was an obvious advantage in the frigid regions where the Beaver was intended to fly.

Renowned for its all-metal construction techniques by the late 1930s, the PZL factory hosted delegations from Romania and Britain, who spent long periods there learning their trade secrets. The Romanians, having licence-built the P-11C for their own air force, spent six months at the Okesie-Paluch plant near Warsaw studying Jakimiuk's design philosophy, borrowing dozens of his engineers, and ending up simply copying the characteristic PZL tail for the IAR-80 series fighters that became operational during the war.

In 1937, engineers from the de Havilland Aircraft Co. of Hatfield, England, arrived for the same purpose and got to know the charming "engineer's engineer," as de Havilland Canada employees of the time remember him.[6] The de Havilland company, the oldest and most prolific aircraft manufacturer in England, had built some of the fastest airplanes in the world out of wood. But for the twelve-to-seventeen-passenger airliner de Havilland had in mind for the late 1930s, all-metal was the way to go.

The DH.95 Flamingo was de Havilland's first all-metal design when it first flew December 28, 1938, in the hands of Geoffrey de Havilland Jr., the son of the company's founder, and George Gibbins. This was easily the most modern airliner built up to then in Britain. A Flamingo was used by Winston Churchill and his advisors for vital trips to France before Dunkirk. Had the Germans invaded Britain in 1940, the royal family would have been evacuated from London in one of the thirteen Flamingos built. An engineering-physics student from the University of Toronto, Dick Hiscocks, was doing his internship at the Hatfield plant.

Jakimiuk's P-11 model appeared later in 1931. While the first prototype flew in August of that year with a Jupiter engine, subsequent pre-production units had the more powerful Mercury IV radials that developed 800 hp for takeoff. Early P-11s were introduced into service in 1935, the year the Bf 109 and Spitfire prototypes appeared.

The P-11C, which reached Polish fighter units later in 1935, featured such small refinements as an exhaust-collecting engine cowling ring that minimized turbulent airflow around the bulky radial. Some P-IIS even carried four machine guns, with the addition of one in each wing panel. The Romanians built seventy P-IIS at their Industria Aeronautica Romana (IAR) plant during 1936–37.

A development of the P-II, the P-24 was an even greater export success for PZL and Jakimiuk. The P-24 had heavier armament, including two 20-mm Oerlikon cannon, and a fully-enclosed cockpit. Greece bought 36, Turkey 60, Bulgaria had received 36 of a 46-plane order at the outbreak of war, and old customer Romania had 50, 44 of them built by IAR.[7]

But P-24s in foreign hands were useless to the Poles in September 1939. With non-adjustable laminated wood propellers that compromised both takeoff and high-speed performance, drag-producing fixed landing gear, and open cockpits, the P-IIS Polish Military Aviation took to war were pressed to exceed 200 mph at anything under 8,000 feet, where most dogfights took place.

By February 1939 Jakimiuk and his team had designed and flown a much more modern fighter, the P-50 *Jastrzeb*, or Hawk. The P-50 had retractable landing gear, a fully enclosed cockpit and, temporarily, an engine in the 900-horsepower class. Eventually, it was to have been powered by Bristol's 1,375-hp Hercules radial. It looked much like a smaller P-47 Thunderbolt or the Italian Sagittario. An initial batch of thirty was under construction in September when the Germans arrived.[8]

With Poland's collapse, Jakimiuk and a number of other distinguished Polish aero engineers made their way west, finding themselves by mid-1940 in Canada.

One account of Wladyslaw Gnys's first combat that morning of September 1939 has him shooting down a Junkers Ju 87 Stuka dive bomber while its pilot concentrated on strafing a column of Polish horse-drawn transport.[9] A subsequent account, published in the same journal by a Polish author, credits Gnys with a much more impressive feat. Actually, Gnys barely survived being shot at by Stukas before he even knew there was a war on, and lived to fight a few minutes later that day.[10]

His airfield, at Krakow, was pounded first by Heinkel bombers, then by Stukas, and finally by Dornier Do 17s. The Do 17 was known because of its narrow fuselage as the "Flying Pencil." Gnys and his buddies sidestepped the bombardment. They had been detached, as a precaution, to a strip at nearby Balice. His unit, 122 Squadron, had not been alerted, and took off only after hearing bombs explode in the distance. Gnys took to the air as wingman to his CO, Captain Mieczyslaw Medwecki.

They had the misfortune to be intercepted on takeoff from behind by Stukas returning from Krakow. A Ju 87 piloted by Sergeant Frank Neubert opened fire on the right-hand PZL, Medwecki's, which exploded in a ball of fire. Gnys, in P-II "5" with an abstract winged arrow ahead of the tail, broke left so violently that his

The PZL P-6 was the prototype of the radial-engine series that led to the wartime P-11c models that first engaged the invading Luftwaffe at the dawn of the Second World War. This one, flown by test pilot Boleslaw Orlinski, performed an aerobatic routine at the 1931 National Air Races, Cleveland, that is remembered as a highlight of the event. PETER M. BOWERS

airplane stalled while barely off the ground. He was fortunate to recover control before running out of altitude.

Soon after, Gnys spotted a pair of the Do 17s about 3,000 feet below him, also returning from Krakow. He attacked one Dornier to the rear, silencing its tail gunner and drawing translucent smoke from its left engine. The second Dornier intervened between Gnys and its crippled mate, and Gnys attacked it as well. After observing strikes from long bursts of fire on the second bomber, Gnys dived steeply to initiate a zoom-climb to overcome his airspeed disadvantage, and lost his opponents when he recovered altitude.

Polish soldiers were stopped on the Trzebinia–Olkusz road that morning in the village of Zurada, whose inhabitants tipped them that two German aircraft had crashed nearby. The soldiers found and photographed the smouldering wrecks of the Dorniers Gnys did not yet know he had shot down. Only one crew member had managed to take to his parachute, but it had become entangled in the wreckage.

Having shot down the first German aircraft of the war, Gnys escaped the collapsing Poland to become an ace with a Polish-manned French Armée de l'air unit. With France's capitulation he joined 302 Squadron, Royal Air Force, with which he fought in the Battle of Britain. He served with three other Polish RAF squadrons, took command of 317 Squadron in 1944, and that same day was shot down for a third time and wounded by German soldiers. His second attempt to escape from his German hospital succeeded. He left the Polish Air Force in 1947 and immigrated to Canada.

By then Wsiewolod Jakimiuk, the man who developed the fighter in which Gnys scored the first Allied aerial victories of the war, was running the design department at the de Havilland Canada plant in Downsview. His introduction to Canada was indicative of the chaotic early stages of the country's call to arms. After a hazardous journey through war-torn Europe from Poland, desperately needed by an aircraft industry not yet capable of building the kind of all-metal designs his PZL establishment had been mass-producing for eleven years, Jakimiuk found himself denied a permanent visa when he arrived in Canada.[11]

In war, as much as any other time, government's left hand seldom knows what the right hand is doing. Despite one department's agreement with the Polish government-in-exile to accept Jakimiuk and his colleagues, another department entangled the engineers over, among other matters, travel costs. These were considerable for the time, although the Poles had hardly travelled first-class.

The de Havilland Company at Hatfield, grateful for Jakimiuk's expertise on the DH.95 airliner project, guaranteed the cost of transportation for him and an eventual total of forty Polish war guests who came to work at Downsview. The total bill, $200,000, was fully repaid by the Poles.[12] Their largely unsung contributions far outweighed the costs of bringing them to Canada, and their talents took them to some of aviation's far horizons after the war.

By the time his colleagues were establishing themselves elsewhere, Jakimiuk, who remained with DHC after the war, was laying the foundations for Canada's greatest line of indigenous aircraft. By the end of 1946 Jakimiuk had already designed what is regarded as the first all-Canadian postwar aircraft, the DHC-1 Chipmunk military trainer, and was supervising the design of the Beaver.

Many of those who were close to the Beaver's design and development process draw a parallel with Jakimiuk's PZLs, which did have a similar layout, if for different reasons. Likewise, the Beaver pioneered all-metal construction for bush planes.[13]

Moreover, "Jaki," as he was known to his growing staff of engineers, had pulled off a personal coup for a newly arrived war refugee and expatriate Pole. With charm enough for three men, Jakimiuk had become a member of Toronto's exclusive Granite Club, not otherwise known as a haven for refugees from overseas, soon after he arrived in Canada. Wartime de Havilland people recall Jakimiuk as "an almost opera-quality bass-baritone, [who could] sing a vast repertoire of songs from arias to folk melodies."[14]

Jakimiuk had the endearing quality of being able to laugh at himself, often by exaggerating his own Polish accent, which had in fact been refined under his wife's influence into the kind of mid-Atlantic speech pattern that would have been at home on the Canadian Broadcasting Corporation of the time.

So the man who by the end of the war was DHC's chief design engineer was a good fellow to have around during or after business hours. Just as he had got his professional break early in his career with the death of Zygmunt Pulawski, Jakimiuk recognized and promoted young talent.

Infected by Jakimiuk's worldly bonhomie and that of the other Poles, Canadian-born engineers like Fred Buller would express their affection for their war guests by lapsing into cornball Polish accents at home and at work. Among the many expressions that originated with the Poles was a line Betty Buller attributes to W. Z. Stepniewski, the aerodynamicist, who, encountering some problem at the Downsview plant, exclaimed within earshot of some of the natives, "It is without any sense." He then shrugged his shoulders and sighed "But anyhow..." and attacked the problem with renewed vigour.

There is something endearing about an aircraft manufacturer's engineering department that, for a while at least, encountered the daily dilemmas of their work by saying out loud, in their caricatures of eastern European English, "It is without any sense," shrugging their shoulders, adding "But anyhow..." and then going at the difficulty with redoubled effort. The Poles did that for DHC, and much, much more.

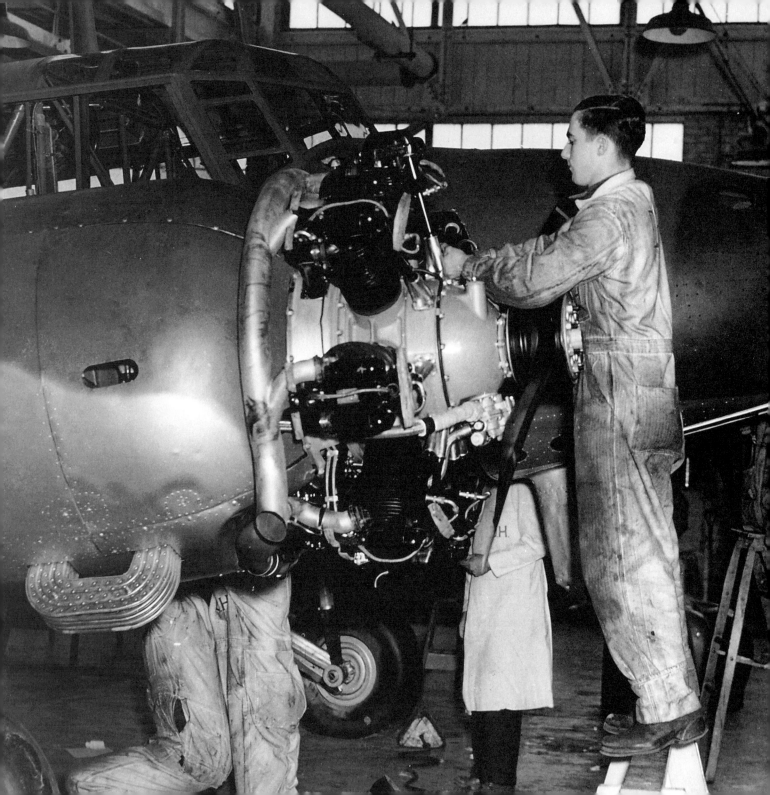

Chapter Three

Downsview goes to war

The de Havilland of Canada organization that Jakimiuk joined had been among the smallest aircraft manufacturers in Canada at the beginning of the war. During the mid-1930s, employment peaked at fifty-two people in the Downsview plant,[1] many of them women who worked in the DHC fabric shop, sewing, gluing and doping linen wing and fuselage skins for the lightweight stick-and-wire biplanes that Downsview's parent at Hatfield specialized in. Even then, de Havilland's aircraft construction methods were falling well behind the times.

The tall, skinny, bespectacled young Dick Hiscocks's experience working for DHC during the summer of 1937 and for the English parent company at Hatfield the following year impressed him mainly by how wilfully backward the company's management was—especially compared with its innovative design staff. A University of Toronto student in Engineering Physics 1938, Hiscocks found himself working eighteen-hour days that first summer assembling the *Globe and Mail*'s "Flying Newsroom," a twin-engine DH.89 Dragon Rapide mounted on floats.[2] The Rapide pretty much summed up de Havilland's design philosophy.

Like the entire DH Rapide small airliner series, CF-BBG was an elegant machine, with slender biplane wings, a minimum of strut-bracing and wires, and good visibility through an almost-continuous strip of windows running halfway back along the fuselage. It was typical of de Havilland products in having evolved through a progression of gradual changes, each of which slightly altered a thoroughly obsolete concept.

Fabric-covered biplanes were already things of the past. Lockheed, Boeing and finally Douglas Aircraft, with its epochal DC-3, had all been building larger, faster, all-metal airliners for years. In fact, wooden wings had been outlawed on commercial aircraft operated in the United States since 1928, when a wood-winged Fokker airliner had crashed, killing, among others, Notre Dame's famous football and track coach, Knute Rockne.

The Dragon Rapide's great virtue was its economy of operation. Like many of de Havilland's small airliners, the Dragon Rapide had found markets as a short-haul commuter airliner and as an executive aircraft for private industry, and would be built in the thousands as a wartime military transport and trainer. The *Globe* intended to share its flying newsroom with a northern mining promoter.

Another attraction of de Havilland designs was that they could be assembled by relative novices such as Hiscocks, who found himself placed in charge of wing assembly for the *Globe*'s Rapide while still in school. The wood and metal parts were shipped from England. The woodwork involved in assembly was considered within almost any employee's capabilities. Nor did the shipments from England include drawings, "which were considered an unnecessary distraction for any competent assembler," Hiscocks recalls.[3]

His foremost qualification for supervising the Rapide's wing assembly was that he had found a picture of the airplane in a copy of Jane's *All the World's Aircraft*.[4] There was constant pressure to finish the job, partly because the pilot had already been hired and had nothing better to do than monitor progress, and partly because the customer had all the patience of those who produce the daily miracle that is a newspaper.

According to Hiscocks's picture, the Rapide's unusual tapered wings had straight leading edges that ran at right angles from the fuselage. That was in accord with Hiscocks's textbooks, which, in those pre-supersonic times, abhorred leading-edge sweepback. The possibility that the de Havilland designer responsible for the Dragon series, A. E. Hagg, might not have read those texts occurred to Hiscocks once the wings were assembled and trial-mated to the fuselage. They didn't fit. The wings' leading edges did have sweepback, after all.

Repairing the damage was all the more difficult because, before the era of bolts with self-locking nuts, the normal practice in assembling bolted machines was to hammer the ends of the bolts to scramble the threads. "It was an effective technique," Hiscocks remembers, "as we discovered when we tried to take those wings apart."

An elaborate and fully reported ceremony was held to christen the airplane when it was finished, and its first flight was highly publicized, especially its subsequent arrival back at the Toronto waterfront on August 21, 1937.

One obvious shortcoming of wood-framed, fabric-covered airplanes was demonstrated that evening, when the flying newsroom returned from its inaugural trip and was being refuelled for the next day's flight. One tank had been filled when a spark from the nozzle ignited fumes from the empty tank into a ball of flame.[5] The flying newsroom burned too quickly to be saved, and "all that could be done was to float it away from the dock and let it burn," recalls Fred Hotson, a DHC employee at the time. Up in smoke went the product of Dick Hiscocks's summer labours.

Hiscocks has often wondered whether the fate of the flying newsroom that summer of 1937 was why DHC was unable to offer him work after he graduated. His visit to Hatfield in 1938, arranged by DHC managing director Philip C. Garratt, was, in its own way, equally disillusioning. De Havilland had its own way of doing things, and the company preferred to train its technicians at its own technical school. These graduates were more highly regarded within the company than engineers from Oxford or Cambridge, who were considered scientists. DH people were hands-on types, hardworking fellows who could use tools.

There were advantages to the way de Havilland operated: the production department was, above all else, flexible. Hatfield could build prototypes cheaply, for almost any market, and could produce short runs of any specific model economically by combining the wing of one type with a new fuselage and powering the result with one of the company's reliable Gipsy engines.[6]

Garratt had arranged for Hiscocks to work at Hatfield on an advanced project—at least, it was advanced for the prewar de Havilland. It was the all-metal DH.95 Flamingo on which Jakimiuk had consulted with the de Havilland design team.[7] Just out of engineering school, wanting to keep himself abreast of the latest developments in aviation, Hiscocks remembers requesting borrowing privileges in the company library. This was regarded as an outlandish request, for which he was paraded before Hatfield's managing director, "no less."

"He wanted to know what earthly use I would have for technical reports, and to his horror I said that there was a lot of good design data in reports from sources such as the Royal Aircraft Establishment. The office of every senior executive in England had a fireplace in those days, and, pointing to this, the head of the company said that government reports were given an 'ignition test' at de Havilland."

Even after the company's leap into high-performance aircraft with the 1934 DH.88 Comet racer, an ancestor of the World War II Mosquito, old habits died hard.

From 1928 to 1939, DHC assembled aircraft using parts supplied from Britain. Here, circa 1933, a two-seater DH.60 Moth fuselage is being overhauled in the foreground while a DH.89 Dragon Rapide airliner fuselage, upper right, awaits its wings. FRED HOTSON VIA DHC

In retrospect, Hiscocks saw in the distrust of scientific credentials and the supremacy of the shop floor at Hatfield a style of aircraft design and manufacture that would cause problems for the company's Canadian branch when it became involved in high-volume production of Mosquitoes during the war.

Canada's potential to contribute aircraft to the war effort was recognized in Britain. Most of Canada's aircraft companies were branch-plants of British armament concerns, such as Vickers. (America's aviation industry was preoccupied with expanding by leaps and bounds to meet contracts placed by the British Purchasing Commission.) But most of Canada's industry—and especially the branch-plants of British concerns—was hopelessly behind the times, assembling aircraft that were patently obsolete under licences from foreign manufacturers.[8]

Canadian Vickers, in Montreal, was building stately but slow biplane Stranraer flying-boats, which, though all-metal, were ten years out-of-date in concept. Boeing of Canada, in Vancouver, was building biplane Blackburn Shark torpedo-bombers even as its parent company in Seattle, 120 miles south, was turning out what was then the most advanced heavy bomber in the world, the B-17 Flying Fortress. A consortium of six subcontractors was organized as Canadian Associated Aircraft Ltd. to build the Handley-Page Hampden twin-engine bomber. Hardly the zenith of aircraft design at the time, it was an instructive all-metal structure, useful for bomber crew training. Associated was having trouble building them satisfactorily.

How de Havilland Canada, among the smallest and most technically outdated aircraft manufacturers in a country that was then an airplane-building backwater, became the biggest in Canada, with 7,000-odd employees who managed to build more than 1,130 400-mph Mosquito fighter-bombers, is by itself an impressive chapter in the annals of Canadian industry.

DHC's growth in size and sophistication was one of those miracles that were routinely accomplished as part of the war effort. But if the word miracle accurately describes the overall wartime picture at Downsview, that wondrous outcome was accomplished by down-to-earth means: equal parts of hardnosed management and the heartbreak that often results from it; a gathering of talent from all over Canada, indeed the world; and exactly the right product. The Mosquito was an aircraft that DHC was uniquely qualified to produce. Among the first of those talented new additions from around the world was W. J. Jakimiuk of Warsaw, Poland.

Barely ten years after having helped found the PZL organization to advance the science of aircraft construction, Jaki Jakimiuk found himself quickly appointed chief engineer of a concern that was building flimsy Tiger Moth biplanes—a huge leap backward technologically.

Installing a 120-hp Gipsy III inverted air-cooled engine in one of the 1,553 Tiger Moth trainers assembled by DHC from 1937 to 1945. Here, Jerome McNamie (left), Ed Loveday and an unidentified worker unite a Gipsy engine with its airframe. FRED HOTSON VIA DHC

DHC's contract from the Royal Canadian Air Force in 1937 for twenty-six DH.82 Tiger Moth trainers was "a rather small piece of the business in a country verging on war," writes Fred Hotson in *The de Havilland Canada Story*, "but everyone at Downsview believed an additional contract would follow in due course... but by the time the last Tiger was delivered on April 12, 1939, no new order had appeared."[9] Layoffs would have occurred at this most unlikely time—on the eve of a world war—if not for an order from the British parent company for 200 Tiger Moth fuselages.

These orders kept DHC alive during the prewar hiatus between the loss of North America's illusion of immunity from the unpleasantness brewing in Europe and the flood of orders that was about to transform the continent within months into the arsenal of democracy. However mundane, the Tiger Moth work was a tribute to the persistent salesmanship of the company's new managing director.

Phil Garratt flew himself to Ottawa almost every week in his personal DH.87 Hornet Moth to drum up business with RCAF procurement officers who as yet had no budget for training aircraft. The Hornet Moth was a true salesman's airplane, the first DH design with a fully enclosed cabin and side-by-side rather than tandem seating for pilot and passenger.[10]

It seems that Jakimiuk consistently saw eye-to-eye with Phil Garratt, who had been involved with de Havilland Canada since 1928, when Garratt volunteered for hazardous work as a test and aircraft delivery pilot "just for the pleasure of it."[11] Like Jakimiuk, Garratt was one of his country's aviation pioneers.

He had been one of the original student pilots at Canada's first flying academy, the Curtiss Flying School, Toronto, in 1915.[12] He soloed in a Curtiss Jenny, received his wings with the Royal Flying Corps in 1916 and spent that summer and fall as a fighter pilot with 70 Squadron. Garratt must have been an accomplished pilot; he was posted as an instructor to the noted Gosport School of Flying for the duration of the war. Like so many First War pilots, he became a barnstormer after he returned to Canada in 1919—in his case, with the Bishop Barker Flying Company.

Despite the cachet of its partners' combined 122 victories in the skies over France (and the Victoria Cross each had been awarded), the company soon collapsed, leaving Garratt clear-eyed about aviation's immediate commercial possibilities.[13] He managed his own chemical company from 1923 until 1936, when the enthusiastic part-timer was offered the general manager's post at DHC. This was an opportunity to become the first Canadian to run the company.[14] By then, it was beginning to look as if assembling airplanes might finally become a profitable business in Canada.

Garratt, pilot, salesman and manager, and Jakimiuk, the engineer's engineer, had a lot in common, including outsized appetites for life. They looked on things from the same six-foot-plus viewpoint. Both were driven by big hearts. Each was, in his way, an aviation pioneer. Both recognized talent and appreciated the value of allowing young engineers free rein.

On December 17, 1939, the British Commonwealth Air Training Plan was launched in Ottawa, and by the following mid-March the first trainees were being taken on strength. Within a year there were sixty-seven training bases and ten advanced flying schools in Canada. The BCATP has been called Canada's most important contribution to the war effort. As a central commitment around which a vast industrial complex had to be built, the air training plan generated activity far beyond the training of aircrew.

At these schools the most numerous aircraft types were the single-engine Harvard fighter trainer being built by Noorduyn near Montreal under licence from North American of Inglewood, California, and the twin-engine Avro Anson, in which bomber crews would be trained.[15] The Anson was the Royal Air Force's first monoplane aircraft with retractable landing gear when it was introduced in March 1936. While it was a total failure as an operational combat aircraft early in the war, it used mainly non-strategic materials in its construction and was widely available.[16]

DHC's experience with the Anson started with the assembly of a used Anson I that arrived from England February 25, 1940, complete with gun turret and camouflage paint.[17] A total of 264 second-hand Ansons, some with bullet-holes, were assembled and distributed to bases across Canada. This supply was suspended during the spring 1940 crisis caused by the fall of France and the evacuation at Dunkirk. The BCATP plan had envisaged that wingless Ansons would be supplied from overseas and fitted with wings built in Canada because of their wood content. Suddenly even fuselages were unavailable.

Canada would have to build Ansons from scratch. Federal Aircraft Ltd. was formed "almost overnight"[18] to build the Anson II, a version with American Jacobs L6MB radial engines instead of the Mark I's British Armstrong-Whitworth Cheetahs and, for climatic reasons, fewer windows along its fuselage. DHC, one of five assembly plants organized under Federal's program, built 375 Anson IIs. They were ideal transitional products for upgrading the skills of the DHC workforce, which nearly doubled to about a thousand workers in 1940.

So important was the Anson to the BCATP that an all-Canadian Anson V, which would use a higher proportion of wooden components, including moulded plywood skin surfaces, was developed by the National Research Council in Ottawa under the direction of the same Dick Hiscocks who had worked for de Havilland as an engineering student at the University of Toronto during the summer of 1937. As an ingenious, thoroughly re-engineered improvement on a proven design, more than a thousand of the Anson Vs were produced at plants other than DHC.[19]

The intense demand for experienced engineers and tradespeople to staff the aircraft plants being constructed, sometimes within weeks, often worked out to DHC's advantage. People were frequently shaken loose from established companies to work for new ones, but some had trouble adapting to workplaces that were being started from scratch.

One such luminary was the former chief engineer of Fairchild Aircraft of Longueuil, Quebec, a respected supplier of bush planes in Canada for many years. Francis Hyde-Beadle was exactly the pioneer of British aviation his hyphenated surname suggests. He was among the first engineers at Farnborough, the cradle of flight research in the U.K.—one of the first six technicians, in fact, to join the British Army's Royal Balloon Factory, the origins of which extended back to 1882. Hyde-Beadle was there when one of the organization's airplane designers and its test pilot was none other than the future Sir Geoffrey de Havilland. The Balloon Factory was renamed the Royal Aircraft Factory in 1911 to reflect Farnborough's increasing preoccupation with powered, heavier-than-air flight.

Hyde-Beadle preferred working on specialized projects that required original design ideas, such as the combination float-fuel tanks on the Gloster racing planes that competed for the international Schneider Trophy, the epitome of air racing until Britain retired it by winning three consecutive times up to 1931. Looking for that kind of challenge after Farnborough ceded its experimental work to Britain's aircraft manufacturers, Hyde-Beadle moved to the four-year-old Fairchild Aviation Corporation of Hagerstown, Maryland, in 1928. He was attracted by Sherman Fairchild's determination to build advanced aircraft. Subsequently he moved to its plant at Longueuil, near Montreal, which opened in 1930 and produced a line of bush planes known for toughness, versatility and the ability to carry five to twelve passengers or a ton of mixed cargo.

In 1938 Hyde-Beadle was hired to head the engineering staff at National Steel Car's new plant in Malton, built to assemble Handley-Page Hampden bombers and manufacture Westland Lysander army co-operation aircraft (it later became the Canadian Avro plant where the first six CF-105 Avro Arrow prototypes were built). NSC's problems building the Hampden had less to do with engineering than with adapting methods suitable for producing railway rolling stock to aviation.

When he moved to DHC, Hyde-Beadle persuaded his right-hand production engineers, the Burlison brothers, George and Bill, to come with him. Like Hyde-Beadle, the Burlisons had grown up with aviation, following their father into Canadian Vickers' Montreal plant. They too disliked the working culture at NSC.[20] George joined the burgeoning production department and Bill became an inspector.

Another distinguished addition from Vickers was Richard J. Moffett, a stress engineer who came to Montreal from England in 1928 and worked on the Vickers

The first Avro Anson I of an eventual 264 assembled at Downsview for aircrew training in Canada. Camouflaged, with gun turrets, they arrived from Britain February 25, 1940 and were assembled that weekend. They flew Sunday and were delivered to the R.C.A.F. Monday. VIA GEORGE NEAL

Vancouver flying-boat program. By mid-Depression, Vickers was down to four employees, but Moffett brought the company to life again in time to licence-build twenty modern all-metal Northrop Delta transports and the twenty outdated Supermarine Stranraer flying-boats that were Canada's bicoastal aerial patrol force at the war's outset. Moffett became Federal Aircraft's general manager in mid-1940 to put together the Anson production consortium, but was unhappy there and resigned twice before being released to become production manager on Anson IIs at DHC that autumn.

"Suddenly," writes Fred Hotson, who saw these changes firsthand, "DHC had a formidable factory management team—their own old-timers plus the cream of the Vickers/Fairchild experience. On his arrival at Downsview [Christmas Day, 1940] Moffett saw that the existing machine shop was completely inadequate, and he had a new one set up and furnished with the very latest equipment."[21]

Hotson recalls that DHC's two new brick buildings, "smelling of concrete and fresh paint," were absorbed so smoothly into the expansion program of autumn 1940 that the company was soon being given such additional contracts as the conversion of another batch of seventy-five Anson Is from Britain to Jacobs powerplants and the assembly of thirty-eight Fairey Battle single-engine bombers, some of which became target-towing aircraft for air training plan gunnery instruction. So far ahead of schedule was the production of Anson fuselages in 1941 that they became airborne without wings, engines or tails: the Ansons were being hung from the factory ceiling, like model airplanes, for storage.[22]

Two of the most outstanding Polish engineers who accompanied Jakimiuk to DHC in 1940 were the aerodynamicist W. Z. Stepniewski and Waclaw Czerwinski, a structures engineer. Aerodynamicist Dick Hiscocks would remember both as "very competent and stimulating people to be with."[23]

Czerwinski, who had designed gliders in Poland, organized a DHC gliding club within the engineering department, members of which built their own glider in their spare time. He also came with plywood-forming expertise that proved invaluable when DHC became committed as a second source for the "Wooden Wonder," the 400-mph Mosquito bomber from Hatfield that became one of the most versatile combat aircraft of the war. A group of the Polish engineers at DHC formed Canadian Wooden Aircraft to manufacture formed-plywood parts, often shaped into complex curves, that replaced parts made from strategically important metals.[24] The Mosquito would eventually bomb Nazi rallies in Berlin with the aid of streamlined formed-plywood drop tanks made at first in a converted piano factory and later at a larger plant on Sorauren Avenue, both in Toronto.[25]

Czerwinski found himself in wide demand. He was involved with several similar projects at the National Research Council to replace metal with wood, including the Anson v, on which he worked with Hiscocks. He joined Avro Canada after the war and was part of the Arrow fighter project.

Stepniewski left DHC after the war to work for Frank Piasecki's helicopter manufacturing company in Philadelphia and became one of the most respected vertical-flight engineers in the world. Piasecki specialized in big, powerful, twin-rotor helicopters in which the torque of one rotor was cancelled out by the other. Without the need to siphon off power to a vertical tail rotor to keep them on course, Piasecki's machines could devote more of their available power to carrying payloads. The Piasecki organization eventually became the Boeing Airplane Company's Vertol helicopter division.

The cooperation between DHC and the National Research Council on the Anson v project was typical of Downsview's practical approach to research and development. Before the war they had jointly developed streamlined ski landing gear for the Rapide. The English company naturally had little interest in equipping its aircraft with skis, so that was the kind of project DHC interested itself in. But with the coming of war, small experimental undertakings only got in the way of the company's mass-production goals.

The answer was to set up Central Aircraft Ltd. in London, Ontario. With the arrival of Jakimiuk and the other Polish engineers at Downsview, Francis Hyde-Beadle was freed to do the work he liked best. Phil Garratt's executive assistant, John McDonough, a former mail and bush pilot who had tested the first Noorduyn Norseman and who was at loose ends after supervising the plant expansion at Downsview, became manager.[26]

It was by joining Central Aircraft in 1943 that Fred H. Buller first stepped into DHC's orbit. Buller, who succeeded Hyde-Beadle as chief engineer of Central Aircraft on the latter's death late that year, had a lot in common with the Englishman. Buller was a pure designer who preferred doing original engineering and was brilliant at it.

The team that would design and manufacture the Beaver was now almost complete. First, though, they had a war to win. Doing so would involve near-cataclysmic changes at DHC. There were Mosquitoes to be built—Mosquitoes to interfere with Adolf Hitler's speeches, Mosquitoes to make Hermann Goering wish for Mosquitoes of his own.

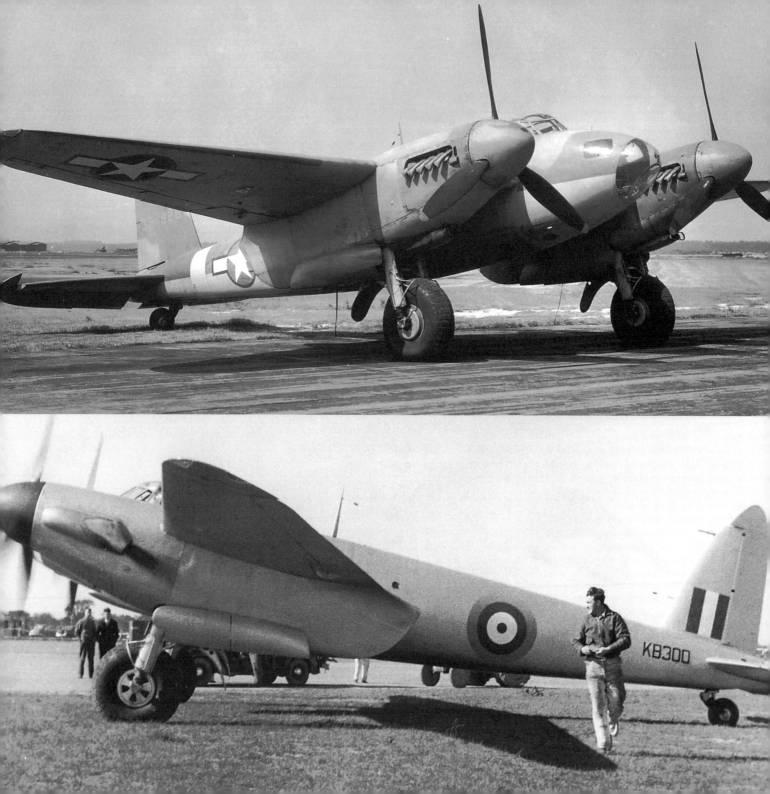

Facing page, top: The U.S. government paid
for Mosquito production at Downsview under
Lend-Lease, partly to have a claim on some
of them as photo reconnaissance machines.
They were known to the U.S. Army Air Force
as F-8s. Downsview built thirty-nine F-8s.
Bottom: The first Downsview Mosquito,
B.Mk.VII (B for Bomber) KB300, the first of
twenty-four of that model built there. It flew
for the first time September 23, 1942. Geoffrey
de Havilland Jr. demonstrated it in Washington
and San Diego. BOTH PHOTOS: PETER M. BOWERS

Chapter Four

One thousand Mosquitoes

The de Havilland Canada that had started the war building Tiger Moths and reassembling used and crated Avro
Anson trainers was not the same company that built
1,133 copies of the world's first operational 400-mile-per-
hour combat aircraft, the DH.98 Mosquito.[1]

The first DHC was a near-cottage industry that had congratulated itself on
designing and fabricating streamlined landing-gear skis for the Rapide and a sliding
cockpit canopy for the Tiger Moth. It was a small outfit with a managing director,
Phil Garratt, who didn't much care for titles and who knew the name of everyone
else in the company.

The second DHC was a fully-integrated industrial organization, primed with
government financing, embracing its own subsidiaries, subcontractors and satellite
facilities, and even an elected local of the United Auto Workers. Several key engineers from Hatfield had joined the Canadian company, including the chief technical engineer since 1925, W. D. (Doug) Hunter, professionalizing DHC's production

methods. It was this second DHC that, by the end of the war, was fully capable of designing and manufacturing the line of Short Takeoff and Landing (STOL) aircraft that began with the Beaver.

Yet the changes that made the company more capable came at a huge price. In wartime, human costs are secondary to the overall objective. By the time DHC had expanded five-fold and was making its contribution to Canada's war effort, there was no Phil Garratt at Downsview. He was sent into exile by the company's new government taskmasters. A number of other company luminaries also left.

The only quibble about Garratt's management style from those who worked for him is that it was a thing of the past. In his eye-to-eye meetings along the production line, which he toured every day, Garratt treated everyone as an equal—at least as much of an equal as anyone facing a man of his size and bearing could feel. He cultivated the wives of his workers, since they were his allies in getting the best out his work force. Phil was a pretty good listener, and by listening carefully he enlisted everyone in the plant in his personal quest to elevate DHC's engineering and manufacturing capabilities. And yet, a management style that depends upon daily personal contact is better suited to a smaller company addressing a market niche with carefully conceived products than to the far-flung industry DHC became during the war.

"Phil Garratt didn't believe in formal organization," aerodynamicist Dick Hiscocks recalls. "He didn't like titles. He said, 'You know what you're here for. Go and do it.'" Hiscocks remembers appealing to him at one point after the war for more of an organization chart in engineering. "He said, 'Your job is to be where you're needed.'"[2]

"He gave us a lot of freedom. We never punched time-clocks. People came in late and stayed later. We didn't ask for time off. Of course, you'd come in on Sunday, too.

"Jakimuk encouraged people to come forward with their ideas—like Fred Buller. I wasn't used to that in a senior man. It was a very co-operative, friendly atmosphere."

A family is the term many oldtimers use to describe the pre-Mosquito DHC. In fact, a lot of de Havilland *was* families. There were, among many others, the Burlison brothers, George and Bill, who, with their father, had worked for Canadian Vickers ever since they were building varnished mahogany-planked Vedette flying boats. Or John and George Neal and their sister Kay, each a pioneer there. John was the first Neal to work at DHC, a distinction in itself. George float-certified the Beaver and took the Otter up for its first flight. Kay Neal's career at DHC personifies the wartime growth of the company. Originally a seamstress, she rose from Betty McNicoll's dope shop, where she fitted snug fabric skins to stick-and-wire biplanes and painted them with dope to form a tough, slick surface, to fabricating bulletproof rubber fuel tank liners for Mosquitoes in a shop filled with potentially explosive fumes. (No wonder Kay eventually became secretary-treasurer of de Havilland Local 112 of the Canadian Auto Workers in 1949.) Phil knew them all before the wartime surge in employment made knowing every employee's name out of the question.

The transition from one type of organization to the other was an intense, painful sidelight to one of the most glorious chapters in aviation history: the often-told story of the DH.98 Mosquito's secret development in an old mansion, Salisbury Hall. How the project persevered despite the determination of British aircraft production czar Lord Beaverbrook to kill it—Beaverbrook is said to have ordered it closed down three times. How the company's test pilots, including Geoffrey de Havilland Jr., overcame with spectacular flight demonstrations the Royal Air Force's early reluctance to embrace the cheeky speedster that would soon interrupt speeches by Hermann Goering and Joseph Goebbels in Berlin, in broad daylight, five hours apart on the same day.[3] Mixed emotions remain with the Downsview veterans from the company's difficult metamorphosis into a prime contractor for what was, until the last year of the war, the Allies' fastest aircraft.

Garratt masterminded this growth. In the year leading up to the decision to build the Mosquito, DHC's staff had grown 140 per cent. By March 1942 the parking lot was being expanded to handle the cars of 2,400 employees, and a new cafeteria had replaced the circus tent in which workers had been lunching. By the end of 1942 DHC's employees had more than doubled once more.[4] Hotson remembers that it seemed at the time that no amount of new square footage would be enough.

Managing that kind of growth requires creativity and the ability to adjust, but as the company grew it became less and less the kind of place where the top banana could walk the production lines every day, let alone know all the employees' names. The organization chart was being revised monthly. It was no longer a family-type operation. Garratt deserves credit for overseeing such explosive growth, which brought with it new requirements for internal communication, personnel and, above all else, training. But a gentleman with the personal touch is not necessarily the right guy to push production hard.

Lee Murray, Garratt's predecessor as DHC managing director, who had since become GM at Hatfield, arrived at Downsview at the end of July 1941 to cast his sympathetic eye over the Canadian outfit's production potential and requirements. "A mound of drawings" is Hotson's aptly vague characterization of the Mosquito production materials that soon arrived from the English plant that had run less by modern methods than by its employees' skills and memories. There would also be shipments of vital parts for twenty-five aircraft and a completed Mosquito Mk.IV to show how it all went together.

Murray's report led to orders a month later from the British Ministry of Aircraft Production for 400 Canadian-built Mosquitoes. These would soon be designated Mk.xx—an equivalent of the Mk.iv bomber version, powered by the American-built Rolls-Royce Merlin v-12, the Packard Merlin 31.

Soon after, Doug Hunter and Harry Povey arrived from Hatfield after a trans-Atlantic flight that was, for that time, a marvel of time management. "[They had left] England on Thursday and begun work in Toronto on Saturday" is how Fred Hotson summarizes their then-amazing experience. After that, however, flying across the Atlantic lost much of its charm for Hunter. He may have thought his luck couldn't hold out indefinitely, or perhaps he changed his mind once ocean voyages became less stressful with the demise of the U-boat threat.

Hunter immediately became chief engineer of DHC, a position fully equal to chief design engineer Jakimiuk's—and, at that moment, more valuable to the company. Hunter was regarded as a typical product of the parent de Havilland company.

"He was a well-educated man. Hunter was not a deep technical engineer but he was a very practical one," in Dick Hiscocks's estimation. "He had mastered the art of getting people to work together. During wartime, things were turbulent and nerves were jangled, and he had a very soothing influence on the more temperamental characters in the engineering department. And, like Garratt, he was a very humane man."

Hunter had begun as a draftsman with one of the original British aircraft companies, the Grahame-White Aviation Co., forerunner of the great Bristol Aeroplane Co., de Havilland's only British rival as a combined engine and airframe producer. George White acquired the land for the U.K.'s post-World War I display flying centre and today's RAF Museum, at Hendon. Hotson remembers Hunter as "always immaculately dressed, spoke quietly, flicked his cigarette ashes over his shoulder, and punctuated every conversation with 'Quite!'"

Hunter's travelling companion, Harry Povey, who had been with de Havilland a year longer than Hunter, was slicked-back and rotund to Hunter's grey-haired and aristocratic spareness. Povey has been described as "an aircraft production engineer without peer." His first move at DHC was to ask for a new plant to build Mosquito fuselages.

The fuselages were formed in halves over concrete forms, using heat-treatment in huge autoclaves to shape the seven-sixteenths-inch-thick plywood left and right sides. Stiffeners and equipment were added before the halves were joined along the top and bottom.

DHC's wing subcontractor was the farm-equipment manufacturer Massey-Harris of Weston, which had supplied Anson wings to Downsview. R. B. (Bob) McIntyre began his long association with the DHC engineering department as chief engineer of Massey-Harris, one of the most reliable suppliers the wartime DHC had.[5] Their record of delivering Anson wings made Massey-Harris de Havilland's first choice for Mosquito wings. They delivered the first set May 9, 1942. Always ahead of schedule, McIntyre and his workers became victims of their own efficiency when changes to the specifications of aircraft on the production line obliged Massey-Harris to modify wings already built but waiting in storage at their plant. McIntyre, who was with DHC by 1944, was a first-rate thinker who became a talent magnet for the company, recruiting, among others, Fred Buller.

Aside from the problem-free wings, the Downsview Mosquito program's early setbacks were all too prophetic. A consistent 2 per cent loss rate for important drawings shipped from England was only the beginning. They arrived as microfilm, which had to be translated into full-size profiles and thence to huge sheets of plywood on the lofting-shop floor in mid-October. Lofting, the process of transferring full-scale drawings to raw materials from which the first parts are made, was a normal part of building any new airplane. It was just that DHC had never done that before. The Mk.IV pattern aircraft, RAF serial DK 287, shipped in mid-September, was delayed and damaged en route. But a fuselage jig did appear from England two weeks before Christmas of 1942, allowing a first fuselage shell and a duplicate jig to be available by mid-March.[6]

By May 5, 1942, Phil Garratt was on his way to meetings in England with a contract for an additional 1,100 Mosquitoes, financed by the U.S. Lend-Lease program. As the Mosquito's impressive speed and load-carrying capacities became known, a bidding process began to assert itself for the ones being built at Hatfield, and later at Leavesden and Standard Motors at Coventry. The pressure to expand production was unrelenting. Every air arm that didn't have Mosquitoes wanted them—even the Luftwaffe. Goering's insistence on a night-fighter with equal performance led to an impressive German twin-engine fighter, built largely of wood, called the Focke-Wulf Ta 154 *Moskito*. Only thirty were built.[7]

Hap Arnold, chief of the U.S. Army Air Force, wanted hundreds of Mosquitoes and was prepared to trade P-51 Mustangs for them. In fact, the Americans were underwriting Downsview production with a view to siphoning off Mosquitoes built to U.S. specifications for themselves. To meet all these demands, the Mosquito became a jack-of-all-trades: fighter-bomber, photo-reconnaissance aircraft, night fighter, Pathfinder target-marking aircraft. Leonard Cheshire, VC, commander of 617 Squadron, the famous Dambusters, wanted a pair to mark targets for his precision-bombing Lancaster colleagues.

With the first Downsview example near completion, Garratt left his meetings committed to turning out eight more Mosquitoes during the rest of 1942, and to reaching a production tempo of fifty per month in a year's time.

Despite the close proximity of its serial number to that of the first Canadian-built Mosquito, KB336 is an indication of how quickly models changed on the DHC assembly-line. This B.Mk.20 was part of the fourth batch, and approximately the 265th Mosquito built at Downsview. It is preserved at Canada's National Aviation Museum, Ottawa. PETER M. BOWERS

The first Canadian-built Mosquito, RAF serial KB300, flew on September 23, 1942. One month later, Geoffrey de Havilland Jr. demonstrated it at Wright Field, Dayton, Ohio, the USAAF's flight test centre; then at Bolling Field, Washington D.C., handy to the Pentagon; and then, that December, at the U.S. Naval Air Station at San Diego. The original Mk.IV pattern aircraft from Hatfield, DK 287, was then made available for intensive evaluation at Wright Field in March 1943.

For the most part, despite Hap Arnold's enthusiasm, the Americans were unimpressed. Most of the American aircraft industry had long since ceased building with wood. The most influential American Mosquito exponent was Colonel Elliott Roosevelt, the president's son, who had flown a Mk.IV on reconnaissance in North Africa. By the time the Americans saw potential in a fighter-bomber that was both faster and longer-legged than their P-38, production at DHC, the North American source, was falling far behind schedule. Lee Murray returned from Hatfield in November 1942, this time to stay.

Garratt was able, nevertheless, to address an upbeat message at 1942's year-end to "the DH Family," as he habitually referred to the company, reporting that during the past year "we have produced 362 Ansons, 550 Tiger Moths, overhauled 119 aircraft and 209 engines; all of this on top of the development work on the Mosquito."[8] That same December, though, only four DHC-built Mosquitoes took to the air.

The problems were not entirely of DHC's or Garratt's making. Twice batches of drawings documenting Mosquito variants were lost at sea. Parts from England were being used to substitute for non-arrivals from subcontractors; when Boeing of Canada was late with horizontal stabilizers, or tailplanes, John Slaughter at Downsview built a couple of sets to keep the project moving. Although the original contract with Britain's Ministry of Aircraft Production called for Mk.xx bombers, the contract was altered to include fighter-bombers, with six-gun noses and different windshields, among other changes. Downsview was also required to engineer its own dual-control trainer version. Then yet another change in the order occurred: aircraft on the line were to be converted as F-8 USAAF recon machines. (Only forty F-8s were ever delivered.) By mid-April 1943 only a dozen Mosquitoes had been produced, with fourteen more on the line.

The aspect of the Mosquito production gap that was unquestionably internal was the issue of who would run a single production line amalgamated from the Tiger Moth (Plant One, under Bill Calder and Frank Warren) and Anson (Plant Two, under George Burlison), with Dick Moffett as overall production manager. Harry Povey's status put him in charge of "all production departments," but neither Moffett nor Burlison approved of his production methods—in particular, the wood jigs that wing man Bob McIntyre of Massey-Harris had already refused to work with.[9]

KA 117 was one of 338 solid-nosed, eight-gun FB.26s built at Downsview. These versatile machines could also carry 2,000 lb of bombs. By early 1945 many Canadian-built Mosquitos had logged 50 sorties over Europe. Photographed in England in November 1945, KA 117 had been converted to a dual-control trainer.

PETER M. BOWERS

Meanwhile, the demand for Mosquitoes grew, Hotson notes, "daily." Ottawa was becoming concerned. Ralph P. Bell was a dollar-a-year man installed as Director-General of the Department of Munitions and Supply on whose desk the buck for aircraft production in Canada stopped.

Bell sent his assistant to look the operation over and—surprise!—found three different men claiming to be in charge of production. In reply, the DHC board of directors expressed its confidence in Garratt's management. Bell told the directors he was holding them responsible for the production holdups.

Two weeks later, lawyer J. Grant Glassco, a government-appointed director of DHC since early 1940, reported his assessment of DHC's board to Bell. The two men went to see C.D. Howe, Minister of Munitions. Howe, the most powerful man in Canada at the time, appointed Glassco controller of de Havilland Canada by a secret order-in-council June 8, 1943.[10] Phil Garratt was out.

Howe brought in as DHC works manager a thin, intense ramrod from his home riding of Fort William, Bill Stewardson. Stewardson "just lived, ate and slept aircraft production."[11] He had spent six years with Canadian Car and Foundry at the Lakehead, most of that time as shop superintendent on CCF's licensed Hawker Hurricane production program. Soon after, Dick Moffett and George Burlison resigned to take other positions in the war effort. That October, Harry Povey was asked to return to England.

It took until the fall of 1943 before Downsview's subcontractors other than Massey-Harris began to produce reliably. The events of that year were hard on morale, and a series of bitterly-fought elections brought the United Auto Workers into the company as bargaining agents. During December 1943, Mosquito production hit twenty per month for the first time.

So popular was Phil Garratt with DHC's oldtimers that his departure was not announced to the workers for nearly a year. In the May–June 1944 issue of *The de Havilland Mosquito*, which appeared ten months after he was replaced by Grant Glassco, an item appeared on the second-last page headlined "CHANGE IN MANAGEMENT." That same month of June 1944 Mosquito production was up to fifty-one, the figure Garratt had agreed to be turning out at the beginning of 1943.

Chapter Five

Fred Buller joins DHC

So Phil Garratt was banished to a grand seclusion on the top floor of what was then the tallest building in the British Empire, Toronto's Bank of Commerce building, with his long-term secretary, Ann O'Neil.[1] It did not seem that way at the time, but his eviction from DHC was in retrospect the best thing that could have happened to him and to the company. The exile was not total: he was able to stay in touch with key people at DHC but he wasn't running the operation any more. Instead, he became the company's strategic planner.

The penultimate indignity for P.C., as most people called him, was that as a preliminary to cleaning out his desk he was called upon to sign DHC's first labour union contract. Three days later he vacated his office. The government and the unions had taken over his near-singlehanded creation. Hatfield backed him up, making him a director of the English company, and making sure, with the office suite that towered high over Toronto's waterfront, that he would be physically comfortable, if no more than that.

As painful as Garratt's exile on King Street must have been for the big-hearted chap who revelled in handing out turkeys on the assembly line at Christmas, this was the fallow period during which the only complete line of STOL aircraft in the world was conceived. Phil Garratt didn't sulk. He used the time well. From mid-1943 to the end of the war, he put together the outlines of a design and manufacturing plan that would win him Canada's most prestigious aviation award, the Trans-Canada (McKee) Trophy, twice.

As Garratt envisioned the peacetime program and Jaki Jakimiuk designed modifications for the Mosquitoes now swarming out of Downsview, and as chief engineer Doug Hunter somehow outlasted the series of production bosses hired to supplant him, the perfect idea man drifted seemingly by accident into the DHC engineering department. As random as Fred Buller's presence in 1943 at the periphery of DHC's Mosquito program might have seemed, nothing about him was the slightest bit haphazard or casual. He had, in fact, invited the government to assign him to a job where his talents could do the most for the war effort. The government had sent him to DHC's Central Aircraft subsidiary to break the Mosquito logjam.

Fred Buller was one of those fortunate few who succeed spectacularly in a line of work that is their second choice in life. To make a living at something other than one's favourite activity is common enough. Most people do it. But only a handful somehow manage to so fully integrate their lives that work feeds on recreation, toil on pleasure, and learning becomes not a task but a lifelong habit—a reflex, like breathing. Fred Buller was one of those. It helped that he had the type of mind that thrives on doing more than one thing at once.

Fred would rather have been designing racing yachts. That was his dream. He once told his wife, Betty, that he had been born fifteen years too early to have had a chance to work in that field. He was born May 25, 1914.[2] During the Depression, there was not much of a market in Canada for the high-performance sailboats Fred was able to design only in his mind until the 1950s.

By then, his success as an aircraft engineer enabled him to indulge himself in small-boat design and racing. Fred understood how boats and airplanes operated in similar environments; water and air behave according to the same principles of fluid dynamics. So you could deduce an airplane's behaviour from experimenting with boats, or vice versa. The time Fred spent racing dinghies along the Lake Ontario waterfront was his informal equivalent of hours spent by other engineers in wind tunnels. This insight into waves and winds was by no means original with Fred; Russia's government aviation research body is called the Central Institute of Aerodynamics *and Hydro*dynamics. But, with Fred, the similarity of water and air as vehicles move through them was only the first and most important of many such problem-solving connections he made, many of them linking totally unrelated fields. In retrospect, Fred Buller, working 120 or so miles away from Downsview at DHC's Central Aircraft facility just east of London, Ontario, was the ideal individual to reinvent the bush plane: just the right combination of idea man and hardnosed can-do guy, handy with tools.

As remote from aircraft design as subjects like astronomy and classical music might seem, they mingled in Fred's fertile mind and were expressed in the economy of those small details of the postwar DHC line of aircraft that, Fred used to enjoy telling his son Christopher, all carried features that had roots in the operating systems of the Beaver.

"He was a genius," says his aerodynamicist partner in designing the Beaver, Dick Hiscocks, "at envisioning something in three dimensions, along with all the angles, bits and all the rest of it. People would say Fred was the most talented engineer ever to work at de Havilland Canada."

Working with any genius exacts a price. With Fred and Dick, the problems were not the usual ones. Communication, for instance, is a common roadblock with geniuses. Not in this case. They understood each other almost perfectly. The problem in working with Fred, Dick says, was that "he was a terror to work with because he never got tired like other people."[3]

Frederick Howard Buller was born in Vancouver to Sarah Jeannette Howard of Boston and one of the city's leading doctors, Frederick James Buller. There was mechanical inventiveness in his background: one of Fred's maternal forebears brought the Gatling gun to Canada in time for the Riel Rebellion.

The Vancouver Fred Buller was born into was a city of big dreams, a city little more than a year past its "Golden Years of Growth," a city that aspired to be "the Liverpool of the Pacific." Vancouver had become the mid-point junction of the most advanced land and sea transportation system in the world, the All-Red (meaning All-British) Route that had cut the time from London to Hong Kong by a third. Vancouver's instant status as a global way station imbued it with a false but persistent belief in the city's centrality in the larger scheme of things. Huge real estate fortunes were made from 1907 to 1913 by those who followed Rudyard Kipling's advice to invest in real estate on Vancouver's Fairview Slopes, with their panoramic views of the Coast Mountains. The decline in lumber prices that had already brought the prewar depression to other logging cities such as Seattle and Portland did not visit Vancouver until just before the war. This three-year delay in the pre-First-War depression's arrival at the Buller doorstep until the eve of his birth was due to British Columbia's status as a protected supplier of lumber to Britain.

Even then, Fred's upbringing was comfortable and happy, and centred on summers at Roberts Creek, a community on the Sechelt Peninsula, more commonly known around Vancouver as the Sunshine Coast. It is not far from Vancouver by

Fred Buller and his crew, Brad Guest, sailing a Buller 14 racing dinghy. Fred carefully observed the behaviour of boats and their sails for insights into aerodynamics.
BETTY BULLER

Beaver, but Roberts Creek nevertheless is sufficiently remote by ferry and road to have been a mecca for back-to-the-land types searching for a magic place into the 1970s. It was accessible when Fred was young only by CPR coastal steamers.

The Sunshine Coast is named for its climate: in the rain shadow of Vancouver Island, the peninsula that runs south from Squamish to enclose Howe Sound is dry, almost Mediterranean, at least compared with Vancouver. Three doctors bought adjoining waterfront properties, and Fred loved the Buller cottage enough to have done a painting of it when he was fourteen. Fred was born with many choices in life and only expanded them as he grew, attacking arts, crafts and sciences with a hunger for knowledge and technique that was unquenchable.[4]

If there was a single element to his working personality that defined him, it was Fred's consistent refusal to be defined. He was an original thinker and a relentless upstream swimmer, never content to be doing just one thing. He watched television with his slide rule in hand, often making notes on graph paper. His education was an unending quest for experience rather than credentials, a way to fill in the time before he could get to work on something worthwhile.

After school, most likely at Vancouver's King Edward School, he attended Pickering College in Newmarket, Ontario, for a year, completing Ontario's Grade 13. In all likelihood, he was there just to experience another part of the country. From there he want to the University of British Columbia in 1932, leaving after the spring term of 1935 without a degree, eager to move on. The specifics of his education are unclear, perhaps because he preferred it that way.

"He was usually a jump ahead of his professors," Dick Hiscocks recalls from his conversations with Fred. "He told me that he got bored at UBC"—in engineering, presumably—"so he went off on a tangent with astronomy. He built his own telescope." There is also a story abroad that at some point UBC added up his credits and decided he had earned a degree. In, of all things, forestry.

Fred Buller always judged others strictly by the quality of their work rather than their titles, as he would have wanted to be judged himself, and he was sometimes abrasive in letting his opinions of others be known. He did no politicking in the workplace. "He seldom smiled," Hiscocks says. "But he was fun at a party." Only one photograph exists of Fred Buller even cracking a grin, although sometimes not laughing was his way of being funny.

His next move was to Edinburgh, where in 1935 the Clyde estuary shipyards still led the world. He would give boats one last chance. Whether Fred was discouraged more by the professional prospects there during the Great Depression or by the dour Scottish weather, he was back in Canada at the end of 1936.[5]

It was at that point that he became fully committed to aviation. He travelled to Oakland, California, to attend the Boeing School of Aeronautics in 1937 and '38.

The school was rigorous and highly regarded in the industry. There was no equivalent in Canada, no institution that offered the same combination of hands-on engineering, first and foremost, backed by the necessary minimum of theory. Whether he was granted a formal degree or diploma by the Boeing school would have been of almost no importance to him. We have no record. Academic credentials meant less than they do today. As was the case in England at de Havilland's technical school, the Boeing school's graduates were more sought-after by aircraft manufacturers than degree-holders from such colleges as the University of California and the California Institute of Technology. California's educational authorities deemed the Boeing institution a trade school and therefore not empowered to award a degree. We do know the reputation of the Boeing school opened whatever doors Fred needed to pass through.

Anyone who had completed the Boeing course had hands-on experience maintaining the associated flying school's aircraft and was capable of stepping into the Federal Aviation Authority's office at the other end of the Oakland field and writing

DHC's prototype Fox Moth, a postwar development of Hatfield's DH.83, which first flew in 1932. The English factory claimed it would carry five people on its 120 hp, but Max Ward seldom carried more than three, including himself. CF-DJC was his first airplane in 1946: $10,000 including wheels, skis, and floats. DHC

the mechanic's examination. Boeing students worked eight-hour days, five days a week, fifty weeks a year. One veteran of the 1940–41 course, Peter M. Bowers, became a Boeing Airplane Company engineer maintaining B-17s in India during the war, was a line engineer for many years at Boeing without a degree or any apparent need for one, designed a homebuilt aircraft that could fly in several configurations (as both monoplane and biplane, with or without floats) and has become one of the most widely published aviation historians in the world.

But the lack of a formal engineering degree was a source of frustration for Fred as the Department of Transport's inspectors more and more often looked for credentialled names on DHC's drawings.

"It kept coming to the surface because we had to satisfy the Department of Transport about the qualifications of the people working there," Hiscocks notes. "The DoT could be very unsympathetic, if you like, when problems arose. They usually wanted somebody with a P.Eng. To get a P.Eng in those days, you had to have an engineering degree. And that was a sore point with Fred."[6]

Fred Buller was a serious man, but not as humourless as his portraits suggest. He simply did not smile for photographers. When he did laugh, the effect was usually contagious. BETTY BULLER

Hiscocks believes that Fred Buller's first job was as a maintenance engineer for the legendary B.C. bush pilot Russ Baker. Unfortunately for the record, Baker was an independent operator whether or not someone was paying his salary. It cannot therefore be said that Fred worked either for Punch Dickins's Canadian Airways or Grant McConachie's United Air Transport, both of which employed Baker during 1938 alone. (Betty Buller thinks not.) Certainly Fred Buller knew all three pioneers of northwestern aviation, and certainly Baker needed all the help with maintenance he could get. Among bush pilots in general, Baker was an unusually ham-handed mechanic. His wife, Madge, called him "a screwdriver and hammer man. If the screwdriver didn't work, he'd use the hammer."[7]

We do know that soon after World War II started, Buller had risen to chief engineer at what is now Northwest Industries in Edmonton, one of the most respected overhaul centres in the aviation-minded city that built the first municipal airport in Canada.

Edmonton was the centre of northern bush flying and home base of such famous pilots as Leigh Brintnell and Wop May, the man Manfred von Richthofen had in his Fokker Triplane's gunsight moments before another Canadian, Roy Brown, shot the Red Baron down during World War I. Punch Dickins was a regular there. Knowing so many first-rate pilots gave Buller an idea of what they were looking for in a bush plane, and working on the wide variety of types in use there, many of them obsolete hand-me-downs from major airlines, gave him a pretty comprehensive idea of the state of aviation art and science.

More specifically, Buller had the good fortune to be working for the bush pilot-businessman Leigh Brintnell, whose Mackenzie Air Services' contribution to the war effort was training Canadian and Commonwealth combat pilots. (Baker had left Brintnell's employ in 1936 after one of those "I quit—you're fired" episodes when Baker blamed his ditching of a Mackenzie plane on faulty maintenance.)[8]

It was while working at Mackenzie's maintenance branch, Aircraft Repair, that Fred met Betty, his wife. She liked his lean purposefulness, the way he always seemed to be in a hurry to get somewhere, and the high standards he set for the technical memoranda she typed for him.

"He never walked slowly. He just strode through the engineering department. I never ever thought our lives would be joined in any way. It was obvious that he was doing what he really loved, which is always attractive. He was always working things out with a slide rule. You could see that he had a bright mind."

Evidently Fred thought she was pretty bright too. Betty was ambitious—she had spent time in Paris at the Sorbonne—but had set aside her plans to be a writer or broadcaster to make a contribution to the war effort. Betty was born in London, England, and with her mother and stepfather emigrated in 1929 to Alberta, where he tried farming and then joined the army. Betty had been at Aircraft Repair for a year or two when Fred showed up there in 1942. She was secretary to the entire engineering department, but as time passed Fred relied on her more and more to help with his own projects.

"He once asked me to go through all the aviation and engineering journals, and list everything that might have a bearing on what we were doing. I worked very hard on it, and I don't think it was five minutes [after she passed it to him] before he had a question. Either something was out of place or possibly it was something that was omitted. He just had an eagle eye and a tremendous memory."

Brintnell's chief mechanic was Ernest Krahulec, who broke in with Mackenzie doing on-the-spot accident repairs along the company's Fort McMurray–Fort Chipewyan–Fort Smith–Edmonton circuit for thirty-five cents an hour. Krahulec (pronounced *Kra*-lic) was trained as a sheet-metal mechanic, his second choice when the local British Commonwealth Air Training Plan course for engine overhaul mechanics he wanted to attend was already filled. (He retired as CP Air's chief maintenance engineer after spending many years personally caring for CF-FHB, the Beaver prototype, owned first by Russ Baker's Central B.C. Airways, and then by Pacific Western Airlines.)

Aircraft Repair refurbished any and all of the various British and American types, with their different specifications, used by the BCATP. Mackenzie itself flew a Norseman, a Bellanca Aircruiser, various Fairchilds and Stinsons, and a big Curtiss

Condor biplane airliner. The work called for versatility. To solve problems, the chief engineer often had to redesign aircraft components and make them buildable by the firm's machinists. Then, because the modification could affect the plane's airworthiness, the procedure had to be documented and submitted to the Department of Transport for approval.

In particular, the main landing gear of the Barkley-Grows was giving trouble. Grant McConachie had lifted three of these streamlined, all-metal, twin-engine transports from Canadian Car and Foundry at the Lakehead after the Barkley-Grow's Detroit manufacturer went out of business. He paid a dollar apiece and a promissory note for the rest. Only eleven were built. The Barkley-Grow looked a lot like Lockheed's hot Model 10 series, three of which founded Trans-Canada Air Lines. For some reason (saving weight, probably) the Barkley-Grows had been designed with fixed and spatted, non-retractable landing gear, a retrograde feature. The Lockheeds' gear retracted. One of McConachie's Barkley-Grows found its way to Mackenzie Air Services before the war and was too valuable with the war on to be scrapped—even with the landing gear struts so loose Fred could move the tire with his foot.

Its designers had built the Barkley-Grow with a stainless-steel firewall in each of the two engine nacelles, or housings. The engine was bolted to the front of the firewall and the landing gear struts behind. It was this hard-working firewall that was loose. Stainless steel unfortunately is hard to machine or drill. Instead, Buller designed an internal system of stiffeners and trusses that took some of the load off the overburdened firewall. That, coupled with a collar for the gear strut, turned the Barkley-Grow's outstanding liability into at least a reliable mechanism. Three of the six eventually acquired by Canadian Pacific Airlines soldiered on into the 1960s on the West Coast, where the aircraft was sized right and could take floats.

Then there was the ongoing problem of access to the Barkley-Grow's air, oil and fuel filters through its then-advanced all-metal skin. Fred had to design and somehow attach openable access panels for an aluminum skin not stressed to take them.

Krahulec remembers: "This was one of the first all-metal airplanes. You couldn't just add a handhold [because the stressed skin was part of the airplane's structure]. There were no drains where there were fuel filters. I wanted to cut a hole so we could get access from the outside. [To strengthen the surrounding metal] he had to put a doubler on with *eight* machine screws.

"Later we got practical. Machine screws at 40-below? Later we used Dzus [one-twist] fasteners and a hinge to make a little door."

Fred was probably best known for designing a ski-wheel landing gear that could be adapted for use on many of the aircraft in Mackenzie's diverse inventory. The forward tips were held up, while in the air, by a rubber strip peeled from an automobile tire that stretched to accommodate the nose-up position of tailwheel aircraft on the ground. To install the ski, the aircraft was simply rolled onto it and the landing gear wheel engaged with a diagonally-mounted fork arrangement that was pinned, at the fork ends, to each end of the wheel's axle. The wheel emerged only slightly through the ski. The system was patented by Mackenzie. Buller also designed a tail ski for the Tiger Moths of No. 2 Air Observer School, Edmonton.

"That was the kind of thing Fred would do," Krahulec fondly recalls. "He would have to do stress analyses. That's part of your submission [for a certification to fly with the modification] to the Department of Transport. But the practical part of it—it's got to do the job. And that was part of the experience Fred got, so when he designed the Beaver, it was a practical airplane."[9]

As an example of a practical, well-designed feature on the Beaver that might have been inspired by his early wartime work in Edmonton, Krahulec points with some satisfaction to its rubber-sprung nutcracker-type wheeled landing gear.[10]

Fred Buller appears in the middle of the back row of this group portrait of Canadians at the Boeing School of Aeronautics, Oakland, in 1939. Dick Fisher, who upon retirement was assistant director of maintenance for CP Air, stands second from the right. The Boeing 247D was on loan to the school from United Airlines. VIA CHRIS BULLER

The Beaver's simple wheeled landing gear, another of Fred Buller's overnight inspirations. Shock absorption is supplied by the stack of rubber doughnuts at the top of the strut. Maintenance consists of replacing the doughnuts every five years or so. DHC

Soon, like such BCATP instructor pilots as Russ Bannock, Fred Buller began to yearn for work closer to the action. He had his own way of finding it. He wrote a letter to Ottawa outlining his background and inviting any appointment that the powers-that-be deemed would take full advantage of his talents.

In late April 1943, the government assigned him to the Crumlin airfield at London, Ontario, where DHC's subsidiary Central Aircraft was the transit-point in delivering newly-built but not fully flight-tested Mosquitoes.[11] As the production rate began to soar, the fifty-five planes a month DHC was assembling by June 1944 began to exhibit flaws. Even near-perfect Mosquitoes overwhelmed the production test crew by their sheer numbers.

Created to design, prototype and manufacture Canadian modifications on Mosquitoes, Central Aircraft, under the direction of Francis Hyde-Beadle, was no more organized for mass-production than Downsview had been. Hyde-Beadle had moved twice after leaving Fairchild in search of original design work, but there were signs that Central Aircraft would be doing it by the numbers, just like Downsview, by the time he died—a genuine British aviation pioneer—eleven days before Christmas 1943.

To this bottleneck in the most advanced combat-aircraft production stream in Canada, Ottawa sent Fred Buller in the spring of 1943. All we know is that the problem was solved, and that, having succeeded Hyde-Beadle as head of Central Aircraft, Buller was one of the small band of wartime additions invited to join the select postwar crew at Downsview by Bob McIntyre. Fred Buller joined the DHC engineering department in mid-September 1944.

Thus it was that a self-made design genius with a wide-ranging mind and a healthy disregard for credentials arrived at a company run, when it was returned to private ownership after the war, by people who did not like organization charts and valued personal initiative above all other qualities. If Phil Garratt liked his engineers to be where they were needed, a bright, restive fellow like Fred Buller, who hated nothing more than sitting behind his desk, was likely to have found at Downsview a permanent home. "He thrived at de Havilland," Betty Buller thought. Fred stayed there for thirty-five years.

Well before the end of the war, Phil Garratt had authorized drawings to be made of his first vision for a scaled-down, peacetime DHC. This was his flying half-ton pickup truck. Mostly through Jaki Jakimiuk's influence, it was foreseen as a neat, streamlined, all-metal, high-wing monoplane with a two-ton all-up weight, built around a new 330-hp air-cooled in-line engine Hatfield was working on, the Gipsy Queen. Jakimiuk was an artist among aircraft designers, and it showed in his scheme for DHC's postwar bush plane.

When people who were there compare the Beaver with the Polish PZL fighters, they are paying tribute to Jakimiuk's finesse in shaping the first all-metal aircraft designed specifically as a bush plane. His scheme was in some ways more advanced than the production Beaver. Certainly it was more elegant.

The nose, in particular, was pointed, and the rest of the aircraft was consistent with this low-drag layout. It was smaller than the eventual Beaver and had a fully cantilevered—that is, internally braced—wing that needed no external strut. It also had teardrop wheel spats, a stylish but impractical feature in the north, where they could become clogged with snow and freeze up.

These drawings were prepared just before the war ended and were being used to promote the bush plane concept by DHC's sales force, headed by A.F. (Sandy) MacDonald.

A photograph of Wes Hurley of MacDonald's sales force and engineer Bob McIntyre, taken in March 1945, shows the two examining drawings of this sleek early design. It was MacDonald who circulated the famous questionnaire asking bush pilots what they were looking for in an aircraft on November 20, 1946.

The answers to that questionnaire are often credited with some of the more thoughtful features eventually incorporated into the Beaver. But the airplane MacDonald was talking about as the war ended was vastly different from the Beaver that made its first flight less than a year after the questionnaire was circulated. The differences can be credited almost entirely to the instincts of Fred Buller and Dick Hiscocks, neither of whom had designed much more than parts of airplanes before.[12]

In the eight months between Hiscocks's arrival at Downsview, just before Christmas 1946, and the Beaver's first flight eight months later, the project then known to its designers as the DHC-X would become a very different airplane.

Chapter Six

DHC-X: Halfway to greatness

Much of the eight-month period during which the
DHC-X bush plane project was transformed was
taken up with finishing the design of the aircraft that
became DHC's first postwar product, the DHC-1
Chipmunk. The Chipmunk went from go-ahead to first flight in seven months
flat. One reason relative youngsters like Fred Buller and Dick Hiscocks were given
their head on the Beaver was the fact that Jaki Jakimiuk was so busy with the
Chipmunk. As much as Phil Garratt looked forward to putting a bush plane into
production, he knew there would be a more immediate market for a basic trainer
to replace the Tiger Moth.

The Tiger Moth design dated back to 1931. Many of its components were older
in origin. Commonwealth air forces—and then there were dozens of them—had
introduced their wartime aircrew recruits to the joys of flight in this fully aerobatic,
easily maintained two-seater. Perhaps the most germane of many compliments the
Chipmunk has garnered is that, with its modern design, it flies much like a Tiger
Moth. And it lasted even longer as a military trainer.

There was plenty of time to introduce the bush plane because immediately after the war commercial aviation, especially bush operators, favoured the cheap war-surplus converted military types that flooded the market soon after hostilities ceased. For those operators, Downsview would quickly resume building the prewar DH-83C Fox Moth, which DHC was able to market for $10,500. This was half the price of a bare-bones Beaver two years later.

The Fox Moth was little more than a Tiger Moth with a bigger fuselage holding two seats in a fully enclosed cabin (while the pilot remained outdoors), and it could be built from Tiger Moth spare parts and engines stockpiled at BCATP bases across Canada. Workers were dispatched from Downsview to scrounge Tiger Moth wings, instruments and mothballed Gipsy Major engines for the Fox Moth. Max Ward bought one.

It was shortly after the first flight of the postwar Fox Moth, CF-BFI-X, on December 5, 1945, that Dick Hiscocks returned to DHC. Like Fred Buller, he had experienced a fulfilling war. There was his work at the National Research Council developing the technology for the all-wood Anson V. Better yet, Hiscocks had been one of the aerodynamicists from Allied countries selected to review captured German wind-tunnel data for possible application to aircraft projects underway at their companies. Most of the research concentrated on the problems of high-speed flight, in which the Germans led the world.[1]

But Hiscocks's fateful lesson happened to concern low-speed flight. It came from Reimar Horten, who, like Jack Northrop in America, was committed to exploiting the superior efficiency of tailless aircraft without fuselages, or flying wings.[2]

Theoretically, having the entire aircraft generate lift allows greater loads to be carried farther. But the problems of controlling such aircraft in flight had not yet been overcome.

Reimar Horten and his brother Walter, a Luftwaffe fighter pilot, had seen a captured P-51 Mustang, the first mass-produced fighter designed with a so-called laminar-flow wing, and had incorporated such a wing profile into one of their flying-wing research gliders. A laminar-flow wing has its point of maximum thickness set well back along its chord, or front-to-back width, with the result that the lift-producing airflow over its upper surface follows the wing surface contours longer. (Behind that point of maximum thickness, the air tends to break away from the wing's surface, causing drag.)

However, the Hortens found that at the speeds the glider was designed to reach, laminar flow was a handicap. At slow speeds, less lift was generated. Laminar flow made it easier for the Merlin-powered Mustang to reach its maximum speed of more than 400 mph, but the reduced lift at slower speeds made the Horten flying-wing gliders almost unflyable. What Hiscocks took home from the Hortens' advice was an awareness of scale effects: that the properties of a fast-flying wing were not necessarily those of a slow-flying, or short takeoff and landing (STOL) wing.

Aero engineers with such strong theoretical backgrounds were in demand at the dawn of the jet age. The new Avro plant at Malton (the government's wartime Victory Aircraft) was working on the world's first jet airliner and would soon start work on the CF-100 fighter project. Avro offered Hiscocks more money. Also, based upon his experience at Hatfield, Hiscocks wondered whether, as an academic type straight from the National Research Council, "I would be more hindrance than help" at DHC.

An intermediate DHC-X bush plane design: the Jakimiuk-Stepniewski scheme with Dick Hiscocks's braced wing in February 1947. In March, it would get the Pratt & Whitney Wasp Junior engine that made it great. DHC

Hiscocks had sat down to lunch in Ottawa with Phil Garratt a year before, in late 1944. By then the two men went back seven years together. Garratt had been sponsoring Hiscocks's career since the mid-Depression, so his invitation to return to DHC carried extra weight.

When he returned from Germany in the waning days of 1945, Hiscocks went to work at Downsview. He remembers being introduced to the engineering staff by Doug Hunter, and that the first individual whose hand he shook was Fred Buller.

Dick and Fred had lunch together that day. Dick felt that he and Fred hit it off "from the word go" because their interests were so similar. They worked together in a small office on the mezzanine floor of a wartime assembly hangar, one of a group of three such hangars, served by smaller ancillary buildings for such specialized functions as painting aircraft, located at the north end of the airfield at Downsview. (DHC, now the Regional Aircraft Division of Bombardier, has been located since the 1950s at the south end of the property.) The mezzanine ran along one wall of the hangar and overlooked the shop floor.[3]

The office itself had plywood walls with wood battens where the sheets of plywood met. It was small, perhaps fourteen by twelve feet. Their desks were set back-to-back. Neither had a drawing-board. Any sketches that came from the office were executed by Fred, often illustrating an idea in three dimensions. He passed them on to the draftspeople below and supervised their translation into parts or assemblies. Dick was responsible for the stress calculations as well as the aerodynamics, and for support he had a small technical team that ranged from three to five people. All of the technical reports required by the Department of Transport to certify the Beaver as airworthy were prepared by this group. Fred had half a dozen draftsmen working with him, as well as the powerplant group, comprising Jim Houston and an assistant. Fred also supervised the lofting department, which was responsible for producing all of the full-scale patterns from which parts were made. The important day-to-day liaison between engineering and the shop floor usually devolved upon Fred, although Dick would become involved if the inspection department wanted an opinion in an area that concerned airworthiness. Dick's main piece of equipment was a desk calculator. Both he and Fred had slide rules, of course—two-foot-long slide rules.

"That was it," Hiscocks recalls fondly. "Pads and pads and pads of paper, of course. And files of technical reports coming out of our ears." The Beaver was designed entirely by hand.

Reimar Horten's advice not to use a laminar-flow wing if he wanted high lift rather than high speed was a lesson Hiscocks began to apply as soon as he joined DHC and found himself working on the bush plane. There was only so much he could do to improve the performance of a design he soon began to think of as a dog. But he could certainly improve the wing.

The limits Hiscocks was dealing with were imposed by the Beaver as it had been designed during 1945. For the most part, Hiscocks had to work within the constraints of an ongoing project about which he had misgivings. He and Fred set up shop in their small office, and the two addressed the bush plane's problems.[4]

The first and foremost of these was power. Because DHC was still a branch of the English de Havilland company, it was simply assumed that the plane would be built to British standards and use a de Havilland engine. The most powerful DH piston engine then under development was the Gipsy Queen 50/70 series, an upgraded version of the timeless and highly efficent Gipsy series of in-line, air-cooled, inverted aero engines that originated with Major Frank Halford's 135-hp prototype of 1927. The Gipsy series was developed specifically for light aircraft. Their in-line layout made for fully streamlined installations. Being air-cooled, they did not require the plumbing associated with most in-line aero engines. Being installed with the crankshaft uppermost allowed most Gipsy powerplants to drive propellers directly, without heavy transfer gears or transmission systems. And they were durable.

When subsequently derated to 100-hp and thus subjected to reduced strain, the Gipsy became "almost certainly the first small engine to be good for a 500-hour time-between-overhauls."[5] An impressive achievement. But would the same basic engine be as reliable pumping out 330 horsepower?

As aerodynamicist, Hiscocks was not responsible for the bush plane's engine; powerplant engineer Jim Houston was. Hiscocks had to be aware of it, though, because the major assemblies of an aircraft are interdependent, and Hiscocks believed it would be underpowered with the Gipsy Queen engine, especially on floats. Even if the engine people at Hatfield could get a reliable 330 horsepower out of this development of their standard prewar motor—and Hiscocks and Buller were skeptical about that—it was clear that the aerodynamicist would have to come up with a wing profile that would generate as much lift as possible to help the bush plane get off the water.

First, though, Hiscocks had to double-check the design work that had already been done. It speaks volumes about the self-assurance of Jaki Jakimiuk's supervision of the DHC design engineering staff that Hiscocks's first assignment as a newcomer was to second-guess the aerodynamic implications of Jaki's beautiful preliminary design.

First, Hiscocks had to determine, should the wing remain high on the fuselage? That was easy. The only real shortcoming of the all-metal Junkers transports, when used on floats, was their low-wing design. Their wingtips were constantly interfering with docks. Low wings could be an advantage when the ice began to melt in springtime: if the skis broke through the ice, most of the airplane stayed high and dry. But why design for disaster? On the whole, the requirement to dock a floatplane without denting its wingtips almost answered the question of high or low wing by itself.

A more fundamental issue was whether Jakimiuk's elegant, fully cantilevered, internally braced wing should remain fully self-supporting. Hiscocks's calculations showed that an internal spar that could take all of the wing loads would be bulky enough—ten inches deep at its midpoint—to restrict the pilot's headroom where it passed through the cockpit. And it would be heavy. Hiscocks recommended the wing be externally braced with a single strut on each side. Weight was a secondary consideration. This rework saved about 4 or 5 per cent of the wing's 450-pound overall weight.

With the wing's location and structural design taken care of, the question of how to improve its lift characteristics now came up. One way would be to take Reimar Horten's advice and do the opposite of what the P-51 Mustang's aerodynamicists had done: Hiscocks would move the wing's point of maximum thickness as far forward as he dared. Rather than take an existing airfoil, such as one of those developed by the National Advisory Committee for Aeronautics, America's foremost aviation research agency (and forerunner of today's National Aeronautics and Space Administration), he would devise the bush plane's wing section himself.[6] He drew the shapes of its upper and lower surfaces to maximize lift, knowing that at the speed the bush plane was intended to cruise, the resulting drag would not be a serious problem. The airfoil was drawn on the basis of calculations of the lift necessary to get an airplane with a 4,000-pound all-up weight off the water, with, he guessed, about 250 horsepower and the relatively small propeller it would drive.

It was an audacious move for a relative newcomer like Hiscocks to replace his supervisor's standard and proven airfoil with one of his own. Subsequent events would make it a master stroke.

All aircraft design engineering consists of compromises between opposing forces, with the balance moved back or forth in accord with other factors. In this case, the other factor was low power. Essentially, Hiscocks was over-designing the wing's airfoil to compensate for the shortcomings of its anticipated engine.

It would also help if the entire trailing edge of this wing could be made to work as flaps, further accentuating the deep curve of the wing's upper surface along the entire span. An airplane's ailerons, the hinged control surfaces at the outboard trailing edges of its wing, regulate its flight in the rolling plane, making turns possible. Usually they work against each other: when one is up, the other is down. The airplane rolls in the direction of the upturned aileron. The trick to making ailerons act as flaps is making them droop together and in conjunction with the flaps at certain times, and then in opposition to each other in turns.

This had been done before. The Noorduyn Norseman was equipped with what are called "drooped ailerons," but they were not considered utterly reliable.[7] Unfortunately, pilots are generally committed to the hazards of takeoffs and landings before they discover whether their ailerons are drooping in unison.

When it became known that Hiscocks and Buller were fooling around with the idea of drooped ailerons, all hell broke loose. Not among their superiors, but among the customers who dropped into the plant like important stockholders. Hiscocks remembers George Ponsford, a potential twenty-five-airplane customer with the Ontario Provincial Air Service, who reacted by saying, "Nothin' doin'. We should make up our minds about whether these things are flaps or ailerons, and stick with it."

Hiscocks had his own reservations. "It was clear to me that with the Gipsy engine, a simple wing would not work, especially with floats. By the end of the day, it was very complex. I was very cautious in selling it. I knew management. If it was, 'These guys in engineering are dreaming up new elaborations....' So I knew what we needed. But I thought the mechanical complexity that would be required would send people running for cover."

Within their joint cubbyhole, Hiscocks soon found himself in more or less the same kind of relationship with Fred Buller that Ernest Krahulec had enjoyed in Edmonton. Krahulec wanted to do something with the Barkley-Grow, and Buller would figure out how to do it.

Hiscocks recalls fondly, "I would say, 'This is what we need to do.' And Fred would say, 'I think we can do that. It's not all that complicated.' And the next day he came in with a relatively simple drawing of a mechanism that would work."[8]

Still, Hiscocks and Buller found it prudent not to broadcast their achievement lest it be rendered stillborn by legions of naysayers. They reached an agreement with the doubtful Garratt and Jakimiuk to leave the drooped aileron system intact for flight testing. That drawing, and many others like it, was stamped Prototype Only—Not for Production.[9]

For Hiscocks, the story of the Beaver's drooped ailerons only goes to show what a major role happenstance plays in the design process. "I decided that, with that power and weight it would be a dog, unless we could do some clever things with aerodynamics. Fred thought of ways to do them. We went to this, quote, complex, unquote, mechanism—by the standards of the day—because we thought that with the original powerplant the plane would be a dog on floats."[10]

The Beaver was becoming less of a dog as 1946 passed. By autumn it was halfway to greatness.

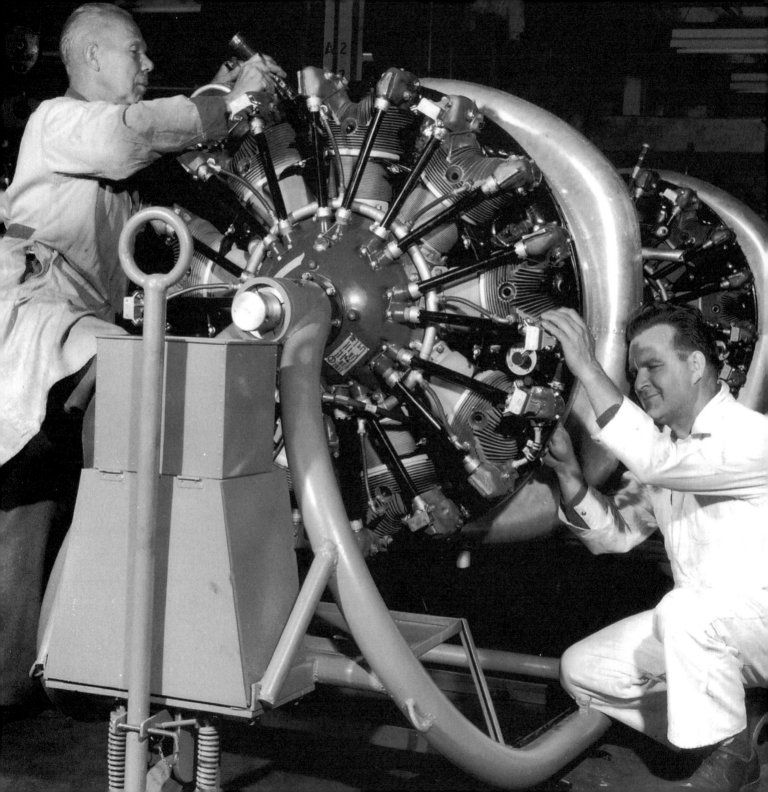

Chapter Seven

Phil Garratt's half-ton flying pickup truck becomes the Beaver

During September 1946 the question of what specifications and performance figures the sales staff could legitimately quote to customers for the bush plane was becoming an issue. Dick Hiscocks, asked by Jaki Jakimiuk to review the predicted performance figures, calculated that the best continual cruise speed that could be hoped for with a 250-hp Gipsy Queen engine was 129 mph. The best maximum economical cruise would be 126 mph—too close for comfort to the specified 125 mph cruise the customers were expecting.[1]

But cruise performance was not the main concern. As Punch Dickins would later put it, for a bush plane "the competition is the dogsled." In his memo to Jakimiuk dated September 12, Hiscocks simply advised that a lower "'quotation' value may be preferable." Just claim a lower cruise speed, was his suggestion. Then he added: "Fast take-off and initial climb prospects are not too good with the proposed power loading [power-to-weight ratio], high engine rpm and relatively small propeller. It is suggested that the specification be made as broad as possible in order to permit alternative layouts in the event that the present scheme should prove inefficient."

In other words, Hiscocks was urging his chief engineer to keep the engine question open as long as possible. Five days after Hiscocks wrote his memo, however, authorization for preliminary engineering studies on the project still known as the DHC-X was given.

That meant DHC was intending to proceed with the Gipsy Queen bush plane. It had the effect of concentrating everyone's attention on a problem that had been for the most part the private domain of Buller, Hiscocks and powerplant engineer Jim Houston, the young men sweating the details.

Hiscocks believes that Jakimiuk was the consummate diplomat, well aware of his engineering staff's reservations about the Gipsy Queen and willing to see whether the proposed beefed-up 330-hp version was going to survive its testing at Hatfield. On the other hand, whether he meant to or not, Doug Hunter became the personification of DHC's determination to use the parent company's engine in the bush plane—at least in the eyes of the young Canadians who were drawing it up. As chief engineer, Hunter's status was at least equal to that of Jakimiuk as chief design engineer, and Hunter's prestige was enhanced by his expertise in the production and manufacturing end of the engineering department. Hunter deserved a lot of the credit for finally meshing the British and Canadian companies' ways of doing things, an achievement that made possible the abrupt increase in Mosquito production during mid-1944.

Hunter's influence kept the Gipsy Queen in the paper DHC-X until after Christmas 1946, when the absence of good news from Hatfield's engine department made him and Jakimiuk decide to take the *Queen Mary* to England to see the new engine on the test-bench for themselves. Hunter left word that nothing was to be changed in their absence. To Buller and Hiscocks, the bush plane, now two-thirds complete as a design and nearly together in mock-up form, appeared frozen in mediocrity.

Much of the work that had already gone into that first conceptual design for the Beaver found expression in the Chipmunk trainer, an airplane as cute and as popular as its name. The same hand is apparent; Jakimiuk, an artistic designer, did the early schemes for both. Move the wing from the upper position on the early bush plane to the lower position on the trainer, install Hatfield's proven Gipsy Major engine and add a two-person sliding canopy, and you have, essentially, the Chipmunk. Fred Buller found common ground with Jakimiuk in arguing for all-metal primary structure, stressed-skin construction on the Chipmunk, and was responsible for detail design of the rear fuselage and landing gear.[2]

Francis St. Barbe, the salesman among the de Havilland company's 1920 originals, was visiting the newly-reinstalled Phil Garratt at Downsview when he spotted a model of the tandem trainer on the managing director's desk and told him if he built it, he, St. Barbe, would sell it to the Royal Air Force. And he did.

Thus the DHC-1 Chipmunk, named after the sprightly little animals that hopped around the Garratt cottage in Muskoka, became the first Canadian military design sold overseas and the first to be licence-built in another country. No fewer than a thousand were built for the RAF at Hatfield and Broughton, England, and sixty more at the Portuguese government's OGMA factory. DHC-built Chipmunks were shipped to India (forty-three), Egypt (twenty-two) and Thailand (eighteen). Chipmunks for the Royal Canadian Air Force were assembled in batches of forty-seven up to 1952 and sixty were ordered in 1956. Five more were sold to flying clubs in Canada.[3] The Chipmunk was only recently retired from RAF service, with many of their examples sold to flying clubs.

Soon after the first flight of the Chipmunk, in the hands of Hatfield's Pat Fillingham on May 22, 1946, production of the trainer became Downsview's first new-aircraft production program since the war. Fillingham was imported from England to make the flight partly as an expression of Hatfield's interest in the Chipmunk, which the English company eventually manufactured in much larger numbers than Downsview.[4] Moreover, Fillingham was an experienced test pilot.

Russ Bannock had arrived during the first week of May and was immediately immersed in flying almost as wide a range of aircraft types as he had as an instructor with the BCATP.

DHC was making ends meet by rebuilding Lancasters and PBY Canso flying boats for the RCAF, and restarting the Fox Moth production line for civil operators. All these aircraft had to be flight-tested, and Bannock came with the backing of the Hatfield organization—St. Barbe in particular—to become chief test pilot and operations manager at Downsview. His first non-flying assignment was to look over the responses to Sandy MacDonald's questionnaire of the previous November to determine which of the suggested features could be incorporated into the bush plane.

From early May, when Bannock joined the company, through mid-June, when the DHC bush plane's rival, the Fairchild F-11 Husky, first flew, through September, when Dick Hiscocks was expressing his concerns about the performance figures for the DHC-X, to the go-ahead for engineering studies September 20, completion of a wooden mockup and the preparation of Sandy MacDonald's questionnaire, sent out November 20 to the bush flying community, Russ Bannock had a ringside seat for the development of what was still Jaki Jakimiuk's design, aerodynamically enhanced by Dick Hiscocks's wing and its lift devices, which were operated by Fred Buller's ingenious linkage. This was the critical moment.[5]

Capt. Clennell H. (Punch) Dickins DFC, an RAF seven-victory ace, joined James Richardson's Western Canada Airways in 1927 and won Canada's highest aviation award, the McKee Trophy, for long survey flights "over unmapped and desolate territory" in Canada's north. During the Second World War he organized the ferry service to fly newly manufactured aircraft to Europe, and joined DHC in 1947. VIA JOHN DICKINS

When he received a copy of MacDonald's letter, the great Clennell H. "Punch" Dickins was pondering the next step in one of Canada's most impressive aviation careers.

Dickins, a seven-victory ace with the Royal Flying Corps and recipient of the Distinguished Flying Cross during World War I, flew some of the first-ever flights to the Far North and the Mackenzie delta. As chief pilot of Western Canada Airways of Winnipeg, he was the second winner of the McKee Trophy in 1928 for his efforts in opening up northern and western Canada to air travel. Too old for combat during World War II, Dickins helped form the Atlantic Ferry Organization on behalf of Canadian Pacific Airlines. Ferrying North American-built bombers to England was still a hazardous trip in 1941, with unpressurized aircraft carrying no creature comforts and no radar.

Like so many other bush pilots who received the questionnaire from Sandy MacDonald late in 1946, Punch Dickins did have opinions about what a new bush plane should look like. Above all else, he thought a bush plane, especially one mounted on floats, should have plenty of power. A consensus was forming in that respect.

Better yet, Dickins was ready to back up his advice with a commitment to sell the airplane if he liked it. Coming from the dean of Canadian bush pilots, that meant Buller and Hiscocks might yet carry the day. Dickins joined DHC on January 10, 1947.

Russ Bannock's best estimate of the exact timing of the climactic events in the Beaver's evolution is that they took place during March 1947. Bannock's estimate is based upon his flight logs, which he does not consider totally reliable as records, but seem to be the only dates available.[6] The few people involved in the Beaver's power-plant decision who are still alive were too busy at the time to keep notes.

In any event, it was Phil Garratt's custom to reserve a suite at the Windsor Hotel in Montreal, and he made a habit of meeting Pratt & Whitney of Canada president Jim Young there once a month. The news from Young this day was that the company had secured certification of war-surplus R-985 Wasp Junior radial engines for civil and commercial use, provided they were overhauled by P&W of Canada from the massive stockpile of parts left from the war. Most of these R-985s were built for wartime use under licence outside P&W's factory.

The Wasp Junior dated back to 1929 but had never really been replaced in the intermediate 450-horsepower class. The R-985 (denoting its 985-cubic-inch capacity) had been used on the Canadianized Avro Anson V. The Wasp Junior was also used in the Twin Beech or Expeditor, flown at the time by many air forces, including the RCAF, and the German Goose amphibian. It was as throughly proven an aero engine as any in use in 1947.[7]

Bannock remembers Young's pitch to Garratt: "You're really making a mistake, Phil. You've got the makings of a fine plane. You're going to power it with an untried engine. Why not put the R-985 in? Put the Wasp in, and you'll have a reserve of power. There were thousands built during the war and you can have them dirt cheap."[8]

It was true. Wasp Juniors still in their crates were going for $35, although, rebuilt for certification, they would cost DHC $9,000 apiece.[9]

The rest is fairly well documented, since so many people were involved.[10] While Jakimiuk and Hunter were eastbound in mid-Atlantic, word came from Hatfield that the Gipsy Queen had broken down on the test-stand. Soon after he read the telegram, Phil Garratt looked out his office window and saw Fred Buller crossing Sheppard Avenue on his way to an early lunch.

Garratt put the telegram down and lit out after Buller. As Fred described it later to company historian Fred Hotson, Garratt came to him as he sat alone at a table staring into a bowl of corn chowder. In fact, Buller and the powerplant engineers were "having more than a little trouble balancing the long engine and positioning the accessories... the conversation soon came around to the new plane and its engine."[11]

When Garratt brought up the P&W radial engine, "Buller was slow to reply. He was inwardly elated that the boss was taking this approach but was exceedingly cautious in view of the directive he had received from Hunter. When he was sure P.C. was serious, Fred Buller admitted that it would be practical to switch to the P&W engine and it could be accomplished even with two-thirds of the aircraft designed. He was told to check out the details and report."

"I do recall," Hiscocks says today, "when Fred and Jim Houston were summoned to Garratt's office to decide whether the idea of switching engines was sound or not."[12]

To begin with, the wider but flat radial needed new engine mounts. Ernest Krahulec believes this was a very early use on a small airplane of dynafocal engine mounts, soft chunks of rubber positioned to redirect the engine's vibration back toward its source, the central crankshaft. He says you can move a Beaver's propeller back and forth some distance because of the softness of its engine mounts.

Hiscocks went to work redesigning the firewall and widening the oval fuselage to one that was more square in section, vastly improving the plane's carrying capacity. With the additional power, it could be a 5,000-pound airplane with the half-ton payload Garratt had envisaged.

The wing was strengthened. Longer landing gear legs were designed to accommodate the larger-diameter Hamilton Standard two-bladed propeller that would take advantage of the Wasp Junior's greater power. (And, incidentally, make the Beaver the operatic performer that it is. The longer propeller blades are, the more likely their tips will go close to supersonic on takeoff, making the unholy racket Beavers are famous for.)[13]

Everything just seemed to fall into place behind the big radial. Not just the hardware of the airplane, but the aerodynamics as well.

One compromise was the position of the radial in the nose. How far forward should it go? Hiscocks's role was to make sure the new balance would satisfy the airplane's stability and control requirements, and to revise all stress and performance calculations, "work I was very happy to do."

The real chore fell to Buller and Jim Houston, the powerplant engineer. They faced the dilemma of moving the R-985 radial engine, which was 50 per cent heavier than the engine it replaced, practically into the cockpit. Needless to say, that was not an option. Garratt, who felt that English cockpits were invariably too small, wanted a cockpit "big enough for a horse." Jakimiuk wanted room for a peasant's—that is, his—feet. "Buller and Houston tore their hair out on this one," Hiscocks chuckles.

The compromise was an engine that often seems to be just the other side of the instrument panel, and the Beaver's characteristic snub-nosed look.

"It was really the combination of high power and high-lift flaps that made the Beaver the first serious STOL airplane," says Hiscocks, sounding more than a little satisfied at the turn of events. By designing his wing to compensate for marginal performance, Hiscocks made the Beaver a world-beater when it was given more power. It is an axiom of aerodynamics that greater lift means more drag. The only way to overcome drag is with more power.

The bush plane became easier to name as the more muscular shape emerged. It had been Garratt's idea to name the trainer the Chipmunk. He proposed continuing to name the DHC line of aircraft after Canadian mammals. "It did not take long to relate the hard-working beaver to the bush plane they had in mind" at the directors' meeting where the name question came up, "and even before coffee was served the decision was made," Hotson tells us.[14]

Punch Dickins is often credited with those thoughtful smaller features of the Beaver that set it apart from all other bush planes, such as the oil spout at the base of the control-wheel stalk that enables the pilot to add oil in flight, and the battery on rails that can be slid out of the fuselage so it can be kept warm overnight. Certainly the crew doors on each side of the cabin that enable the pilot to exit without climbing over the cargo load, no matter which side of the aircraft ends up nearest the dock, and the big cargo doors on both sides of the cabin that can take an oil barrel rolled aboard on its side, were simple and logical responses to frequent bush-flying situations. They simply made sense, even if they had not been done before.

For Hiscocks, the various doors that were cut into his and Fred Buller's fuselage were raising questions about what, in engineering terms, they would be left with. In addition to the doors on the prototype, a floor hatch for agricultural purposes and a roof hatch for emergencies were added at the request of customers. The military then added windows over the cockpit.

"On a strength-to-weight basis, a shell is great—consider an egg, for example— until you put a hole in it," Hiscocks points out. "The shell of our airplane seemed to require an alarming number of holes.... This went on until the skin was punctured in so many places that the structure was neither shell nor truss. No one knew where the loads went and we had to do a lot of ad hoc testing to prove to ourselves and the Department of Transport that it was in fact a structure and not a mechanism."[15]

Chapter Eight

But will it fly? Testing the Beaver

Russ Bannock's unscheduled dead-stick landing after the Beaver's abbreviated first flight was a tantalizing glimpse of the bush plane's potential. He had noted its impressive power and, of course, had glided it back down with the Wasp Junior barely ticking over. No test pilot expects to examine a prototype's power-off performance during a first flight, although that is always a possibility. The Beaver's ability to glide was one preview of its short-landing-and-takeoff behaviour. Things could have been worse.

"As I was in the air only about twenty minutes, I was reluctant to offer much comment about the Beaver's characteristics, other than to say, 'It was very pleasant to fly.' I chose to wait until I'd had a more detailed first flight," Bannock recalls.

"I went back to my office. After only about an hour Doug Hunter phoned me to say we were ready to go again. It turned out that the oil system had been purged and checked the previous day and a non-return valve had been reinstalled upside-down, which caused the oil to siphon out as soon as I became airborne. As I had shut down while there was some oil left in the system, there was no engine damage.

"I took off about noon for either a continuation of the first flight or a second flight, lasting about an hour, during which I went through the preliminary flight envelope we had agreed upon. One of the things I noticed quickly was that we were shy of elevator. (We added chord, or width, to the elevators.) I carefully did some approaches to stalls. I felt the controls working on the approach to landing—whether there was an abrupt drop when I lowered the flaps, that sort of thing.

"On landing I recall that my first comment to Phil Garratt and the engineering team that was on hand was, 'It is a delightful aircraft to fly and I do not think we need to make many changes.'

"I had made some comments, noted speeds, temperatures and so on, on a knee pad, so we had a full debriefing in the engineering department. I recall some comments were:

"The aircraft is very noisy inside, even at cruise power;

"The elevator is not in harmony with the ailerons;

"Brake pedals will need adjusting;

"There is considerable elevator buffet during approach [to landing] when flaps are lowered. . . ."[1]

Not much changed from the Beaver prototype to the production models, aside from special equipment for certain customers. The airplane was pretty much right from the beginning.

"The first flight was pronounced a great success," Hiscocks recalls, "as all first flights are if they terminate in anything less than disaster. When I congratulated the pilot on his landing, which was more in the nature of an arrival, he grabbed my arm and dragged me to the tail, where the hinge wire in a control tab had backed out and partially jammed the elevator. . . ."[2]

Fixing the hinge wire did not completely cure the problem, so an early change was to increase the chord of the Beaver's elevators, making them broader and more responsive on takeoff and, once in the air, in pitch (that is, nose-up, nose-down longitudinal manoeuvres). A servo tab added to the elevators' trailing edge helped make them more responsive.

The top of the windshield, which consisted of flat sections of Perspex that extended back and out into the wing's leading edge, was changed for airflow reasons during a series of test flights that winter by George Neal, who took over the Beaver's certification program at the end of September, when the airplane was put on floats. It immediately looked more at home sitting high and level without the wheels.

Once this ascetic, nearly-anonymous prototype was proven to be flyable, it became slightly more resplendent. By the time it was being tested that autumn on floats over

Toronto's Lake Ontario waterfront, some decoration had been added: a yellow speed line, outlined with a black pinstripe, starting several inches wide at the front of the engine cowling and diminishing to nothing under the tail. To harmonize with this addition, the black fin stripe was repainted a matching yellow edged with black, with CF-FHB-X rendered in bolder black lettering.

It was as if, having proved itself, the Beaver could dress up and make a statement. From then on, it looked almost sporty. It had begun to earn its stripes.

Bannock could have come to de Havilland Canada with no better backer than Hatfield's Francis St. Barbe, the English de Havilland salesman extraordinaire and a longtime exponent of the Canadian market who had maintained close ties with DHC since urging its creation in 1928. St. Barbe continued to have a strong influence at Downsview, almost guaranteeing the success of DHC's first all-Canadian design, the DHC-1 Chipmunk. The DHC-2 Beaver was DHC's second postwar design.

Even then, Bannock was much more than an ace flyboy with a silk scarf and a headful of war stories. He is one of those rare people who seem to do better at each successive challenge in life.

The Beaver in its element: George Neal takes off in CF-FHB-X from Toronto Harbour, October 1, 1947. The Toronto skyline is dominated by the Royal York Hotel and the Bank of Commerce Building where P.C. Garratt sat out the last two years of the war. FHB has yet to be equipped with a ventral fin. DHC

He grew up in Edmonton, the centre of Canada's early arctic bush flying. His plans to become a geologist and mining engineer were derailed by the war. But one aspect of that career strategy, learning to fly, had got him a job with Yukon Southern Air Transport in Edmonton.

In Bannock's lifetime of impressive referrals, none carried more weight than being recommended to the wartime RCAF by Wilfrid "Wop" May, the greenhorn Sopwith Camel pilot who escaped the Red Baron. May had gone on to score thirteen victories in World War I and become Edmonton's outstanding bush pilot.

Scheduled to go overseas with the RCAF's 112 Squadron and the 1st Canadian Division when France fell, Bannock was diverted to the British Commonwealth Air Training Plan and spent three years making his contribution to the war effort as a pilot instructor. An experienced pilot whose prewar experience had enabled him to easily win his air force wings, Bannock, like many of his instructor colleagues, was frustrated by the policy of having the best pilots beget other pilots instead of feeding their irreplaceable skills into the front lines. Most BCATP instructors wanted to fly in combat but were exiled in Canada by their talents.[3]

Not Bannock. Even then he had finesse. He conducted his own quiet but persistent campaign for a posting to an operational unit until his efforts paid off in 1943, when he was sent to Greenwood, Nova Scotia, to learn to fly the de Havilland Mosquito fighter-bomber.

In his book on twelve Canadian fighter aces, Don McCafferty calls Bannock "a cool professional," an apt description of a man whose total is more than the sum of his parts. McCafferty goes on to call him "Canada's second-highest-scoring ace of World War Two." By McCafferty's calculation, Bannock comes second only to George "Buzz" Beurling, a ranking the author bases on his unique method of adding Bannock's aerial victories against Luftwaffe aircraft as a night intruder over German bases—at least eleven—to his kills of V-1 buzz-bombs, of which he had nineteen.[4] All Bannock's victories came at night.

McCafferty is right to emphasize the value of each V-1 prevented from reaching London. Dozens of civilian lives, in some cases hundreds, are likely to have been saved by the elimination of each V-1. Bannock became known in the British press as "the Saviour of London" for his prowess at dispatching them.[5] The pulse-jet buzz-bombs, put-putting along like two-stroke motorcycles, were fast. It took special techniques and deadly aim to catch and dispatch the small flying bombs.

The idea was to patrol near the V-1 launch sites, spot their exhaust flames against the night sky, push the throttles through the stops and try to stay ahead and above until the faster buzz-bomb caught up. For Bannock, the hard part was holding opposite rudder to counteract the torque forces of two Rolls-Royce Merlins at full chat. Once the V-1 passed underneath, the intercepting aircraft would switch on its navigation lights to warn other aircraft, dive and shoot at this small target from at least 300 yards astern, to avoid the blast from its one-ton warhead. It helped to be able to track the low-flying buzz-bombs against the English Channel's waters, bright with reflected light, although for some time pilots who shot v-1s down over land got more credit. There was considered to be a boost to morale in civilians' seeing the demise of the doodle-bugs, as they were often called.

Bannock was a deadeye night hunter whose success was immediate. He and his navigator, Flying Officer R.R. Bruce, shot down a Messerschmitt Bf 110 twin-engine night fighter during their first operational sortie, June 14, 1943. They then bombed its airfield. Four days later, on their first try, they blew up a v-1 over the English Channel. The night of July 3 they caught three v-1s not far from their launch-point at Abbeville, France. Three days later they accounted for four within an hour, and the next night two more.

By early September Bannock had himself a Distinguished Flying Cross. Bruce got his own DFC, and Bannock added a bar to his after a night in which they shot down two Bf 108 trainers but had an engine disabled and flew at treetop height over six hundred miles of German-held territory—a seven-hour and fifteen-minute trip and a remarkable navigational feat—to make their base at Holmsley South.

Just under four months after his first mission, Bannock was promoted to wing commander, given control of 418 Squadron, and then of 406, which became the most effective night fighter squadron in RAF Fighter Command. Bannock scored 406's first intruder victory himself, with a new navigator. He shot down his last victim, a Ju 88, April 23. In recognition of both his own virtuosity and his ability to motivate his squadrons by example, he was awarded the Distinguished Service Order.[6]

His achievements, if less publicized than those of characters like Beurling, are nevertheless impressive, and they extend far beyond his service career. Few wartime aces have much of a life when the excitement dies down—certainly Beurling didn't—even when they stay in the military. Bannock rose to become director of air operations for the RCAF in London, then was posted as air attaché to Moscow. He preferred Toronto, arriving there in May 1946 and looking up Grant Glassco, the former controller at DHC, to offer his sympathy over the death on Mosquito operations of Grant's younger brother Hugh. Glassco urged Bannock to consider the aircraft industry. When the ex-wingco expressed interest, Glassco wrote to Geoffrey de Havilland at Hatfield. St. Barbe, de Havilland's right-hand man, did the rest.

"What is amazing about Bannock," at least in McCafferty's estimation, "is that he doesn't seem to care about his lack of fame. He was the classic citizen-soldier who performed his duty, and, like Roy Brown, simply got on with life."[7] Quite a life.

CF-FHB-X in January, 1948. As a result of flight-testing, a new dorsal fin, the anti-spin strake on the leading edge of the left wing, and the final windshield are all in place.

DHC VIA PETER M. BOWERS

One change Bannock wanted made on the Beaver from the moment he first switched on the Pratt & Whitney R-985 Wasp Junior radial the morning of August 16, 1947—it took two batteries to get it going—was to make the airplane quieter. And that was the one complaint nobody wanted to hear.

Radial aero engines, like most air-cooled motors, are inherently noisier than water-cooled powerplants, which surround their cylinders with extensive plumbing and cast metal. The R-985, as installed in the Beaver prototype, had its nine cylinders exhaust into nine pipes that were collected into five outlets, so that three emerged from the right side of the engine cowling and two from the left, all of them just in front of the cabin. This arrangement minimized back-pressure, conserving power.

"As far as I was concerned," Bannock says, "the more power the better." But the noise made flying the Beaver tiring.

On September 27 he took Jaki Jakimiuk up to hear the noise. No chief engineer likes making changes to his newborn baby. Jakimiuk had been resisting this one for five weeks. Back on the ground, with the engine switched off but the radial engine's *taketta-taketta* still hammering in his brain, Jakimiuk screamed at the top of his lungs to Bannock over the racket he thought he was still hearing, *"It's not noisy!"*[8]

Two days later Bannock took Phil Garratt up. The Beaver concept was his, but Garratt had less personal investment in the specifics than the chief engineer. The key to the amount of noise any piston engine makes is its exhaust arrangement. Although a quieter and therefore more restrictive exhaust system would cost a few horsepower, Garratt saw Bannock's point.

The answer was cheap, easy and fairly near to hand. Canadian Vickers in Montreal had assembled the plywood-fuselage Anson V that Dick Hiscocks had been involved with, and engineered a Wasp Junior powerplant installation that offered more power than the Jacobs L6MB engines on the Anson IIS that DHC had built. The Anson V exhaust arrangement collected the pipes from each of the Wasp Junior's nine cylinders and merged them into one long pipe that not only deposited the noise a few feet further back in the slipstream but provided hot air to the cabin to boot. With everything DHC had gone through to redesign the Beaver around this new engine when the design was two-thirds complete with the earlier Gipsy Queen, cutting a few decibels seemed to Garratt a simple-enough task. Not that a radial-engined Beaver will ever sneak up and take anyone by surprise.

Bannock checked out George Neal on the Beaver on September 27. Neal would take over test-flying duties with a very specific, occasionally dangerous agenda: certifying the Beaver to fly with floats, seeing how quickly it could climb, trying takeoffs and landings in crosswinds, figuring out its forward and aft centre-of-gravity limits to govern loading, and finding its maximum dive speed. Whatever snags appeared along the way would have to be ironed out.

One of these was already known. The Beaver's tail tended to shake with the flaps down—in other words, when it was landing or taking off. In fact, from that point onward almost anything that could go wrong with CF-FHB, short of an actual crash, did go wrong. It was just as well George Neal was at the wheel to save the ship.[9]

Bannock was too busy as director of operations to continue with one project.[10] Not that Bannock was concerned about turning the airplane over to someone who just might have been a better experimental test pilot than he was.[11] He trusted Neal implicitly.

"He just said, 'Go ahead,'" Neal recalls today. "I knew the engine. I'd been flying the engine for years (with the BCATP, in Ansons).

"What could he tell me? It's an easy-flying airplane. Approach [to landing] 75 miles per hour and flaps at 30 degrees. When you put the flaps down you'll get a lot of buffet [Russ told me]. There were flat corners to the windshield that caused turbulence, and that carried back to the tailplane and elevators. We finally came up with a fix for it.

"I just went ahead and flew it. I learned every time I flew in it."

George Neal was elected to Canada's Aviation Hall of Fame in 1995 for what must be the most widely ranging set of achievements in Canadian aviation. He has been a pilot, an instructor, a mechanic, an airframe rigger and a builder of vintage aircraft replicas. Neal started flying while he was an automobile mechanic at a Toronto garage whose owner was a member of the Toronto Flying Club. He soloed in a Gipsy Moth. His first job with DHC in 1937 was as an engine mechanic, although with time he worked his way through every shop in the company. The

1939 re-engineering of the Anson to take its second powerplant of the war, the Jacobs L6MB, involved Neal, who was photographed installing its predecessor, the Cheetah, in an Anson that year; the picture shows a handsome kid with a perfectly-combed part, every bit a test pilot in the making.

Two years later he was flying Ansons, along with Tiger Moths and Stinsons, at Air Observer School No. 10, Chatham, New Brunswick. He amassed more than 2,000 flying hours on Ansons alone. He did post-maintenance test flights at Chatham during the war, and returned to DHC July 14, 1945, test-flying an Anson V. He flew his own personal Cessna Crane after the war.

Neal believes that having built engines and airplanes himself made him a better pilot, certainly a better test pilot.[12] He would need every smidgeon of his instinct and inside knowledge to cope with testing an airplane designed to deal with the worst bush-flying conditions.

Neal did only one familiarization flight, on September 30, after his checkout hop with Bannock, before getting down to the business at hand.

"We were very brave in those days," Neal marvels, noting from his RCAF log that he had only six hours in the Beaver, some on wheels, some on floats, before the floats came off for the winter freeze-up and he started doing the dive tests. Each of these configurational changes made the Beaver a different airplane, of course. Neal simply had to adjust.

Whether it was on wheels or floats, FHB had a nasty habit of dropping a wing as it stalled. Bannock had approached the stall on his first flight (or second, depending on how you assess the events of August 16), and had fully stalled it as part of his 150 hours of early development tests, noting that the airplane wanted to roll as it went into a stall.

An airplane stalls when its airspeed drops below the minimum necessary to sustain flight. Airflow over the wings stagnates and becomes turbulent, lift at the tailplane decreases because of the downstream turbulence, and the nose comes up. At that point, the airplane is about to depart from controlled flight. The Beaver's tendency to roll at this point only added one more priority to a swiftly lengthening list of things to do for the pilot.

Neal and Hiscocks were looking for a fix that would give the pilot a warning before he or she lost sight of the horizon. A stall, left to develop, can become a spin, which requires another set of corrective measures. Making stalls easily recoverable prevents spins.

The fix was a stall bar, a v-shaped piece of metal riveted to the leading edge of the left wing. A simple-enough solution, but one arrived at only after many flights with differently-shaped stall bars positioned at various points along the wing's leading edge. It worked by causing turbulence over the wing *before* the stall was imminent, so that the tail buffet became a warning, not a symptom. The stall bar also cured the tendency to drop a wing as part of the stall behaviour.

The Beaver's float certification trials were the key to making it a true bush plane. The search for the prototype's fore and aft centre-of-gravity limits was intended in part to provide guidance for pilots for whom the Beaver's characteristics on the water would be critical.

First, though, the question of the aerodynamic effects of the floats themselves had to be answered. Adding mass and drag, as floats do, always has a consequence for the stability of an airplane. This is usually cured with some sort of extra vertical surface, such as a fin underneath the tail. The size and location of the Beaver's ventral fin had to be calculated, and it had to be fabricated and mounted, test-flown and modified. In time, vertical finlets were added to the horizontal stabilizers of many Beavers to further correct the destabilizing effects of floats, and, in many cases, to allow removal of the ventral fin, which often struck docks.

George Neal's hairiest adventure in FHB occurred during the fore-and-aft centre-of-gravity or CG testing. It was right out of the movie *Test Pilot*. In that aviation classic, Clark Gable is the dashing flyboy who gets the girl, and Spencer Tracy is the sidekick-mechanic. George Neal would have been qualified to play both roles, of course.[13] But the unfilmed DHC 1948 version co-starred flight-test engineer Gene Dowell. The Beaver was on wheels during the winter of 1947–48. In the film, the Gable and Tracy characters are testing an early version of the four-engined B-17 Flying Fortress, loaded with sandbags for ballast. They fly as high as they can, Gable suffers oxygen-deprivation and loses control in the thin air, they go into a spin, and the sandbags break loose from their restraints, throwing the Flying Fortress out of balance and making the spin unrecoverable. Tracy wakes up in the mountains with a terrific headache.

In the Beaver version, the sandbags are not even tied down. The idea was for Dowell to move them, one by one, to the back of the Beaver's cabin to establish the airplane's furthest-aft safe centre-of-gravity. The very idea sounds so insane Neal can't tell the story with a straight face. But it made sense then.

"They weren't tied down, because Gene had to move them. I would set it up, with a certain degree of elevator or whatever, I forget the power settings; we did it at various flap settings too. Gene would get out of his seat beside me, pick up a bag, and move it back to the back of the cabin. He had to set it in his marks on the floor.

"And he kept doing that, and I would see how much elevator I had left to push the nose down." Neal chuckles. Nobody would do anything remotely like this today.

The first production Beaver, CF-OBS, bound for the Ontario Provincial Air Service, mounted on floats and delivered April 26, 1948. OBS is retired to the Ontario Bushplane Heritage and Forest Fire Educational Centre, Sault Ste. Marie, Ontario. DHC

A routine dolly takeoff. Once a death-defying act, taking off on floats from Downsview became a normal part of the delivery process once the dolly was perfected. CF-HJW, the 590th Beaver built, leaves the plant probably some time in 1953. DHC

"We were doing this, everything was going fine, and he picked up another bag and did exactly as he had done before. But he must have moved *himself* back, with the bag. And guess what happened. The nose came up and I yelled, 'Come back! Come back!' The nose just kept going up and up and up.

"He realized what was going on, and he just moved ahead. And, as he moved ahead, the nose began to come down, bit by bit. It did come down. We didn't stall."

The most famous story to emerge from George Neal's early-production Beaver flight-test and delivery period was the saga of the dolly.

Engineering had been detailed to design a wheeled cart on which the float-equipped Beaver could be mounted at the factory. (It would alight on the water at the air harbour then located at the foot of Yonge Street.) But the experimental shop decided that all the formalities of designing the dolly, issuing drawings and having such a simple device go through the engineering department rigmarole would be a waste. Bill Burlison's shop produced a three-wheeled dolly with the tailwheel fixed so it ran straight until the pilot took off.

The flight test crew were concerned about what the cart's directional behaviour might be as the pilot used his rudder on takeoff to counter the torque effect of the propeller. And they would have liked to see brakes, linked to a bar that would release as the aircraft lifted away, bringing the dolly to a safe halt. As it happened, the first dolly takeoff, into a brisk wind, was accomplished without incident by Russ Bannock in the first Ontario Provincial Air Service Beaver, CF-OBS. With a 20-mph headwind, Bannock was airborne before the dolly could do anything. No changes were made.

There was, alas, not much wind when Neal made the second dolly takeoff. "Wouldn't you know it," Neal recalls, "the next dolly takeoff, clear, no wind, and of course all the VIPs were there." Most of the engineers came to see how this thing worked. Neal was at the controls of the second OPAS Beaver, CF-OBT.

This time, the absence of headwind made the whole arrangement that much less adequate. As Neal approached liftoff speed, he had very little rudder and, of course, no brakes. The dolly suddenly veered off the runway to the left. Neal waited until the dolly reached a ditch that ran parallel to the runway. When the cart got to the ditch, Neal gave the Beaver full elevator and full takeoff power, barely managing to get airborne as the cart dropped into the ditch, came up the other side and rambled over the grass. There could have been no more dramatic demonstration of the Beaver's STOL performance.

This time the dolly was modified by the maintenance engineering department. The tailwheel was stiffened. A total of thirty-four floatplane deliveries were made with the cart, seeming to prove that the small modification had worked. With production well underway, Neal was taking off on a delivery flight in CF-OCK, another OPAS Beaver, June 9, 1950.

There were VIPs this time too, including Phil Garratt and a potential investor who later became chairman of the company, Doug Kendall.[14] Garratt had parked his brand-new Studebaker on Runway 27, near the point where Downsview's three runways intersected. Neal was taking off from Runway 33, to the left and almost squarely tangential to the Studebaker.

Neal left the dolly and the ground much sooner than the visitors could have expected in a classic demonstration of the Beaver's STOL capabilities. "Oh, what a marvellous way to do this," Phil Garratt's son John remembers him saying.

Garratt, excited at how smoothly everything had gone, was pitching the Beaver's market potential to Kendall, his personal guest. Kendall, looking over Garratt's shoulder, was transfixed by the dolly as it rumbled down Runway 33. That is what it was supposed to do, but as it careered into the intersection of the three runways, it began to deviate very slightly from its course. Almost imperceptibly at first, it began to turn slightly to the right. John Garratt remembers the tableau:

"The cart's turning...," Kendall kept saying.

"Look at that takeoff...," P.C. marvelled.

"Look! The cart's turning...," Kendall said as he tried to divert Garratt's attention from the airplane's spectacular climbout. But the managing director was transfixed by Neal's takeoff, which used perhaps one-quarter of Runway 33.

"The dolly's taking a cycle...," John Garratt remembers Kendall saying. "It looks as though...it might...."

"No," the elder Garratt said. "Look at the plane. Isn't it beautiful?"

As the dolly slowed, its rate of turn increased. It crossed both Runway 04 and Runway 27, and appeared to be circling around the shiny Studebaker. As its turn radius tightened, the dolly turned inward, toward the car it had appeared to be missing. It rammed the Studebaker and raked it front-to-back. The car was a complete writeoff.

Then Neal made a low pass across the airfield, showing OCK off for the VIPs. It was clear to him at a glance what had happened. "I thought, 'Oh God.'"

What was Garratt's reaction? Neal telephoned from the waterfront to find out. "He just laughed," Neal remembers.[15]

Engineering then built a four-wheeled takeoff dolly, equipped with brakes triggered by a spring-loaded rod that was released when the airplane lifted off. It was a simple task for a department just embarked upon the million-dollar gamble of starting production of the best bush plane in the world, made all the more critical by the delay that cost Garratt the minor price of his new car, rather than George Neal his life. The first Beaver to take off from this dolly on June 28, 1950, was CF-GQJ, number 84 off the line, for Saskatchewan Government Airways.

As for the protype the most useful part of its life would seem to have been over. FHB had been thoroughly wrung out, coming within a hair's breadth of disaster more than once. It had been modified in various somewhat crude ways. Prototypes are often kept around engineering and flight-test departments as engine testbeds or to try out new wrinkles of one kind or another. They become factory hacks, seldom accorded the honours the forerunners of great lines of aircraft deserve. FHB looked to be on that road when it was refurbished for use as DHC's Beaver demonstrator, and Punch Dickins set out to show it off across the West in the spring of 1948.

Dickins may or may not have known when he set out on his sales tour that, of Central B.C. Airways' two Junkers airplanes, CF-ASN had been wrecked and CF-ATF had suffered damage assessed at $5,000. Under severe financial pressure, Russ Baker and Karl Springer, CBCA's financial backer, were at odds over who controlled what was left of the airline. The stakes in their dispute were high: the airline was being offered a 1948 B.C. Forest Service patrol contract amounting to a minimum of $45,000, a 50

per cent raise over their 1947 fee. Springer was threatening to withhold any further operational funds, when suddenly he wrote a cheque for $27,809 to buy CF-FHB.

Nobody was as shocked by the sale of the Beaver prototype to CBCA than the engineers who built and tested it. FHB went on to another thirty-two years of service, much of it in the hands of the crash-prone legend of northern B.C. bush flying, Russ Baker.

"We didn't really want to sell it," Dickins told John Condit, author of *Wings Over the West: Russ Baker and the Rise of Pacific Western Airlines,* "but Russ was so anxious to get one after he'd seen the performance that he insisted we deliver him that one."

FHB was the making of CBCA. The airplane "greatly pleased the B.C. Forest Service," in Condit's words, impressed competitors enough to make them ripe for takeover, and opened the pockets of B.C. timber baron H. R. MacMillan, "who exercised a benevolent influence on the airline's financing." Baker also used it to take Pierre Berton and his writing colleagues aloft, "streaming columns of print from junkets all over B.C."

FHB was delivered to CBCA June 2, 1948, making it the sixth Beaver delivered, and was part of the Beaver fleet of that airline and its successor, Pacific Western Airlines, until March 1966. It moved on to Northward Aviation and B&B Aviation, both of Edmonton, until April 1969, when it was acquired by North Canada Air (Norcanair) of Prince Albert, Saskatchewan, which operated it until the National Aviation Museum, Ottawa, bought it in 1980.

Amphibian CF-PCG, the 1,000th Beaver, was registered as DHC's gift to P.C. Garratt in 1955. The porthole window is attributed to his wife Jessie, who, riding in the rearmost seat of FHB, is said to have asked "Isn't there a window for me?" It is now in service with Seair Services (1990) Ltd., a charter outfit in Vancouver. DHC

Chapter Nine

Russ Bannock takes the brass fishing

In a world where military aircraft manufacturers routinely lavish expensive favours on the procurement staffs of air forces, the success Russ Bannock enjoyed in generating orders by the simple sales technique of taking the brass on one-day fishing trips in a Beaver has a homespun innocence to it that speaks well of the product itself.

Of course, he took them to places inaccessible even by Jeep. And, while getting there was impressive enough, getting out with the additional weight of fat trophies from virgin streams, over tree lines on mountain slopes, usually closed the deal.

From then on, it was usually just a question of proving through formal channels what the brass-hat fishermen already knew. This was all Bannock ever needed—a chance to demonstrate the Beaver. Once a requirement was formulated around the Beaver's capabilities, the resulting competition was, in a perfectly legitimate and aboveboard way, a foregone conclusion. No other aircraft ever came close.

"The real turning point in the history of the Beaver, and de Havilland itself," Bannock believes, "was getting it sold to the U.S. Air Force and the U.S. Army." Once the Beaver had found its military niche, a market followed for each larger STOL transport DHC produced.

In time, de Havilland Canada products became a kind of cult in the American army by virtue of their ability to operate closer to the battlefield than other fixed-wing aircraft, while having superior load-carrying capabilities to the helicopters of the time.[1] In offering qualities that battlefield aviation theorists had not thought to ask for, the DHC Beaver, Otter, Caribou and Buffalo created their own tactical roles. A STOL technology that was developed to make aircraft safer, rather than with any military application in mind, made itself indispensable under fire.

So successful were the later DHC designs—especially the DHC-3 Otter and DHC-4 Caribou—that the U.S. Air Force, the first military organization to appreciate the Beaver's charms, looked upon the achievements of its successors in U.S. Army service with mounting dismay. By the late 1960s, the USAF had resorted to congressional action to reclaim for itself a battlefield transport role it never, up to then, had shown much interest in. If the air force couldn't have these nifty lifters, neither could the army. Thus ended a golden age of army aviation and a front-line tactical transport role that was filled almost entirely by DHC products.

During May 1949, an item in a copy of *Aviation Week* jumped off the page at Bannock as he read it in Edmonton on a demonstration tour. The 10th Search and Rescue Group of the Alaskan Air Command, United States Air Force, based at Fairbanks, was looking for a seaplane/skiplane with STOL performance, a 500-mile range and a 1,000-pound payload. The 10th SAR's requirement notice was written by the polar aviation pioneer Bernt Balchen, now a colonel in the USAF. It read like an operational description of the Beaver.

Bannock was by then DHC's manager of military sales. Production of the Beaver was well underway to fill orders from the Ontario Provincial Air Service, which had initially ordered twelve, and for another dozen from various energy companies involved with the Leduc oil discovery. Bannock had simply parked a Beaver at the Calgary airport for five or six weeks and invited executives and pilots to take rides. With the Beaver, an oil executive could take off from Calgary, visit his drilling sites in farmers' fields and be back in a matter of a few hours.

During 1949 the Beaver program was looking to be a steady, if unspectacular, three-a-month supplement to Chipmunk production until the specifications of the larger one-ton version the RCAF was interested in, known at Downsview as the King Beaver, could be finalized.[2] It became the Otter.

Bernt Balchen's announcement changed all that. Bannock left Toronto on July 13

in an early-production floatplane Beaver, CF-FHS, for Alaska. Hopping to Kenora, Winnipeg, Prince Albert, Edmonton, Fort St. John and Whitehorse, he was at Fairbanks four days after leaving Toronto. Along came a writer-photographer team from *National Geographic,* who wrote about the trip for the magazine. At Fairbanks, Bannock met Charlie Babb, the biggest war-surplus aircraft dealer in the U.S. and American agent for the Beaver. Together, they met the legendary Balchen and his superior, Brigadier-General Dale Gaffney, deputy commanding officer of Alaska Air Command.

Balchen, as Bannock well knew, was one of the great but largely unsung heroes of aviation history. A Norwegian by birth, he first came to American attention when, as a member of Roald Amundsen's rival expedition to reach the North Pole by dirigible, Balchen helped repair damage to the skis of Commander Richard E. Byrd's Fokker F.VII3m trimotor for his 1926 attempt to fly over the North Pole. Balchen did most of the piloting of Byrd's aerial crossing of the Atlantic June 29, 1927, five weeks after Charles Lindbergh's New York–Paris solo flight, and he also flew Byrd's expedition over the South Pole in 1928. These flights were made in commercial aircraft rather than purpose-built flying gas tanks, like Lindbergh's Ryan NYP.

In addition, Balchen was one of several pilots who flew to the rescue of the three-man crew of the *Bremen,* the first aircraft to cross the Atlantic east-to-west

U.S. Army 51-6266, ready for delivery to the Army Field Forces Board, was one of the first six YL-20 service test Beavers. As of the end of January 1962 the Army inventory included 641 L-20As. Later, U.S. military Beavers were redesignated U-6As. DHC

but marooned on Greenly Island, Labrador, April 12–13, 1928.[3] For these and a number of subsequent pioneering flights, Balchen deserves more recognition than he received.

Part of the reason he wasn't recognized seems to lie in the complex, egocentric personality of Byrd, considered during the 1930s the equal of any explorer in history. Byrd was a U.S. naval officer who could never quite bring himself, as leader of three important aerial expeditions, to credit fully the accomplishments of any pilot other than the one who either did or did not take him over the North Pole, Floyd Bennett, whom Byrd regarded as "a real man, fearless and true—one in a million."

Byrd understated not only Balchen's accomplishments on his behalf, but slandered Tony Fokker, the builder of the Fokker trimotor transports that carried him on two of his three flights of exploration. Balchen's retiring personality did not permit him to reply, but Fokker, a multimillionaire industrialist backed by General Motors, spoke for both.

In his 1931 autobiography, *Flying Dutchman,* Fokker rated Charles Kingsford-Smith, conqueror of the Pacific Ocean in a Fokker F.VII3m trimotor similar to Byrd's, as "the greatest flier in the world today," with Balchen "perhaps comparable to him, but only in the cockpit."[4] By that, Fokker, a pretty good pilot himself, meant only that Kingsford-Smith had "the advantage of being a great commander as well as flier . . . the best organizer for success I know. . . ." In retrospect, Fokker can be forgiven for overrating Kingsford-Smith as an organizer. Four years later the charismatic World War I ace would disappear in an ill-advised attempt on the England-to-Australia record.

Balchen, on the other hand, was a former Norwegian air force officer who had assisted in Amundsen's flight in the dirigible *Norge* over the North Pole and subsequently become a test pilot for the Fokker Aircraft Company in the U.S. It was Fokker who urged Byrd to take Balchen on his trans-Atlantic hop rather than rely on Bert Acosta, who was not qualified for instrument flying.

"Balchen," Fokker wrote, "flew [Byrd] to the South Pole, after having put Byrd firmly in his debt by saving the lives of the *America*'s crew with his hours of 'blind flying' and remarkable landing in the surf off the rocky beach of Ver-sur-Mer. . . ." *America* was the name of Byrd's Fokker trimotor.

For these services, the sole acknowledgement in Byrd's account of the flight in his autobiography, *Skyward,* was that, when the time came to ditch, "Balchen happened to be at the wheel."[5]

"Happened to be at the wheel," Fokker italicized in his own book, his fury at Byrd's slight fairly leaping off the page. "Balchen set the ship down on the flares [previously dropped to illuminate the water and show wind drift and altitude], so accurately did he land. One of [the flares] actually flew into the observation cabin. The impact tore

off the landing gear, of course, but Balchen had landed so skilfully that the great ship settled comfortably on the bottom, with the sea running just awash of its wing."

"His extraordinary modesty shames the shrinking violet" is the poetic conclusion to Fokker's hymn of praise to Balchen. The shrinking violet continued to serve his adopted country during World War II in the obscure but vital theatre of Greenland, an important refuelling stop for combat aircraft being ferried over the Atlantic to England. Balchen was involved in the capture of outposts in Greenland held by the Germans and used to direct faulty navigational information to Allied trans-Atlantic fliers.[6] The aerial armada that pounded the Third Reich by day consisted largely of aircraft ferried to their English bases over the Atlantic, a generally safer route than by ship through U-boat-infested waters.

But the most critical evidence of Balchen's qualities as an airman is the fact that, after a lifetime's flying in the worst of conditions, he was still flying in the north, still saving lives, and, considering his exploits, still alive himself to meet Russ Bannock and the Beaver almost twenty years after his flights of exploration. No man was better equipped to appreciate what the Beaver had to offer.

Bannock used the best sales pitch available to him—letting the Beaver do the talking to pilots in Fairbanks and Anchorage. Fairbanks is built on an arctic plain, but Anchorage, surrounded on three sides by mountains and exposed to the south to powerful, changing Taku winds whistling over the Kenai Peninsula and up Cook Inlet, was one of the most hazardous places in the world to fly before the advent of radar-assisted landing systems. Any pilot who flew the Beaver was sold, but sometimes a memorable demonstration was in order.

It was a measure of the impression the Beaver had made that Bernt Balchen and Brigadier-General Gaffney asked Bannock whether the plane could get them to their favourite fishing spot. It was located about thirty miles south of Northway, itself just off the Alaska Highway not far from the Alaska–Yukon border. Normally the air force officers flew to Northway and took a Jeep from there. So Bannock offered to fly Gaffney, Balchen, Babb and two others, a total of six, with all their fishing equipment, to fish for arctic grayling in a river—a stream, really—too small to have a name.

They arrived at about noon. With the Beaver's drooped ailerons, which effectively give it full-span flaps, Bannock was not all that worried about getting in. He circled and flew low, looking for sandbars in the crystal-clear current.

"It looked okay," Bannock recalls. And it was. But there would be no sport for Bannock, except for the adventure of taking off.

Instead, he spent the two hours while the others fished cutting stakes, which he used to mark out his takeoff channel, pounding one every fifty yards on each side of

The first U.S. Army YL-20 Beaver, delivered to the Chief of Army Field Forces by then-Lt. Col. Jack Marinelli and Maj. John Oswald in March 1951. It was used for testing for much of its service life, including a period at the Transportation Aircraft Test and Support Activity (TATSA) at Fort Rucker, Alabama.
PETER M. BOWERS

a twenty-foot-wide channel that avoided sand and gravel bars. There was less than a half-mile between bends in the river, but he figured there was an eight-knot current he could use to give him a rolling start. By going in the downstream direction, though, he would have to make a turn on the climbout to clear the trees.

"Anyway, I had no trouble getting off the river. This was extremely impressive to Balchen and General Gaffney."[7]

Suddenly fishing trips in the Beaver became a recognized hobby for officers of Alaska Air Command, America's first line of defence against the nuclear might of Russia. Bannock did more such trips out of Anchorage, always an interesting place to take off from in any direction. Balchen, a quiet but agreeable companion, usually managed to go along.

Just to be scientific, though, Balchen arranged some measured takeoff tests, pitting the Beaver against the airplane then coming into service with the 10th SAR Group as a light utility type, the Cessna 195 on floats. Cessna's vice-president of military sales came north from Wichita to prepare the 195. Both airplanes carried the same payload. Bannock forgets the actual takeoff distance. What he does remember is that where the Cessna first broke from the water, "I was already at 300 feet in the Beaver."

Two USAF L-20As 52-66105 and 52-6112. The left-hand aircraft, 105, appears destined for Alaska, judging by its high-visability red wingtip, elevator and fin panels. 112 is the Nellis AFB aircraft, and is also the number of Beavers the USAF ordered in 1951. DHC

Balchen forwarded a request to Washington for the relatively paltry order, in Pentagon terms, of twelve Beavers for the 10th SAR Group. But pilots are not the ones who buy airplanes for the U.S. Air Force. The turning point for de Havilland and the Beaver was not quite at hand.

When he learned about the order, Bannock went to Washington to do further demonstrations for members of the Deputy Chief of Staff, Requirements and Operations. Then he flew on to Langley AFB, Virginia, where he flew the Beaver for Tactical Air Command headquarters there. The immediate result was to add a hundred Beavers to Balchen's order for a dozen for Alaska.

A 112-airplane order for a foreign design in peacetime was bound to attract interest from the world's largest aircraft industry, an industry still undergoing a postwar shakeout. Suddenly American aircraft company executives who had hitherto never heard of de Havilland, Downsview or Beavers that could fly had a target to shoot at. They demanded a competition and in August they got it. A flyoff would be held during October and November at Wright-Patterson AFB, Dayton, Ohio, home of the USAF's Air Materiel Command.

Bannock's subscription to *Aviation Week,* already de Havilland's most productive executive expense, paid off again in late summer 1950. The U.S. Army Aviation Section Test Center at Fort Bragg, North Carolina (part of the U.S. Army Artillery Board), was looking for a tough STOL utility aircraft capable of carrying six people for a radius of 200 miles and able to "land anywhere."

Bannock immediately wrote to the test centre's commander, Colonel Louis Compton, offering to demonstrate the Beaver, and received a polite reply during October: Yes, at your own expense and liability.

The army was cool to the Beaver, which was a little bigger than the types then in use for artillery spotting, liaison and general utility, such as the Piper Cub, Aeronca, Stinson L-5 and the two-seater Cessna L-19 that was just then coming into service. But it was just that load-carrying difference that made a big impression on Compton.

The key demonstration came on the second day at Bragg, in the form of Compton's request for transportation to a drop zone where artillery was to be parachuted from Fairchild C-119 Flying Boxcars. Compton asked to be taken to the test-range airstrip, where he and his four staff officers would transfer to Jeeps for the three-mile leg to the remote DZ.

Bannock asked, "Is there any place I can land at the drop zone?"

"There is a road there, but you wouldn't want to land on it," was the answer. The soil was soft and sandy, ideal for parachute landings but not for fixed-wing aircraft.

For Bannock, this amounted to an invitation. "Can I take a look?" he asked. Sure.

"I took the five officers and landed on the sand road at the drop zone." This time, the hazardous part was to execute a nice nose-up flare and three-point landing. Getting out would be a comparative piece of cake. Bannock doesn't remember the specifics—the trip seemed fairly routine—but as he watched the drop with the artillery men, he realized he might have underestimated the danger.

"The thing I remember is, a 105mm howitzer came out of a Fairchild c-119 Flying Boxcar, the parachute didn't deploy properly, and the piece disappeared in the sand...."

The upshot was an invitation to bring the Beaver back to Bragg after the air force competition to repeat the tests carried out at Wright-Patterson. Now the stakes were double or nothing for the Beaver.

Thirteen American types appeared at Wright-Patterson for the air force competition. They included such illustrious names as the Beechcraft Bonanza (an early version of the model still in production) and Beech's prototype Twin Bonanza, an early Aero Commander, a Republic Seabee amphibian, Cessna 185 and 195, Ryan Navion, the first Helio Courier and an Atlas four-seater prototype. Edmonton's Northwest Industries (Fred Buller's early wartime company) brought a Bellanca Skyrocket. There were also a couple of prototypes of aircraft that never achieved production. Most of these competitors had been designed for general aviation, rather than the more rigorous demands of the military, although the Courier had been optimized for STOL with even more lift devices on its wings than the Beaver—including leading-edge slats—and was the forerunner of a line of impressive short-field performers. Bannock was there in Beaver CF-GQO.

The USAF was nothing if not thorough. The competition lasted into January of 1951, with a break for Christmas. Six test pilots did flying evaluations of each entrant, and a painstaking engineering evaluation was carried out for maintainability, craftsmanship, durability and simplicity. Only the Courier had come close on STOL performance, but its enviable takeoff and landing capabilities were bought at the expense of its flyability.

By late January the Beaver was declared the winner, and designated the L-20A. The 112-airplane order was reinstated, to be followed soon by an order for a further 100.

For Bannock, the USAF and subsequent army competitions were summed up by an incident at Fort Bragg that showed how closely the Beaver's engineering, intended for rugged bush operations, happened to coincide with military requirements.

Despite having won the Wright-Patterson flyoff, Bannock continued to perfect his personal STOL technique. The short-landing tests at Bragg were comparatively simple: a string between two poles was set at fifty feet and made more visible with tassels. Each competitor was to clear the barrier, land and be measured for ground run from the barrier.

At first Bannock practised making his approaches by lowering the Beaver's nose, the conventional technique. Then he found that by coming over the barrier right at the stall and beginning to mush—that is, flirting with losing control—he could apply the Wasp Junior's power halfway down to avoid landing too hard and could finish his runout in barely 600 feet! This was phenomenal. The small aerodynamic gains made by George Neal and Dick Hiscocks helped: the leading-edge spin strakes and curved windscreen added as a result of experience with the prototype were now paying off in low-speed control.

Not that any of these refinements made much difference to the contest results. The Beaver was competing with itself. How true this was occurred to Bannock only when the Beechcraft pilot asked him how he was achieving ground runs of less than 1,500 feet. This difference—the Beech was taking more than twice as far to get down and stopped—shows how great the Beaver's edge was. Bannock briefed him in careful detail, leaving out nothing.

The Model 50 Twin Bonanza, which had flown for the first time less than a year before the competition, on November 11, 1949, seemed a good candidate to duplicate the Beaver's feat with the combined power of its pair of 260-hp Lycoming engines.[8] But when the very capable Beech pilot tried the same stunt, the Twin Bonanza stalled, landed hard and ran one main landing gear strut up through its wing, smashing the wheel. Overnight, the Beech team and DHC's Beaver technical representative, Norm Davis, repaired the damage, using a Beaver wheel to replace the Beech prototype's, which was, of course, not yet in production. The effort paid off. The Twin Bonanza's landing gear would not retract, but the airplane was still in the hunt. DHC won the competition, but both Beechcraft and de Havilland landed four-plane evaluation-series orders for very different roles.

The Twin Bonanza, as the YL-23/U-8D Seminole, became an army personnel and staff transport, winning orders totalling 115 by 1954. The Beaver's follow-up army order, after tests on the first four, was for fifty. By the time those aircraft were delivered, the USAF realized the army could take better advantage of the Beaver's work habits and turned their first 200 over to be painted khaki. The aircraft were not passed to the army, though, until all 200 had been accepted. Beavers supplied to the U.S. military eventually numbered 976.

"And I know," Bannock says, "the air force kept four or five Beavers at Goose Bay, Newfoundland, to take officers fishing." Many of the rest went directly to Korea.

Jim Spilsbury of Queen Charlotte Airlines, the "Accidental Airline," scoffed when Punch Dickins offered Beavers at $31,000 to replace his WW2 types in 1949. Six years later Spilsbury bought CF-ICL, only weeks before he received an offer he couldn't refuse from his bitter rival, Russ Baker of PWA. DHC

Arthur Fecteau got "da Beaver fever" from Russ Bannock and soon had more than a dozen of them. CF-JAC, Beaver number 937, was built in 1955. For Fecteau, Beavers not only outperformed his Norsemans; they could go almost three times longer between engine overhauls. DHC

During mid-June 1951, not long after the Fort Bragg competition, Bannock was in Ottawa with a recent-production Beaver, CF-GQI, to demonstrate its performance on floats to Laurentian Air. A call came from sales manager Sandy MacDonald: a brand-new Norseman V of Arthur Fecteau's had burned while being refuelled at his dock at Senneterre, Quebec.[9] Fecteau's base was 320-odd kilometres north-northwest from Ottawa, past Val d'Or, near the northernmost Canadian National Railways line. It was situated on a river that flows north into Lac Parent, itself a long ribbon of water running northeast from the base. Fecteau's outfit operated Norsemans and a prewar Junkers W34, using the river as a taxiway and the lake as a runway.

Bannock left Ottawa June 20. On his landing approach, Bannock estimated that the river was 300 to 400 yards wide, and he noted a strong wind from the east.

Fecteau was planning to replace his Norseman with another Norseman, and he was too busy to see Bannock when he arrived. But Bannock had no difficulty rounding up four or five pilots for a quick hop in the Beaver, which was still a novelty. Bannock left the dock in GQI and headed straight across the river without bothering to turn left. As it began to dawn on the pilots that he—and they—were committed to taking off *across* the river, instead of taxiing north to the lake, Bannock heard more than one voice asking, "What are you *doing?*"

They were off the water before general panic could set in. Bannock allowed them to take turns at the wheel and had a planeload of converts when he alighted, again across the river, and taxied straight to the dock. Taking off and landing across the river had caught Fecteau's attention. He was interested.

But not fully convinced. At Fecteau's insistence, he and Bannock taxied to the lake before taking off, and Fecteau flew the Beaver himself. Normally a garrulous man, Fecteau was quiet when they returned to his base. After some time with no reaction from his sales prospect, Bannock noted that it was getting late, and broke the silence by asking Fecteau whether he might not like to take another demonstration flight before the light failed completely. Fecteau said nothing. Apparently he did not want to go up again. *Was something wrong?* Like any good salesman at the moment of truth, Bannock waited. He remembers seeing Fecteau seated on a bench in his office, head in his hands.

"*Son*ofabitch," Fecteau finally exclaimed in his backwoods Québécois accent. "Hi got de Beaver fever."

He had it bad. As Russ Baker had with CF-FHB when Punch Dickins showed him what the Beaver prototype could do, Fecteau wanted the very airplane he had flown in, GQI.

DHC liked Fecteau's line so much the company built an advertising campaign around it. As for Fecteau, there was no lowering his temperature where the DHC-2 Beaver was concerned. A month passed before GQI was ready for commercial service. Eventually he operated fourteen Beavers, becoming for a time the largest commercial operator of the type.

Arthur Fecteau's Beaver fever was never really cured. It could only be treated. At a little less than $30,000 per treatment, floats included.

Chapter Ten

Fort Rucker, Alabama, to Wanganui, New Zealand

Just as Russ Bannock's demonstration Beaver, CF-FHS, replaced Jeeps for the final run-ins to that arctic grayling stream near the Alaska-Yukon border and the drop zone at Fort Bragg, the Beaver, or L-20A as it became known to the U.S. Air Force, took over many of the Jeep's vital frontline tasks in Korea and Vietnam.[1] The Beaver could fill the single role ground forces in battle value most in an aircraft: to fly in and out of unprepared spaces at the very edge of the fighting.

In retrospect, the Beaver's arrival as a higher-capacity utility aircraft than the Cessnas the U.S. Army had been using ushered in a second heyday of army aviation.[2] In Britain, a 4,000-pound all-up weight limit had been imposed on army aviation, limiting the Army Air Corps to its wartime Air Observation Post (AOP) Taylorcraft Auster light planes, rough equivalents of the Piper Cub. By the early 1960s, the British Army wanted to do more than just go up and look around.

By then the Beaver had demonstrated how much more it could do than the light aircraft and early helicopters then coming into service. Fitted out with fibreglass litter straps that ran from ceiling to floor behind the pilot and co-pilot's seats, Beavers became flying ambulances that could carry twice as many wounded soldiers, in greater comfort, than the Bell Sioux M·A·S·H helicopters that did the same medevac job. Most U.S. Army Beavers were equipped with small underwing bomb shackles, not for bombing, but for dropping supplies to beleaguered outposts or for running radio-telephone wires from position to position.[3]

The battle honours of these aircraft, designed and built for peacetime uses in remote corners of the world, have been largely forgotten by all but those whose lives were saved because Beavers were there when the shooting was most intense. Pilots remembered too, and jumped at the opportunity when larger de Havilland STOL transports became available.[4]

One battle honour the Beaver earned in Korea that strains credibility was the movement in four hours of an entire regiment, about a thousand men, over a mountain range that would have taken trucks three days to cross. It took fifty Beavers to do it, but the airlift showed how much more important STOL characteristics were to a shuttle operation than sheer carrying capacity. More than anything else, the feat pointed in the direction of the larger subsequent DHC battlefield STOL transports, the Caribou and Buffalo.[5]

Perhaps the weightiest compliment for the thousand Beavers that were eventually supplied to the U.S. military came from those in a position to pick and choose their mode of battlefield transportation, and preferred the Beaver. To them, the Beaver was known as the "General's Jeep."[6]

It was at Fort Rucker, Alabama, that the newly promoted Captain K. Randall Mattocks of the Royal Canadian Army Service Corps finally got to fly the de Havilland Beaver, an aircraft that was by then being used by the military air arms of several countries and had long since become legendary among bush pilots back home—but was never bought by the Canadian military. His job was to fly the DHC-2 well beyond any limits Downsview's engineering staff had in mind when it was designed. Not even its DHC test pilots had subjected the Beaver to anything like the U.S. Army's Hard Landing Program.[7]

Fort Rucker was home of the Army Aviation Board, a test-flying unit being run during the summer of 1961 by Colonel Jack L. Marinelli, who had delivered the U.S. Army's first L-20 Beaver in 1951, and was very happy to see someone who he assumed had spent much of his career flying Canadian airplanes like the Beaver, its bigger brother, the Otter, and the twin-engine DHC-4 Caribou.

Rucker was a prestige career-building posting for Mattocks, who had been groomed with a succession of flying assignments, fixed-wing and rotary, and staff positions in Ottawa, before being ushered into the epicentre of army aviation

K. Randall Mattocks, promoted to major in 1965 after his eventful posting at Fort Rucker, the home of U.S. Army aviation. It was in Alabama that this Canadian army pilot first flew such Canadian-built aircraft as the Beaver and Otter. K.R. MATTOCKS

Randy Mattocks often flew in the right-hand seat of Royal Canadian Air Force DHC-4 Caribous, such as this one in UN peacekeeping service at Sharm el Sheikh, Gulf of Aqaba. As an army officer, though, he was not supposed to have flown such large types. K.R. MATTOCKS

worldwide just as its revival was underway. His arrival at Rucker was attended with certain understandable expectations.

"Marinelli said, 'Oh, good. My Canadian has arrived. I want you to take on survival kits.'

"I said *eh?!?* Yes, the same mentality that has Americans bringing skis across the border at Windsor in July. So I took on survival kits. And there *was* a need.

"I was embarrassed down there. About the second thing they said to me was, 'Of course you're conversant with the Beaver and Otter, and we have a Caribou here....'

"I thought, *Don't talk to me about the Caribou. The Caribou's been taken away from me by the RCAF....*"[8]

The Beaver was, of course, out of the question. And, it so happened, Mattocks had not yet flown an Otter, which was in service with the Canadian Army, Royal Canadian Air Force and Royal Canadian Mounted Police.

"So I said, 'Really not, you know.'"

"And they said, 'Oh, wow, sonofagun.'"

So it was that Captain Mattocks, a rising star of Canadian army aviation, first flew the Beaver, Otter and Caribou, all of them designed and built in Ontario, in the blue skies of Alabama. He did things in them that they were never intended to do.

Army aviation in Canada had not come far when, as a Korean War veteran, Lieutenant Mattocks learned to fly at the Light Aircraft School in Rivers, Manitoba, in 1953. Rivers is situated near the Saskatchewan border, at the end of what was then the Canadian National Railways grain run from Winnipeg.

Rivers had been a BCATP base during the war, and had since expanded to become the Canadian Joint Air Training Centre, a tri-service facility that trained paratroopers, provided an air-to-ground rocket-firing range for F2H Banshee fighters from HMCS *Bonaventure,* and converted Royal Canadian Air Force aircrew to several of the many transport and utility types the RCAF operated at the time. Rivers was an exciting place to be in the 1950s.

For Lieutenant Mattocks, though, it was as if nothing had happened in army aviation since 1945. The instructional staff at Rivers' light aircraft school consisted mainly of World War II-veteran AOP pilots, flying pretty much the same little Austers, Cessnas and Piper Cubs as they had then, and still teaching their vital but arcane specialty of directing artillery fire from the air.

But Mattocks was in on the ground floor of a military phenomenon. Army aviation in Canada was about to explode. There was much more to be done than watch where shells were landing. By the late 1950s the Canadian Army had decided to become more involved with aviation. The army's needs were being neglected, and no operational void that large stays unfilled for long.

The RCAF, in common with most leading air forces, was preoccupied with developing big transport aircraft and supersonic, or at least trans-sonic, fighters. Bigger

An L-20 is swallowed by the hold of a Fairchild C-119 Flying Boxcar. DHC

and faster were the twin thrusts of military aviation during the 1950s. By default, there was a growing niche for aircraft that could perform such ground-oriented aerial tasks as the rapid movement of small units of troops, artillery-spotting and casualty evacuation. The RCAF still used Norsemans left over from the war, but was looking for something bigger.

This question of equipment was only then being addressed by the army, as well. While Mattocks was at Rivers, the military characteristics of the airplane the army would buy were being worked out. The service corps, to which Mattocks belonged, had decided it needed a flying truck with a three-ton load capacity, a 500-mile range, equipped only to fly visual flight rules—a clear-weather aircraft, in other words—with STOL capabilities. This requirement was the beginning of the Canadian military's interest in the first DHC twin-engine transport, the Caribou. Once ordered by the army, though, the Caribou was judged to be of a size operable only by the RCAF.

Meanwhile, the helicopter was only beginning to be accepted as a vehicle for army aviation. After Rivers, Ottawa decided to send Mattocks to Fort Sill, Oklahoma, to learn to fly the U.S. Army's transport helicopters, the Sikorsky S-51 and S-55 series. These were the first really useful military helicopters, only then coming into service with the U.S. Army.

By the mid-1950s Mattocks was a staff officer on the army aviation staff at Department of National Defence (DND) headquarters in Ottawa. Next they sent him to the epicentre of the army aviation world—Rucker:

"They sent me to the Army Aviation Board, which is a service-test-flying facility. Service test meaning, 'Okay, the manufacturer has built the airplane or equipment to our specifications—now, does it fit into our system?' So you test the equipment under a contrived operational situation to see if it will work.

"When I went down there I saw more airplanes than I'd ever seen before. More in their *museum* than we had in our inventory. We had the D-model Huey [at Rucker], the Bell UH-1D Huey, which was just in service test then."

Mattocks was given a number of projects to work on besides developing a compact, lightweight life-support system that could be comfortably carried in aircraft like the Beaver for army flyers downed in places like Alaska. Some of these projects had an almost bizarre quality to them.

One was the Range Extension Kit. Most army aircraft had limited range, which made it difficult to ferry them over long distances. The proposal was to have Goodyear Rubber make L-shaped fuel tanks incorporating 12-volt pumps that sat strapped on the seats of aircraft being ferried long distances. They were connected by wires and pipes to the fuel system, one tank for each empty seat. By placing the tanks where human beings would normally sit, the aircraft's centre-of-gravity was not affected, and the internal placement did not interfere with the aircraft's aerodynamics. On the other hand, you were flying with several hundred-pound Molotov cocktails as your co-pilot and passengers.

"There were only two problems with it," Mattocks remembers. "First, anybody who smoked, you know, was in *real* trouble. And the second thing was U.S. Army aircraft didn't have relief tubes. (Relief tubes enable male pilots to urinate while in flight.) And, God, you know…what *we* had to do *was* check these things. So if the engineers said this system was designed to fly for fourteen hours, you had to go and fly fourteen hours—longer if you could. So I did. I broke all sorts of informal records, how long you could keep any particular type in the air…."

Among the types he endured such testing in was the Beaver. The U.S. Army stretched the Beaver's limits in a number of directions; this one came at the cost of occasional excruciating abdominal pain for pilots such as Mattocks.

The third test program was the most intriguing of all for the exchange pilot. This was the Hard Landing Program. A chronic problem with military aircraft is rough-and-tumble use. It happens, but is seldom reported.

"They'd had a lot of trouble out in the field with people not reporting hard landings. So they had taken a piece of existing equipment, a strain gauge, and they said, okay, maybe we can mount these strain gauges on aircraft and have the mechanics look at them after the landings and see if a needle pops up or there is a number or something so we'll know that they've exceeded the G-rating.

"These strain gauges would be mounted on the landing gear. As for the gauge readout itself, they said, 'Okay, where will we put these things?'

"The gauges were installed, for convenience I guess, back here, on the floor behind the pilot's seat in the Beaver. I developed a mirror on a stick. There I was, rolling down the runway after a hard landing, looking behind me to see what this thing was reading…."

Two world wars and battle honours such as Vimy Ridge and Dieppe have given Canadians a certain reputation within other nations' military organizations. This reputation rewards officers and men such as Mattocks with choice assignments on exchange programs.

"They said, 'Mattocks, get out there and see whether the strain gauges work.'

"And I said, 'What sort of criteria?'

"They said, 'Well, obviously don't break the airplanes.'"

So Mattocks spent six weeks abusing eight different aircraft types, including the Beaver. Far from Canada, flying an airplane built in Downsview, he developed a healthy respect for the design and craftsmanship of the Beaver.

Gift-wrapping Beavers. Pakistan was yet another mountainous nation where the Beaver found gainful employment. One Beaver, AP-AKQ, sold to the Pakistani government in early 1958, served with that country's Department of Plant Protection. DHC

"All I'd do is go out in each one, tell the tower what I was going to do, and then spend a half-hour doing circuits and bumps, but *hammer* 'em in every time. Drop 'em in.

"It looked curious from the outside. The guys in the tower didn't be*lieve* at first what was happening. Like, I told them, but they didn't believe it. I'm told there were informal pools in the tower—he'll do it to*day*, won't he?"

An unusual task for the Rucker Beavers was to fly support for the base's attempt to break world helicopter records with their new Bell UH-ID Huey. The U.S. Army was very proud of the Huey, which in Vietnam extended the role of the battlefield helicopter well beyond anything previously attempted. So Mattocks also flew the Beaver back and forth from Rucker to the Bell Helicopter plant at Fort Worth, Texas. This is a long flight for a Beaver, even with the Long Range Extension Kit.

Exactly how far was this? "A-bout seven hours. Chug, chug, there's the Mississippi River, chug chug. . . ."

The army wanted to break time-to-climb and 100-mile closed-circuit speed records with the Huey. The record attempts were done at night, when the cool temperatures and thicker air were conducive to high-performance rotary-wing operations. This may be one of the few recorded instances of Beavers being used as chase planes.

The sole Mk.2, a might-have-been better Beaver. With an additional 100 horse-power, three-blade prop and ample tail, this prototype offered more of every-thing the Beaver offers. Sent to the United Kingdom for evaluation, it did not achieve production. DHC

Mattocks's job was to circle not far from Longview, Texas, and watch for the speeding Huey. The idea, of course, was to fly as slowly as possible. Mattocks had done this in the Auster at Rivers and in the Cessna L-19, then the U.S. Army's stan-dard spotter plane. But those are much lighter aircraft than the Beaver. The Beaver wouldn't fly at 45–50 mph as those aircraft would—"at least," Mattocks says, allow-ing for the possibility that the Beaver could do one more amazing thing, "not that I'm aware of."

With the Beaver, he had to fly in the 75–80-mph range with full flap and a lot of power. "For that sort of job, when you're cruising and on a taxi route just wait-ing for something to happen, you want to make the best use of your fuel. Certainly it wasn't at high cruise. You wouldn't be counting the blades going by, but it would be lower rpm. If he [the Huey] squeaked, I could light his area so he could land somewhere safely."

Fort Rucker was a demonstration of how highly the U.S. Army thought of the Beaver. There were seventy or eighty Beavers used for instrument flying training there, and Mattocks had been qualified for the Huey record attempt by passing this instrument-flying course.

"I don't know that it's the best aircraft for instrument flying training, because it's single-engine. There's an aspect to instrument training flying, that most aircraft that are used for instrument training have a multi-engine capability. Later on, when you start losing engines, you're supposed to be able to cope with the problem under the hood." Instrument flying training is conducted under a collapsible hood that shuts off any visual cues for the student, forcing him or her to fly solely on the information available from the instrument panel.

"So if you're teaching instrument in a single-engine aircraft, it leaves you with something that you can't teach." But using the Beaver for instrument training did say something about the U.S. Army's regard for the DHC-2's single-engine reliability.

Most U-6AS, as the Beaver became known to the U.S. Army, had long since been sold off and refinished in brighter civil colours by the late 1980s. But the handy size and STOL performance keeps at least three Beavers still serving with the flight test facilities of the U.S. Navy and Air Force. It was notable enough when former Army U-6A 150191 was photographed in 1974 at the U.S. Naval Air Test Center (NATC), Patuxent River, Maryland, on wheels.[9] Of all the aircraft in the NATC inventory—everything from F-4 Phantom fighters to four-engine NC-121K Warning Star patrol planes—the oldest of all, the Beaver, best demonstrated the STOL experience for future evaluators of naval aircraft. That U-6A was one of several that have served there, including U-6A 164525, still active at NATC, and 164526, DHC construction number 851, stored for parts. Just as remarkable, U-6A 53-2781 (c/n 562) is flying with the Test Pilots School at Edwards Air Force Base, a museum piece teaching twenty-first-century test pilots its fifty-year-old but seldom-duplicated short-field specialty. That U-6A recalls a time during the early 1950s when the U.S. Air Force bragged that the Beaver was the slowest airplane in its inventory.[10]

Great Britain possessed an empire on which the sun was only beginning to set during the late 1950s. It was still an empire that required armed maintenance in both desert and jungle conditions. The British fought wars over oil (the Suez Canal crisis), over rubber (the insurrection in what was then Malaya) and because the wrong sorts of chaps were trying to take over (Kenya). In 1957 the Royal Air Force had reluctantly disposed of its AOP Austers, leaving an operational gap the Beaver could more than fill, although not at the 4,000-pound all-up limit the War Office had imposed for the army liaison-utility role. As had already happened in the U.S., a special dispensation was granted to allow the Army Air Corps to order forty-six Beavers, delivered from 1960 to 1967.[11] No other type had been considered.

A British-built Beaver had been considered as early as 1952. The parent company at Hatfield took the thirty-sixth Beaver built, G-ALOW, as its sales demonstrator in

1949. Downsview still being part of Hatfield's worldwide scheme of things, a version built to British specifications, possibly with a British engine, had made sense almost from the beginning.[12]

A radial engine that offered 100 more horsepower in exchange for 96 pounds additional weight, a worthwhile trade, had been in service with the RAF's Percival Provost trainer and Pembroke twin-engine communications aircraft. This was the 550-hp Alvis Leonides. One example was shipped to Canada for testing on a Beaver. Besides adding to the Beaver's length, the experimental Leonides installation in CF-GOE-X involved redesigning the vertical tail, giving it straight leading and trailing surfaces and a larger dorsal fin. The Alvis engine drove a nine-foot, three-bladed propeller. George Neal flew the Leonides Beaver on March 10, 1953. Takeoff and landing distances were shortened, the latter due partly to new Goodyear disc brakes, and higher time-to-climb and top speed figures were recorded.

But the cost of the conversion did not fully justify the performance improvements. The British Army Air Corps bought standard Wasp Junior-powered Beavers built to almost-exact U.S. L-20A specifications. As part of their test program, the AAC landed a Beaver on a Royal Navy aircraft carrier deck.

Even in military service with a British Army involved in small conflicts around the globe, the Beaver was a civil aircraft, a builder rather than a destroyer. One AAC Beaver was stationed at the British Embassy in Laos at the peak of the war in Vietnam, and survived a total of 1,343 hours on everyday missions in those dangerous skies. British Army Beavers supported an expedition under Lieutenant-Colonel John Blashford-Snell, whose party explored the sources of the Zaire River during 1974–75. The team could be supplied only by para-drops or by operating Beavers from jungle clearings. In the searing heat of equatorial Africa, 700 miles south of Khartoum, Beavers supplied 32 Field Regiment, Royal Engineers, as they built bridges and carried out exercises with indigenous forces. Often the distinction between the Beaver's civil and military roles blurred. It was not unusual for Beavers to work as both swords and ploughshares, especially in the Third World.

The British Army Beavers were present for a major shift in the global balance of power as they oversaw the end of empire or protectorates in, for instance, the jungles of Borneo and the sands of the Arabian Gulf states. Beavers served with a number of air arms in parts of the world with dangerous or primitive flying conditions, such as Argentina, Cambodia, Chile, Colombia, Cuba, the Dominican Republic, Ghana, Finland, Holland and its overseas possessions, Kenya, Laos, Pakistan, Peru and Zambia.

But no Beavers worked harder or longer than the ones that were eagerly sought to make the arid Australian Outback bloom and New Zealand's upland pastures

Although most Beavers can be flown from either front seat with it Y-shaped control column, this agricultural model, most likely to be used in New Zealand or Australia, comes complete with right-hand drive. Flying from that seat puts the pilot behind the white panel regulating the fertilizer's rate of drop. DHC

greener. The most famous of the dozens that did tours of duty Down Under, and the only one in New Zealand to wear air force roundels, was the military Beaver that paid the ultimate price in the most peaceful of operations, the Commonwealth Trans-Antarctic Expedition of 1956–58. Antarctica added a new dimension to the Beaver's reputation for flying in the worst of conditions. Both Australia and New Zealand, along with most of the other countries that participated, chose Beavers to equip their Antarctic teams.

Beaver NZ6001 started its career with a number of claims to fame. It was bought by public subscription and named *City of Auckland* after most of its cost was raised there. So it was something of a celebrity from the start. It was also a case of mistaken identity, with an already-distinguished serial number inadvertently borrowed from the Meteor III that had recorded the first jet flight in New Zealand on February 11, 1946. Decked out in a high-visibility orange-red paint scheme with the standard sporty DHC speed line in black running from cowling to horizontal tail (with the name Beaver in neat contrasting white script on the crew's doors), the DHC trademark Mosquito-silhouette badge high on the fin, and Royal New Zealand Air Force roundels in the usual positions, NZ6001 arrived at Wigram, near Christchurch, in time to be photographed in 1956 before it went to Antarctica. In early 1958 it returned intact and, the serial duplication having been discovered, was renumbered NZ6010. In 1959 it once again "went south," as they say in the most southerly temperate part of the world.

In January 1960 the Beaver was written off in a whiteout on the Beardmore Glacier. Both pilots escaped the crash unhurt. Under conditions of near-zero visibility, the fliers were spotted from an Auster by Flying Officer W. T. Cranfield and rescued. Cranfield was awarded the Air Force Cross for his bravery in finding them.[13] The Beaver was replaced, by the way, with a DHC-3 Otter.

NZ6010 was gone but by no means forgotten. The worldwide warbird movement restores aircraft with military service records, often painting them in the markings of famous examples of the type. Although the Beaver does have an impressive record of service in Korea and Vietnam, it was never designed as a combat aircraft. (Beavers were assigned to U.S. Army special warfare units, so they may have undertaken more aggressive duties than we are aware of.) But the Beaver distinguished itself mainly as a battlefield utility transport and air ambulance in, for the most part, humanitarian or communication roles. Nonetheless, in 1983 two Beavers were in the hands of the world's foremost warbird enthusiasts, the Confederate Air Force, a group of Americans well equipped to re-fight World War II in the air.

Such is NZ6001's renown in New Zealand that not one but two privately-owned Beavers have been given the markings of the aircraft known in that country as, simply, the Antarctic Beaver.

The first Beaver to memorialize "NZ6001" was ZK-CKH, which has an interesting history of its own. Many of the Beavers imported into New Zealand and Australia during the 1960s came from other parts of the world, rather than from the factory, which was preoccupied meeting its delivery schedules with the U.S. military.

One of 50-odd Beavers operated at one time or another by Agricultural Aviation. This one, VH-IMF, is being loaded at Armidale, New South Wales, in 1982. Beaver number 1452, IMF was built for the Ghana Air Force, and appeared on the U.S. register as part of a group of ex-Ghanaian machines, several of which were bought by AA. PETER ROSS VIA STEVE TODD

CKH was flown in Canada, England and Sierra Leone before being brought to New Zealand as a top-dressing aircraft by Air Services Wairarapa in 1965.[14] After the usual hardworking life of twenty-odd years in agricultural aviation, CKH came into the hands of an Auckland syndicate which had it refinished in the Antarctic Beaver's 1956 paint scheme (authenticated from an original access panel) and afforded the aircraft a fairly relaxed retirement at Ardmore and on the summer airshow circuit, where its expenses were partly defrayed by its ability, unusual among warbirds, to carry joyriding passengers—"rather more practical," as New Zealand vintage aircraft author John King puts it, "than a Harvard [two-seat World War II trainer]!"

The second impersonator of "NZ6001" is the subject of an Antarctic diorama at the RNZAF Museum, Wigram, where the original was based before it went to the south polar icecap. Painted with every feature of the 1956 aircraft except the DHC Beaver script door and Mosquito outline fin trademarks, this Beaver is resplendent in its bright colours and complete with underwing bomb shackles, carrying under the port wing a beautifully restored and varnished sledge, a collector's item in itself.[15] This Beaver, donated by Fieldair Holdings, once the aerial top-dressing outfit with the most Beavers in New Zealand, is still registered as ZK-CMU, Beaver number 1590.

Unlike many Agricultural Aviation Beavers, this unit arrived direct from DHC in 1964, and was photographed at AA's Bankstown, NSW, HQ in 1966. It subsequently served in British Columbia with Airwest Airlines as CF-AWB (Air West Beaver) and two other operators. VIA STEVE TODD

Almost every Beaver in Australia and New Zealand was used, and used hard, for most of its time there as an aerial top-dressing aircraft. Top-dressing is not quite the same as crop-dusting. Usually it involves dropping nitrogen fertilizers in the form of pellets on pastures in Australia or New Zealand. This agricultural technique is almost exclusive to that part of the world.

Understandably, this was not a market the brains trust at faraway Downsview had considered. When an expression of interest was forwarded through New Zealand's de Havilland affiliate from Rural Aviation's Beryk Dalcom not long after the Beaver went into production, "the wires between Wellington and Downsview ran hot with cables about superphosphate's specific gravity, angle of repose, angle and rate of normal flow, and the required dump rate."[16] Of course, the only individual at Downsview likely to fully understand such factors would be a powerplant engineer.

Jim Houston, who had masterminded the change of engines in the Beaver, now went to work modifying the aircraft for a new role. He was a versatile hand, having started, like Dick Hiscocks, as a young Canadian at Hatfield during the Depression, when there were few jobs in aero engineering in Canada. He was working in de Havilland's thriving propeller division when the onset of war made DH's acquisition of a licence to build propellers using the Hamilton-Standard hydraulic constant-speed governing mechanism something of a bonanza: Britain's fighter force was still equipped with obsolete fixed-pitch wooden airscrews during the Battle of France.

After the war Hatfield decided the propeller was an anachronism and converted its propeller facility into a missile division whose products did not find a market with the Royal Air Force.[17] By then, of course, Houston had returned to Canada. He was presented with the challenge of creating a new Beaver for an especially useful role.

Very quickly Houston designed a hopper that could carry a ton of dry phosphate fertilizer, all of which could be jettisoned in one-and-a-half seconds. This system could be adapted to carry the same weight of liquid chemicals in a drum-type container that sat sideways, poking through the freight doors. The modified aircraft, one of the first fifty manufactured, was registered as ZK-AXK, and was in New Zealand in November 1950. It was demonstrated by DH New Zealand test pilot John Kerr, who made such an impression that more orders flowed in than Downsview could handle. For seven years top-dressing companies waited for aircraft that were going to the U.S. military or found their Beavers elsewhere. Fieldair, the company that donated "NZ6001" to the RNZAF Museum, had the largest fleet in New Zealand: nineteen. In Australia, Aerial Agricultural Aviation operated up to fifty Beavers at various times in the top-dressing role into the 1980s.[18] Other companies that operated Beavers included Air Contracts, Wanganui Aero Work of New Zealand, Rural Aviation and Superspread Aviation of Melbourne.

Dick Hiscocks considers Houston's aerial agriculture devices to have been an important highlight of the Beaver's development. The equipment never gave any trouble, except when overloaded.

Of course, like pilots everywhere, top-dressing fliers routinely overloaded their Beavers. In the vast open spaces of the Australian Outback and New Zealand's remote high alpine sheep-grazing meadows, they were more likely than most to get away with it. Like so many other specialized roles the Beaver excelled at, aerial top-dressing is about to join the leather flying jacket and the silk scarf in a golden sunset glow.

The decline of aerial top dressing over the past ten years, and the Beaver's replacement by Fletcher agricultural aircraft, has meant that, for the pilots at least, the work is a lot less enjoyable. It was a hard grind, spreading as much as sixteen-to-eighteen thousand tons of fertilizer, not an uncommon annual total for a pilot twenty years ago. That total could only be realized by dropping eighty to a hundred tons a day, with, say, an average load of 2,200 pounds of fertilizer, an overload of 400–500 pounds—"plus fuel and a pilot" a veteran top-dresser, David Salter, points out entirely without bravado, "well beyond the legal limit." Spreading that much fertilizer entails making eighty to a hundred landings and takeoffs—hopefully, as the old aviation adage dictates, the same number of both—on a good working day. Reloading typically takes twenty seconds, usually from a front-end

DHC called this "the Supply-Dropping Beaver," and fitted two 250-lb (113 kg) racks under each wing with switchgear for salvo or individual drops. In New Zealand they were used for dropping fenceposts, in Ontario for supplying forest rangers and firefighters. DHC

loader on the back of a truck, with a fuel tank between the loader and the truck cab. Each cycle takes five or six minutes.

"Mind you," Salter adds, "I've never done quite that much. I've only done fourteen-thousand. . . ."[19]

Many pilots in many places have asked the Beaver to do things it wasn't meant to do. The Australian contribution to this art form was "bunting" it. Salter says that of course he never did any such thing. But it is widely believed that a grounding of top-dressing Beavers in 1952 was caused by pilots who, finding themselves unable to drop because their hopper doors were jammed, would dive and abruptly pull out in an effort to free the doors. Salter doesn't believe that was happening; he says the problem was simple overloading. Of course, the doors could have been jammed by overloading in the first place—or, more likely, by fine-particle dry chemicals that tend to form solid lumps at the hopper's discharge chute. Whatever the cause, the connections between wing strut braces and wing spars were failing. One way or

Beavers have often been assigned to spiritual tasks, but few have been blessed with the pageantry of this Buddhist ceremony accorded one of Japan's International Geophysical Year Beavers in 1957. Tokyo newspapers used Beavers to distribute copies to the suburbs. DHC

another, the Aussies were flying the wings off their Beavers. Salter points out that these fittings were reinforced on the assembly line with aluminum; today stainless steel plates are used.

In one respect it doesn't really matter whether the Aussies were bunting their Beavers or grossly overloading them to the point of structural failure. Either way, they were, in their own devil-may-care fashion, endorsing the bush plane's strength factor. Overloading it or aerobatting a workhorse like the Beaver says something about the confidence it gives those who fly it. It can be done. The Beaver can take it. Top-dressing "does get monotonous," Salter acknowledges. One does want to vary the routine.

It certainly helped to be flying an aircraft that could give you an honest 4,000 feet, even heavily loaded, over alpine areas. Salter knows. His ranch, a hundred miles inland from the east coast of Australia, between Sydney and Brisbane, is 4,000 feet above sea level. He is that high when he takes off. (The Beaver's top-dressing replacement won't fly that high, although it does carry that 2,200 pounds of fertilizer legally.) It also helped to be flying an aircraft with a roomy, dust-free cabin upholstered in leather. A Beaver was considered to have an airframe life of ten-thousand hours before overhaul doing this intensive, high-wear work. Top-dressing pilots didn't consider the Beaver perfect: they found it noisy and often flew with earmuffs. (Salter wore both earmuffs and earplugs; his Beavers had their noise insulation removed to save weight.) But flying the Beaver, even back and forth and in straight lines, was fun.

"Few would rather fly anything else for aerial top dressing," writes Kiwi John King in his book on vintage aircraft in that country.

"It's a real pilot's aeroplane," says Salter. "That's why I've been sitting in one for twenty-three years." Aussies like Salter preferred the Beaver less for its carrying capacity than for its flying qualities, although he appreciated the ton-and-up useful load when he left Aerial Agriculture with six of its Beavers, first to take over part of that company's business and then to start his own outfit. As opposed to the purpose-built agricultural aircraft that have largely replaced the Beaver in that role, "the beauty of the Beaver is you can do other things with it."

Which is why the Beavers that were once so important Down Under are migrating back to North America. Salter still owns and flies two Beavers. On a recent holiday in North America, he visited Seattle, Ketchikan in Alaska, and Minneapolis, among other places. It was a kind of cook's tour for him: all three cities are centres for Beaver restoration and modification. Six former Aussie Beavers were at Bob Whiplinger's facility in Minneapolis alone. At Kenmore Air Harbor on Lake Washington, near Seattle, parts of thirty-odd Beavers, white tails with blue numbers and white cowlings with blue stripes, all of them from Aerial Agriculture's once-proud fleet, are stacked in an open warehouse, a priceless collection of artifacts from Australia's aviation history that await incorporation into the restored Beavers that now command up to $400,000 American. Salter finds the Beaver top-dresser plane drain a little sad.

The growing of foodstuffs is a cornerstone of civilization, and the Beaver's contribution to agriculture is not confined to Australasia. In East Africa, the Desert Locust Control Organization operates eight standard Wasp Junior-powered Beavers, including 5Y-KOU and 5Y-KRD, and a Pratt & Whitney PT-6 gas turbine Turbo Beaver, 5Y-DLC, modified by Viking Air Ltd. of Victoria, Canada.[20] This Beaver, one of sixty Turbos built at Downsview between 1965 and 1967 (see chapter 11), was extensively modified for its work, which can involve flying through swarms of locusts or flocks of grain-eating birds. A filter system worth $40,000 is fitted to protect the engine from these hazards, along with a new oil cooler system and reinforced wing and tail leading and trailing edges. This Beaver carries wing droptanks the size of those on some fighters. It was purchased for the organization by Germany, one of the seven countries that support it.

Sometimes the Beaver's boon to humankind consists of nothing more than making basic transportation available to those with no other means of getting around. Six Beavers, including the 500th built, VP-FAE, went to the Falkland Islands, where two became casualties of the 1982 war. They were replaced by two more Beavers. African Central Airways used their Beavers for the same purpose they are used for in the Falklands or North America's Pacific Northwest: "To go where," the airline promises, "only Beavers may fly."

Chapter Eleven

The Turbo Beaver

The origins of the Pratt & Whitney Canada PT-6 go back to 1956, when the Montreal subsidiary of what was then the leading aero engine builder in the world decided to design its own products. So Jim Young's company set up a gas turbine design group. A new engine always suggests new possibilities for airframe manufacturers like de Havilland, but in this case—the most successful aircraft powerplant ever developed in Canada—de Havilland Canada was involved with the project before the engine ever flew.

It was the same versatile DHC organization that had modified a dozen-odd World War II types for the RCAF who devised a flying testbed for the PT-6 in 1960. Several piston-engined twins were considered before the Beech 18 was adopted as being the right size to take the small gas turbine in the nose and become a piston-turbo trimotor. Expeditor HB109 was "borrowed" from the RCAF much as one once borrowed a cigarette: with very little likelihood of its being returned. The Beech continued to fly in the colourful RCAF markings of the time, complete with a red lightning bolt running the length of its natural-metal fuselage. It made 719 flights, logging 1,068 hours between its first flight in this configuration May 30, 1961, and its last, June 3, 1980. (It became an instructional airframe at L'École aéronautique, St. Hubert—a more instructive airframe, indeed, than most.)

The Twin Beech and the PT-6 were a good fit. Only 23 pounds of ballast were required to balance out the installation, although the word balance is used loosely in this context. HB-109, later CF-ZWY-X, required constant attention from the pilot, especially with all three mills lit. But it amazed air traffic controllers by climbing as high as 26,000 feet in the hands of DHC's Bob Fowler and P&WC's John MacNeil.[1]

So Downsview was somewhat more familiar with the small turbine before it went into production than other potential customers alerted to it by P&WC's sales force. In fact, DHC's interest in the PT-6 went further back than that, to early 1959. At that point, Downsview and the Defence Research Board were at least a couple of years into a program to investigate "the outer limits" of STOL performance. The chosen vehicle was a heavily-modified Otter, again borrowed from the RCAF, with a taller vertical tail, oversized flaps, and rugged landing gear suitable for steep approaches. This landing gear consisted of very strong box-section bars, mounted like floats, with wheels mounted on thick lever-action forks at their rear extremities to take the initial shock of steep landings, and smaller, steerable straight-oleo struts and wheels at their forward ends.

The airplane was tested, first at low altitudes, by George Neal, and then upgraded with a J-85 jet engine exhausted through moveable nozzles at each side of the rear cabin, making its first flight so configured in the hands of Bob Fowler in September 1961. A lever-type control in the cockpit enabled the pilot to direct the jet's thrust ahead or astern, allowing Fowler to examine in-flight reverse effects and slipstream deflection. This DRB-DHC experimental aircraft recorded speeds in controlled flight of as little as 48 mph and a landing roll of less than 500 feet over a 200-hour test program. The next step was to explore the effects of propeller thrust over the wing surfaces which, theoretically at least, would augment lift at low speeds. RCAF Otter 3682 was once again redesigned to take a piston engine on each wing panel.[2]

P&W Canada, learning of this change, suggested using PT-6s instead, and offered to fully support those engines on the DRB-DHC research Otter. Bob Fowler flew this aircraft on May 7, 1963, and its program of test flights lasted more than two years. In addition to providing data for the agencies that had sponsored it, this first twin-engined Otter became a second PT-6 testbed for P&WC. This was by no means a prototype for the eventual DHC-6 Twin Otter; Fowler says the two aircraft flew entirely differently.[3] Nevertheless, "one suspects," wrote the authors of *Power: The Pratt & Whitney Canada Story,* "that it also had some bearing on DHC's later thinking about the forthcoming Twin Otter."

But that was not the PT-6's first application in a DHC production aircraft. DHC chief engineer N.E. "Nero" Rowe, Fred Buller and the rest of the engineering staff were quick to conclude that if their best-selling Beaver had done well with 450 hp from the Wasp Junior and shown real potential with an additional 100 hp from the Alvis Leonides, getting that same extra punch from a more aerodynamic engine with 35 per cent less installed weight than the Wasp Junior might be that much better.[4]

If DHC hadn't thought of the idea already themselves, they were prompted by such Beaver users as Pacific Western Airlines.[5] PWA wanted to know whether the conversion was feasible, and, if so, sought DHC's help in converting their Beavers to turboprop power themselves. The Ontario Department of Lands and Forests estimated that "they would be able to add dozens of smaller lakes to their northern duties and ordered a study on converting their Beaver fleet," Fred Hotson recalls.

A Kenmore Air Harbor Turbo Beaver struts its stuff. Kenmore owns the last Beaver built, Turbo number 1692, N9744T. DHC's new owners, Hawker-Siddeley Aviation, closed down the Beaver line in 1967, causing Russ Bannock to resign. C. MARIN FAURE

The prototype Turbo Beaver, registered CF-PSM in honour of its project engineer, Peter S. Martin. It first flew December 31, 1963, in the hands of Bob Fowler.

VIA STEVE TODD

"It was thought that an engine change for the Beaver would be a simple project," says Dick Hiscocks, who remembers the mid-sixties as an exceptionally busy time for DHC—so busy that had anyone in management known what would be involved, the project likely would not have gone ahead.

Downsview was converting to turbine power across the board. The DHC-4 Caribou twin-engine transport was becoming the turbine-powered Buffalo. As difficult as that project was, the Buffalo was a military project, and the speed, field-performance and load-carrying improvements that were anticipated excited the U.S. Army, then embroiled in the Vietnam war. The armed forces seemed eager to pay for those improvements (although, as it happened, the U.S. bought only a handful of Buffalo test models). But would the bottom lines of feeder-line operators support the costs of turbine power for the Beaver?

"We had argued for a long time about whether the engine change would make sense," says Hiscocks. "It burned at least 50 per cent more fuel per hour. So the range would be drastically reduced. That would have made sense if we could have made the Turbo Beaver 50 per cent faster. But of course we couldn't do that. So there was resistance to putting the turbine in.

"On the plus side, the turbine needed much less maintenance. It started in cold weather without any of the fuss and bother of removing oil overnight and heating it in the morning.

"Management was disappointed it wasn't a quick-change job. Especially with the new engine weighing 330 pounds when the original, with accessories, weighed eleven-hundred-plus. So the nose had to be lengthened for balance. The cockpit was pushed ahead of the wing. We took the opportunity to stuff in a couple more seats. We needed a big fin. The increase in power was only one hundred horsepower, but we were still concerned that the swirl from the propeller would interfere with longitudinal stability." The engineers were right. The big vertical tail, borrowed from the Leonides-powered Beaver for the prototype, got bigger, more squared-off, and became swept-back to cope with the increased power.

From a purely esthetic point of view, the Beaver emerged from this latest redesign a more angular, squared-off airplane, at once more streamlined up front and blunt at the tail. Functionally, it is still the ultimate Beaver. And the most expensive.

The P&WC PT-6 turboprop powerplant increased horsepower by 100 over the R-985 Wasp Junior, to 550-shaft-hp (the measure of gas turbine power). This installation was much smoother than the piston one, the impression of easy power augmented by the turbine's three-bladed, full-feathering, reversible-pitch propeller that shortened the Beaver's already impressively-short landing runs with its braking effect. From 160 mph (257 km/h) for the piston Beaver, maximum speed increased to 170 (273 km/h) for the Turbo Beaver Mark III, as the PT-6-powered Beaver was officially designated (the Leonides-powered Beaver having been the sole Mark II). More important, cruising speed was up to 157 mph (252 km/h) from 130 (209 km/h) at 5,000 feet (1,524 m).[6] Although the Turbo Beaver was not at first certified to carry higher payloads than the piston version—the loaded weight of both, unmodified, is set at 5,100 lb (1,254 kg)—the Turbo's empty weight is 275 lb lighter, while its fuselage is 28 inches longer, the additional length being added behind the pilot's seat. That means two additional passengers, 157 lb more payload, more fuel capacity, faster climb and a higher service ceiling at 20,500 ft (6,250 m). One operator of the Turbo, Kenmore Air Harbor of Seattle, claims a service ceiling of 23,900 feet, which enables this Beaver to "vault the summit of any mountain in North America," in the words of Gerry Bruder, a Kenmore pilot.[7] The prototype Turbo, CF-PSM-X (for project engineer Peter S. Martin), first flew on the last day of 1963, in the hands of Bob Fowler and flight engineer J.G.H. (Jock) Aitken.

All these performance improvements came at a cost: $253,000. This was an excessive price tag for small operators, especially in comparison with the well-equipped ex-U.S. Army Beavers then coming on the market. Sixty Turbo Beavers were built at Downsview. Of those, seventeen went to that old reliable DHC customer, the operator that launched the piston Beaver and Otter, the Ontario government. Their first Turbo was delivered June 4, 1965.

One role the Ontario Department of Lands and Forests had in mind for the Turbo Beaver was in the quickly evolving technique of water-bombing forest fires. Aerial surveillance of large wooded tracts began in Canada after World War I, when Curtiss HS2L flying boats were used to spot fires and then haul men and equipment to the scene to fight them. Canada's provincial air services were founded to cover the huge forest lands of the second-largest country in the world.

In Canada's largest province, Quebec, which produced more than one-third of the country's newsprint by the mid-70s, more than half its 600,000-square-mile area, stretching from the United States border to the Arctic Circle, is covered with forests. Much of this resource was unreachable, even by aircraft, because of the lack of suitable places to land. Even flying-boats and amphibians were limited by their inability to get in and out of smaller bodies of water. Various types were tried, including the largest production flying boats of World War II, the Martin JRM Mars 'boats still at work for Forest Industries Flying Tankers in British Columbia. The most numerous big water-bombers were the impressive conversions of war-surplus Consolidated PBY Canso flying boats that began to flow from Field Aviation of Malton, Ontario, in 1961. But they were unable to fill this specialized quick-response need. Perhaps a smaller, slow-flying single-engined aircraft could get to fires earlier and achieve more accurate drops.[8]

Ugandan aerial prowler: the 1,672nd Beaver built, 5X-UVU was registered CF-WSD in 1967 at Downsview and may have been part of the backlog that convinced Hawker-Siddeley to close down the line. Only 20 more were built. VIA STEVE TODD

The first type so converted was the DHC-3 Otter, in 1957. At the urging of an Ontario Provincial Air Service pilot named Tom Cooke, an Otter was modified with open-topped, cylindrical tanks within its floats that could be rolled sideways by means of a cable release to empty their water on the fire below, and a probe to pick up water while taxiing. Cooke made an impressive demonstration of the Otter's capabilities that July, when he singlehandedly held a mile-long fire at bay until crews were able to arrive to finish the job.[9] Within a year all OPAS Beavers and Otters were so equipped. Piston Beavers could carry ninety gallons in their floats.

Long before it flew for the first time, the Turbo Beaver's potential as a water-bomber was obvious. While its float tank capacity was 140 gallons, a worthwhile improvement over the piston Beaver's (compared with the Otter's 230 and the PBY Canso's 800), the Turbo Beaver picked up its load in five to eight seconds in a run of only 400 feet—two-thirds of the Otter's pickup run. Although experience has confirmed that a variety of aircraft types should be available for use in fighting fires, and the turbo-powered DHC-6 Twin Otter has replaced the Turbo Beaver in this role, the Beaver Mk.III pioneered the quick pinpoint-response technique of fighting forest fires before they spread out of control.

In the midst of a sales slowdown that had a number of Beavers awaiting buyers in 1967, DHC's then-parent, Hawker Siddeley Aviation, shut down the Beaver assembly line. A number of DHC board members resigned over the decision, including Russ Bannock.

By the late 1960s the profile of northern bush flying had changed. Every native settlement had a mile-long gravel runway, and many northern cities had fully-equipped all-weather airports. While the need for STOL performance was less acute, the change to turboprop engines, with their more efficient long-distance cruise characteristics and easy cold-weather operation, made the Turbo Beaver and its successors, especially the Twin Otter, ideal for the new northern reality. If anything, the Turbo Beaver was slightly ahead of its time.

On the West Coast, the more economical short-hop low-altitude characteristics of the standard Beaver makes it the continuing choice of such operators as Vancouver's Harbour Air Seaplanes and Nanaimo's Baxter Air. For them, the Beaver was pretty much perfect as it was originally designed. For the customer who wants that extra margin, however, Victoria's Viking Air has certified a new Turbo Beaver for the 1990s.

Viking Air's Turbo Beaver is an improvement over the Downsview original by the simple virtue of the passage of thirty years since the original was designed. To begin with, Viking offers a more powerful version of the PT-6, the -27, which, while

offering only a projected 620 horsepower for takeoff, 70 more than the PT-6s installed at Downsview, develops that power with less strain, enhancing mechanical durability and reliability.

Viking also offers a complete avionics package with its Turbo Beavers, an all-new electrical system, a cabin extension licensed from Sealand Aviation with its two-part, top-hinged Alaska cargo door, steel-fixture lifetime wing struts, and, for floatplane or amphibious operation, Wipline floats cleared for operation at a 6,000-pound gross weight.

Viking summarizes the improvements it can make to any Beaver by calling its Turbo the "Six-Thousand Pound Turbo Beaver," certified to carry ten persons or 2,450 pounds of freight.

It is still expensive, although its price has increased only by a factor of three over a period during which many durable-goods prices have increased tenfold.[10] On the throttle-propeller-fuel quadrant, the new Beaver identifies itself as a DE HAVILLAND–VIKING TURBO BEAVER 6000.

Bill Whitney, Kenmore's chief pilot, installs a fresh-water rinse-out fitting in place of one of the PT6A-135's igniters prior to flushing the engine after a day's operations in salt water. Kenmore's Turbo Beavers and Otters are powered with the new-technology 750-shp -135s, both for the power and for the improved rinse-out system. C. MARIN FAURE

Chapter Twelve

Adventure stories from the moody Pacific Coast

Of all the world's cities, only a few offer an air show every rush-hour, right downtown. They are port cities with harbours surrounded by mountains, like Sydney, Seattle, San Francisco and Vancouver. Those cities' harbours are downtown runways for floatplanes. The preferred floatplane is the Beaver. More and more, the Beaver has become a combination bush plane and uptown plane.

It is only mildly ironic that an airplane designed for the wilderness now spends much of its time ferrying executives between urban cores. To begin with, a city like Vancouver is situated at the edge of pristine wilderness. And the flying is just as spectacular. Sometimes a final approach into the prevailing wind involves clearing a high bridge, then dropping like a stone to a lake in a bowl formed by high surrounding hills, as is the case with Lake Union, Seattle's downtown floatplane terminal.

In Vancouver the fly-past can best be seen from Brockton Point in Stanley Park. Moments after you arrive, the air show headliner is right in front of you: a glistening white Beaver, showing you its gracefully-curved de Havilland-trademark tail and red stripes on the tops of its squared-off wings as it banks toward you, turning hard from left to right toward the Nine O'Clock Gun, a ceremonial artillery piece that once warned fishermen it was time to return to their moorings.

This Beaver is a gleaming representative of the Baxter Air squadron of Nanaimo—"the nicest Beaver fleet on the coast," says Jack Schofield, editor of the *West Coast Aviator*. An experienced eye, watching the Baxter Air Beaver rounding Brockton Point, notes the way the control surfaces move on the trailing edges of the wings, reflecting the morning light. The Beaver's prop is still pulling hard, keeping the power on.

The Beaver's next move might not seem as impressive as air show aerobatics, but, in its own way, it is. Only the most experienced pilots try it. Most pilots, even flying Beavers, simply continue east, taking advantage of a liquid runway that extends a mile or so east to the end of the downtown Vancouver waterfront at the Alberta Wheat Pool, if necessary, and then taxi back. But that takes time.

Instead, this pilot is turning sharply around Brockton Point, executing a very tight descending turn toward the Baxter Air terminal in Coal Harbour, losing airspeed while maintaining the right balance of engine revolutions to descend on a rectangle of water about a big as an aircraft carrier deck, and crosswise to the prevailing west wind—but in the lee of the park's giant Douglas firs. Several seemingly contradictory things are happening at once: the plane is slowing as its engine keeps the power on in case of an overshoot, and the Beaver rolls into its descending turn.

Inside the cockpit, the pilot is furiously pumping a lever between the front seats to generate hydraulic pressure and lower the flaps on the inboard trailing edges of the wing. The flaps drop at the rate he pumps. Now they are down, and so are the ailerons out by the wingtips. Dick Hiscocks's all-moving trailing edge, operated by Fred Buller's ingenious operating mechanism, can either give the Beaver more lift or, as now, function as a larger airbrake as the flaps move through 15 degrees toward 30. The Beaver's power and size, along with the skills pilots develop flying in and out of the north Pacific Coast's misty mountain inlets, are also its safeguard against sudden crosswinds and heavy chop on the water.

The Beaver swings around behind the trees, heading south toward the towers of downtown Vancouver. It levels off and finally swoops down into its final approach to the harbour, practically floating in air to a foamy touchdown inside the Burnaby Shoal marker due east of Brockton Point. It taxis past the three boat-refuelling barges at the entrance to Coal Harbour at the waterfront's west edge.

Up in the Harbour Control tower, atop the waterfront office tower known as 200 Granville, with visibility an easy hundred miles in every direction but north, the air traffic controller who cleared the Baxter Air Beaver for landing as it flew over the Lion's Gate Bridge, watches it far below and almost straight ahead as we face north. It leaves a white v-shaped wake coming toward us. The tail drops and its floats settle into the water as the pilot cuts the throttle.

Why do only experienced pilots do this?

"Because," controller Ron Ulmi explains, speaking from behind twin reversed images of Vancouver's waterfront convention centre, Canada Place, on the bottom halves of his government-issue Nicolet sunglasses, "if you have to go around"—that is, abort your landing and try again—"you fly straight into all these buildings."

There is a story about the Beaver that is legendary not because it didn't happen, but because it happened so often. It would have happened in the 1950s, a time when pilots and Department of Transport inspectors played what both sides acknowledged was a cat-and-mouse game, and a likely location would be Campbell River, then the floatplane capital of the world. Celebrities like Bob Hope and Bing Crosby drop in to fish for salmon. A Beaver at the aviation dock is so heavily loaded its floats are almost submerged. The pilot is stowing a few last-minute items in the cockpit when a stranger ambles up, obviously impressed.

"Must be a good airplane if it can carry all this stuff. . . ."

"Oh yeah," the pilot says. "Put *any*thing in there, it'll go."

Maurie Mercer once alighted at Kelsey Bay with a diesel engine aboard. He actually strained the airplane's fuselage from the dead weight without digging his floats into the water, an impressive feat of airmanship. Of course, he says, digging your floats in can cause the airplane to cartwheel, which, he points out in his laconic pilot's storytelling mode, "is not too good on the physique."[1]

Maurie Mercer, who once went inverted in a Beaver to escape a logger's chokehold and glided CF-CAT six miles over water to convince a sceptical passenger the Beaver is a safe airplane. MAURIE MERCER

. . . So the pilot at Campbell River, feeling expansive about flying the greatest bush plane ever built, was explaining how it was routine to fly overweight in Beavers.

"But those floats are under water," the stranger said.

"No problem. Just keep the nose up."

How much did he think he was overweight this time, the stranger asked.

"Oh, maybe 500 pounds."

"Well," the stranger says, taking out his Department of Transport inspector's ID, "you take everything out of there and weigh it."

The pilot had been optimistic—a hazard brought on by flying Beavers for any length of time. The cargo came to 800 pounds over the Beaver's authorized gross takeoff weight. The pilot was grounded for a month.[2]

Only *eight* hundred pounds over? That's nothing these days. Many Beaver floatplanes working the B.C. coast are cleared to carry 1,000 pounds more than the

1,700 pounds that was their original useful load. There are dozens of bays and inlets along the coasts of the mainland, Vancouver Island and the Queen Charlottes where the only express supply link, ambulance and one-day connection with Vancouver is by Beaver. In places like Texada Island's Blubber Bay, with crosswinds and a two-foot chop on the water, a Beaver is the only aircraft a thinking pilot would try to get in and out with.

Gerry Bruder, a pilot and author who flies for Seattle's Kenmore Air Harbor, quotes a colleague who flies B.C.'s temperamental Inside Passage to Alaska as saying, "You can't get me out of a Beaver in bad weather."

"Few roads or airports await the traveller in this network of waterways that weaves among islands and mountains for one thousand miles along the coasts of western British Columbia and southeastern Alaska," Bruder writes in the April 1988 *AOPA Pilot* magazine. "This is floatplane country. Famous for its beauty, the Inside Passage is notorious for its rain and gales, but the Beaver's thick, high-lift wings and big flaps let a pilot who is straining to see where he is going slow to a comfortable 60 knots despite the airplane's legal 5,090-pound gross weight. And when a 30-

Not for novices: a technique for getting unstuck in calm water with little wind.
C. MARIN FAURE

knot wind whips the water, sturdy construction and hefty floats (usually 22-foot-long Edo 4930s) allow a Beaver pilot to take off and plop down safely flight after flight while the Cessnas spend the day drydocked. . . .

"Those 450 horses provide enough power for the prudent Beaver pilot in virtually any scenario. In fact, since the supercharger lacks a wastegate, firewalling the throttle below 5,000 feet results in too much power. Every once in a while, however, a wind shift or a miscalculation puts the airplane into deep, undulating ocean swells at a point the pilot thought he'd safely be in the air, or a sudden downdraft shoves the airplane towards the treetops during a climbout. In this context, intentionally overboosting the engine beyond the 36.5-inch manifold pressure takeoff limit is akin to withdrawing funds from a savings account earmarked for the kids' college educations; you do what you have to do in an emergency and be thankful that a way out is available. Back in town, of course, you tell the mechanics about it as a courtesy to whoever flies the airplane next. . . ."

Beaver pilots have a studied nonchalance about all this. Men and women who fly it every day see the Beaver as a basic tool—a handy, well-broken-in, everyday appliance. They don't exactly take it for granted, but they don't compare flying it with sex either. An everyday appliance is exactly what Phil Garratt had in mind when he envisioned it in 1945 as a flying half-ton pickup truck.

"It's like your basic Kenworth tractor on the highway," says Larry Langford of Campbell River's Vancouver Island Air. "You use it, you hardly think about it, you maintain it. Durable, reliable, easy to work on. What else is there?"[3]

"With a Beaver you can get into tighter spots, smaller bays, higher lakes," says Frank Roberts, also of Campbell River, a thirty-five-year Beaver driver, "because of the performance. It's a great old pickup truck."[4]

"Just a tremendous aircraft," says Tom Baxter, who with 5,000 hours on Beavers uses five of them to maintain an eleven-flights-daily harbour-to-harbour schedule between Nanaimo and Vancouver, sometimes with two or three Beavers at once to handle all the business.

"They pack the loads and they do the job. Lumber, sheets of plywood. Canoes. That is amazing—and they fly. You just get a bond for them. It's just like a fungus growin' on ya."[5]

"No airplane can compete with it," says Harbour Air's chief pilot, Bill Pennings. That's why Harbour Air Seaplanes had fourteen of them in 1996—three more than they had the year before.[6]

Pilots feel so safe in the Beaver they have been known to gently mock their passengers' fears of flying in it. Campbell River's Lee Frankham, who has flown Beavers from there to Newfoundland, used to pull the nose up and jerk a string to release a few nuts and bolts that would rattle back along the floor from the vicinity of the engine mounts. The passenger's reaction was invariably colourful. "Oh," Frankham would say, "don't worry about it. . . ."[7]

Maurie Mercer was a corporate pilot with a heavy-equipment supplier from 1960 until 1979. It fell to Mercer, prize graduate of Vancouver U-Fly, to become one of the first corporate pilots to work out of the South Airport—a job to kill for today. A few years later he was at Downsview to accept the factory-fresh, amphibious Beaver CF-CAT, with wingtip tanks for seven hours endurance, at the then-astronomical price of $65,000. He soon developed oodles of confidence in CF-CAT.

Mercer often carried a company salesman who was terrified of flying. Mercer remembers him saying things like "If that engine fails, we're doomed."

On the contrary, Mercer told him, if the engine failed the aircraft would glide. Even airliners would glide, he said. He offered to show the salesman how far a Beaver could glide.

"He was against it," Mercer grins. "I said, 'It'll reassure you.' Six miles out over the Strait of Georgia, I cut the engine and glided into Vancouver Harbour. Air traffic control wondered what I was doing, but we made it. Could've gone farther, in fact.

"My scariest moment in a Beaver?" Flying a hung-over logger to Jervis Inlet, Mercer was grabbed from behind and held in a choke-hold as the logger mumbled, "If there's anything I hate, it's pilots."

"I remember thinking to myself, 'How are you going to get out of this one?' I did the only thing I could under the circumstances. I turned the airplane over into a deep bank, and he sure let go in a hurry."

"Adventures?" repeats Bill Pennings. "Man, every day of my life is an adventure. But I never had any close calls with Beavers. I've had close calls with other airplanes. But the Beaver has never put me in a position where I've had a close call." That's in *ten* thousand hours.

Some pilots go out of their way to refute what one calls "the myth that the Beaver is perfect." No pilot, other than Pennings, ever calls any airplane perfect. A perfect airplane would require less airmanship.

"The only thing about the Beaver," Maurie Mercer says, "it has a small tail. When you're throttled-up"—as on takeoff—"you need full rudder to fly straight. If you don't, you'll be running along the sand on the shore." The torque created by the spinning prop tends to turn the Beaver to the right under full power—an effect exacerbated on floats. Then too, the airplane with enough tail for all of its pilots has yet to leave the ground.

Accessible only by Beaver: Walker Nature Preserve, Spatsizi Plateau, Coldfish Lake. Five hundred miles from the nearest post office. GRAHAM OSBORNE

Larry Langford of Vancouver Island Air says, "The Beaver has some bad flying qualities, contrary to popular opinion. It has a very high stall speed"—the speed below which an airplane stops flying under control—"at 60 degrees bank, with a full load and no flap." Under those conditions, he says, the Beaver will stall at about 105 mph.

Langford was describing a fatal accident involving a Beaver in northern B.C. in which an inexperienced pilot tried a turning climbout and caught a float on a log. At a 60-degree bank, fully loaded and without flap, at barely more than 100 mph, the load on a Beaver's wing is 8,800 pounds, equivalent to an overload of 3,700

pounds. On the other hand, Langford adds, "It does well with the flaps down," as the pilots rounding Brockton Point on their way into Vancouver's Burrard Inlet harbour demonstrate during any weekday rush-hour.

Even the age of the average Beaver reassures some pilots. The last piston-engined Beaver was built about thirty years ago. "Every time I get into one of the damn things," says Lee Frankham, himself aged sixty-five, "I think to myself, 'It's not likely that anything's gonna fall off while I'm in it. One thing about a Beaver, everything that's gonna fall off has fallen off. Anything that's gonna go has already gone.'"

A Pacific Coast veteran pilot, possibly the pilot with the highest time when he died, was the late Leo Doucette. He became the late Leo Doucette in an aircraft other than the Beaver. If anything, the Beaver he was flying when its wing folded up with an almighty *Craa-a-ck!* just outboard of the bracing strut joint prolonged his life by continuing to fly.[8] Internal corrosion is always a possibility in an aircraft flown mainly around salt water, and extra maintenance is usually part of the routine for Beavers operating in the North American West Coast environment.

One reason Beavers from elsewhere are brought to the Pacific Coast is that there will be less corrosion in aircraft operated only on fresh water, such as the lakes of Ontario or Quebec, where many early Beavers, and a few of the later ones, were operated for much of their useful lives. Mike Quinn, of Whistler Air, bought one of the last ones built, CF-SKZ, number 1,594 off the line, from Sault Ste. Marie lumberman Frank La Jambe. It had 7,000 hours on it when he bought it in 1995. Flying out of Green Lake, near the Whistler Mountain resort, it still often takes off from fresh water. SKZ has been modified for sightseeing with a Sealand cabin extension kit installed in Campbell River that gives seven window seats instead of the usual five. The giveaway from outside is two rectangular windows behind the rear door on each side. Quinn compensates for the rearward centre-of-gravity shift by using only his forward gas tank and limiting the weight of the passengers on the new rearmost bench to 200 pounds. A battery shift forward is a normal part of such a modification, which incorporates the old battery compartment into the bigger cabin. Quinn calls the modification "fine-tuning" an otherwise 95 per cent perfect airframe.[9]

One task the Beaver was not designed for is flying heavy loads at an altitude of much more than 5,000 feet. Its supercharged Wasp Junior engine develops full power up to that altitude. So it will forever be a mystery to Jack Schofield how he found himself taking a charter to the 8,000-foot level over a glacier in Beaver CF-JFQ.

The Beaver floatplane's listed service ceiling is around 18,000 feet, but in practice fully-loaded Beavers seldom get halfway to that height. At 12,000, after any

Facing page: Kenmore Beaver on approach, Chutine Glacier, June 1987.
C. MARIN FAURE

length of time, a pilot begins to exhibit the effects of oxygen deprivation, and the Wasp Junior that got him there will be gasping for breath as well. And the floats are no help. The ones on CF-JFQ were, like those on Maurie Mercer's CF-CAT, amphibious. The extra weight of floats combined with amphibious landing gear reduces payload by about 35 per cent, and the drag reduces whatever ceiling that particular Beaver is actually capable of reaching. With the more than two-hundred-pound additional weight of their retractable wheels, any altitude higher than a mile in an amphibian is as accessible as the gates of heaven.

Why, exactly, Schofield and his two passengers were about to climb over the mountains near the intersection of Wakeman Sound and Kingcome Inlet had not been made known to the pilot when he took off on a beautiful morning from Runway 07 at Port Hardy. He did note that his passengers, who had never seen an amphib Beaver before, were vastly amused at the furious hand-pumping Schofield was doing to raise the wheels into the Beaver's floats. They had no idea.

Schofield knew only that they would have to be at 5,000 feet when they reached their intermediate destination, and then climb steadily up the Kingcome Valley to a glacier marked by his passengers with an x on his map. The elevation of that glacier was indicated in bold print as 8,050 feet—well above the altitude at which the engine develops its peak power.

"My estimated time-to-climb worked out pretty good," Schofield says, "and we arrived at the corner of Wakeman and Kingcome at about five grand and still climbing. I felt a little sorry for the engine along the route and had levelled off several times to permit those hard-working cylinders to cool off.

"In addition to my two passengers, the Beaver was carrying a fair load of equipment and foodstuffs, principally canned goods, packed in small, well-secured bundles. A single seat had replaced the three-passenger rear bench seat and the round camera hatch in the aft belly had been removed prior to takeoff. The load parcels were all small enough to go through the hatch. . . .

"The aircraft was showing signs of reluctance to climb, and time to gain the next 3,000 feet was greater than the first leg. I persevered in pampering the engine to that height, where it became essentially tapped-out, with the throttle to the wall, turning up sea level cruise manifold pressure and rpm."

Along the way, Schofield asked his passengers what all this was in aid of. They explained that they planned to climb this glacier to the 8,050-foot peak, then descend the other side and transit several other peaks before reaching their eventual goal.

"We, of course, were to drop their food caches along the route. To my question of, why were they doing this, their answer was simply, 'Because it is there to be done.'"

JFQ, very much at home at 50 feet above sea level, was flying like a pig at 8,000. Schofield's co-pilot-seat passenger brightly indicated the route from the peak of the glacier to the base, "where they wanted me to fly while they pushed the parcels out the camera hatch.

"It would take more than one pass to get rid of all this stuff. Which meant another endurance climb back up to eight thousand."

"We would like you to be as close to the glacier as possible when we drop the food," called out the passenger as he unbuckled and climbed into the back to help his friend.

Schofield is a sea level pilot. The mushy response from the Beaver's controls was giving him a headache. So they wanted him to pull out as close to the glacier floor as possible. Glaciers generate their own downdrafts—Katabiatic winds, or Taku Winds, as they are known in Alaska. Cold air whistles down the glacier's flanks like an invisible avalanche. Other factors, such as accelerated cooling of the Beaver's cylinders during the rapid descent, came to mind.

It was at this approximate moment that he thought of Chuck Jenson's bent de Havilland Otter. What a story that was! It had been driven onto the ice of a similar glacier. It tobogganed down the slope on its floats until it reached flying speed and became airborne again. With struts bent, floats punctured, fuselage twisted, Chuck had nursed the Otter home, but it never flew again. And an Otter is bigger and more powerful than any Beaver.

With all these thoughts parading through his fully-alert mind, Schofield figured now was the time for "a professional decisive approach. I turned around and yelled to my passengers over the rush of air from the hatch: 'I won't go lower than 300 feet above the ice and we *will* climb out of the descent before reaching the bottom of the glacier. . . .'

"I don't know where I got those numbers. At the lowest point of the descent I was circling a few feet above what geophysicists call a cirque. It is hard to say who was the more reluctant to climb back and do it again—me or the airplane—but JFQ did what was asked of her once more. She handled like a marshmallow. I was terrified. JFQ wanted to go home and so did I. We just barely got out of that canyon.

"I never heard from those climbers again. But I've got a hunch they're still up there on that glacier, digging like maniacs, trying to find their lunch."[10]

Facing page: The DHC-2 tech manual and the restored ex-Karl Springer Beaver at Al Beaulieu's Pacific Aircraft Salvage hangar, Vancouver South Airport, 1984.
ALEX WATERHOUSE-HAYWARD

Chapter Thirteen

Beavers better than new

The wrecks arranged in neat little piles around the war-era hangar of Al Beaulieu's Pacific Aircraft Salvage at Vancouver's South Airport are mute testimony to the truth of an old flying adage: aviation in itself is not inherently dangerous, but, to an even greater degree than the sea, it is terribly unforgiving. One of these wrecks was—still is, maybe will be once again—CF-OMI, Beaver number 1204, a missionary Beaver which belonged to the Roman Catholic Church. It landed upside-down in the Queen Charlotte Islands, a frequent, if temporary, graveyard for Beavers.

These piles of aluminum are often so grotesquely twisted or compressed that it seems inconceivable that any further use can be found for any of them, let alone making them fly again. Had the wreckage been part of almost any other type of aircraft, it would long since have been melted down into ingots.

The South Airport, Vancouver's air terminal until it was replaced by a bigger one during the early 1960s, is the kind of aviation backwater that is now a hive of aircraft repair and maintenance activity. It is a low-rent conglomeration of obsolescence, an ex-Trans Canada Airlines Viscount here, a CF-100 fighter there. In other words, the perfect environment for a pure entrepreneur and craftsman like Beaulieu.

Not all the Beavers that pass through Beaulieu's hangar have crashed. Some were merely abandoned. Not every corner of the world has the means to maintain the 1929 technology of the Beaver's engine. So some aircraft were left to moulder away as worn-out, obsolete, useless artifacts. One man's refuse is another man's treasure. If anyone could retrieve NZ6010 from the Beardmore Glacier and make it fly again, it would surely be Al Beaulieu. This hangar is one portal through which some of the thousand-odd Beavers still flying have passed on their way to becoming airworthy again.

Drawing from his steady supply of crashed or abandoned Beavers, Beavers from forgotten airfields being reclaimed by jungle or pulled out of salt water—five of them lined up wingless and without engines across the back of his hangar—Beaulieu turns out three or four Beaver recreations a year. He obtains these raw materials by means he declines to specify; this is, after all, his most important professional secret. One Pacific Northwest pilot calls him "the artist." A couple of hangars down the road they just roll their eyes when his name comes up. Like any artist, he is often misunderstood and his name invariably mispronounced. "Al Bolio?" says one of his skeptical neighbours. "He still in business?"

Such a dealer in the remains of airplane crashes and their attendant mortality cannot but develop, wreck by wreck and hulk by hulk, a philosophy, a personal outlook if you will, on the human folly that caused them. This philosophy must be consistent with the fact that Beaulieu has dedicated his working life to this airplane, the Beaver, that he first flew and fell in love with in a way he has fallen in love with no woman, before he had a pilot's licence. It must be a philosophy that takes note of the Beaver's design faults, of which he feels it has its share, without blaming the machine itself for whatever happened to bring it to his hangar. His insights must take account of the fact that Beavers he has rebuilt and put back into service with his own small northern British Columbia airline have crashed. "Ninety-nine-point-nine per cent of the Beaver crashes were caused by fuel starvation," he declares. "Pilot error, mostly."

The five fuselages lined up at the back of Beaulieu's hangar, none of which show evidence of ever having crashed, form something of a Beaver museum in themselves. One, CF-JAA, is the sixteenth Beaver, Beaulieu says, sold new to Frank Beban, the man who logged most of South Moresby, one of the Queen Charlotte Islands. (Beaulieu doesn't find these early-series Beavers all that impressive: "We've had number four in here," he says. That would be CF-OBU, one of the original Ontario Lands and Forests batch.) The next, CF-CDT, was a beautiful Kenmore

Beaver number 135, about to be brought back to life. Donated to the French Red Cross and abandoned during the early Vietnam War as F-OAKK with low hours on the clock, it was one among five Beaver fuselages ranged across the back wall of the Pacific Aircraft Salvage hangar in 1994. ALEX WATERHOUSE-HAYWARD

rebuild from Seattle—Beaulieu often compliments his Beaver-rebuilder competition in Seattle—that hit a rock landing at Haki Pass on Calvert Island, sank, and was wrecked in an attempted retrieval. The third is number 135, donated to the French Red Cross as F-OAKK just before Dien Bien Phu, used briefly by Air Viet Nam, and made a museum exhibit in Hanoi with so little air time that the finish on the varnished wood rubstrips around the doors is intact, as are the simple, early-series Model A-style door handles. The fifth is a former U.S. Army Beaver, "built just a little bit stronger."

Dick Hiscocks has been here. This hangar is a personal museum for him, too. Beaulieu remembers the Beaver's aerodynamicist shaking his head at the wonder of it all: a design that was considered a stopgap until the bigger Otter went into production, being rebuilt for commercial use nearly fifty years after its first flight. "He says he just couldn't believe the planes would go so far," chuckles the man who makes them go on and on.

In front of Beaulieu on this day in 1994, gleaming in the sunlight at his hangar's open door, is a 24-*thousand*-hour Beaver—"one of the highest-time Beavers around"—in gleaming lemon-yellow with forest-green markings. It crashed near Prince Rupert, British Columbia. It is now what is known as a zero-time airplane. It is Beaulieu's current masterpiece, the twelfth Beaver built. It once belonged to the late mining magnate Karl Springer, who was the money behind Russ Baker's Central B.C. Airways. Ernest Krahulec, FHB's mechanic, also maintained this one after CBCA was absorbed by the company that became CP Air (and is now Canadian). Having run up 24,000 hours at the time of its first demise, the ex-Springer Beaver might be said to have simply died of old age, except that Krahulec insists there is no such condition for a properly-maintained airplane—especially when he was the one supervising its maintenance—and of course he is right. For all intents and purposes, it is now factory-fresh.[1]

No, Beaulieu says, better than that, "25 per cent better than when it came out of the factory. At least 25 per cent better. We say 100 per cent better, but it's at least 25 per cent...."

Among the improvements are stronger floor mounts for the seats—a modification derived directly from crash experience—and a new instrument panel that puts the engine-performance gauges, such as the rpm indicator, up in the pilot's line of sight on takeoff. It has skylights, as the military Beavers did. Moving the cabin

Surplused U.S. Army Beavers seldom rest for long. This is the raw material from which restoration shops such as Kenmore build Beavers better than new.

GREGG MUNRO, KENMORE AIR HARBOR

bulkhead back two feet creates a more spacious cabin, and a bigger, domed window can be added behind the door for better shoulder room and visibility for passengers. (The Sealand extended cabin installed in Whistler Air's Beaver moves the bulkhead back even farther, at the cost of range.) Relative weak points, such as the junction between the wing bracing strut and the wing itself, are given double skins. A three-blade propeller cuts down on the noise.

Like all Al Beaulieu Beavers, this one is cleared to carry that extra half-ton of freight that Beavers have been carrying all along anyway, making it an honest-to-goodness one-ton truck of the air. Exactly what Phil Garratt had in mind fifty years ago. Sometimes perfection takes a little longer. Having outlived at least a couple of owners, the ex-Springer Beaver could be called immortal.

"A lot of planes, as they get older, the regulations tighten up," Beaulieu says. They are permitted to carry less and less weight. "This plane's still getting heavier."

So even once the worst has happened, few Beavers get to rest in peace. The increase in value to ten times what they cost new from the factory has made it worthwhile to rebuild Beavers, often from little more than pieces of crumpled aluminum and the factory identification plate. A quarter-million dollars still pays for a lot of highly skilled metal handwork. A rebuilt Beaver can cost even more than that, depending on avionics, or whether it was among the thousand-odd built to military specifications, which are especially prized.

Inflation doesn't account for all of the increase in value. Dozens of little improvements have made it a better airplane. Today's Beaver is cleared to carry more weight than it was coming out of the factory. There is no direct competition. For the most part, aircraft for general aviation stopped being manufactured more than twenty years ago, when the insurance premiums for civil aircraft manufacturers became prohibitively high. If a Cessna Caravan sounds like a new, single-engine equivalent to a Beaver, its $1.5 million price tag is likely to put it out of reach for a coastal bush operation.

Pacific Aircraft Salvage is one of several companies in the Pacific Northwest that together have formed a small industry working on Beavers. Each of these operations has its own style, its own markets, its own secrets for transforming wrecks, hulks or just plain tired airframes into Beavers that are better than ever.

One reason Beaulieu has such respect for Beavers that have passed through the Kenmore Air Harbor facility on the shores of Lake Washington, near Seattle, is that Kenmore originated many of the modifications he carries out to make the Beaver at least 25 per cent better. He has also sold Beavers to Kenmore. To visit Kenmore's base is to complete a pilgrimage to one of the founts of Beaver wisdom. Most of the

Kenmore modifications were developed before the 1980s, when certifying changes to existing aircraft in the United States became a case, as Kenmore chief engineer Jerry Rader puts it, "of having to have a full page of paper for each word's worth of engineering."

Kenmore was started by a wartime Pan American Airways mechanic named Robert B. Munro in 1946 with a hangar and a 36-hp Aeronca-K. It was soon operating a Seabee and two Norsemans, the latter having been "the best workhorse on floats in the '50s. Then we discovered the Beaver...," as Kenmore's catalogue states. "When another operator tried to use their new Beaver to lure one of our most important charter customers away in the early '60s, we began shopping for our own. Our love affair with the Beaver continues to this day."

A two-man team did most of the Beaver modifications then. Preston Dickson was the engineer and Dick Ulm test-flew the modifications. "They engineered things through common sense," Rader says. Was the main cause of floatplane noise in the toney neighbourhoods around Lake Washington the Beaver's near-nine-foot prop? Okay, let's put a smaller-diameter three-bladed propeller on.

"That does three things for you," Rader says. "It improves the noise level considerably inside the airplane. It's a different kind of noise. Less fatiguing. It improves the structural integrity of the airplane and the instruments. Before we made this change, we constantly had to repair cowling fixtures and cracks in the cowlings themselves. Once we put three-bladed propellers on, all this disappeared. The third thing is greater clearance to the water. The blades don't get chewed up. And there's no detriment to performance." There is also a weight saving of 56 to 61 pounds.

Another weight saving results from removing the battery from its sliding rails behind the normal cabin bulkhead and moving it behind the engine. This can save as much as 72 pounds when a smaller battery of comparable power is substituted. The former battery hatch becomes a luggage space. A new alternator system can save a further 33 pounds. Every pound saved on the airframe is another pound of payload.

Often you can recognize a Kenmore Beaver by the bubble rear-door window, which gives better vision downward for passengers. A rectangular window in place of the porthole behind the passenger/freight door reveals that this Beaver may have had its cabin extended.

The most frequent visual giveaway for a Kenmore Beaver is the pair of endplate fins on the horizontal stabilizers, replacing the original floatplane Beaver's ventral fin, which tended to strike docks. For former military Beavers, a three-passenger bench seat goes behind the two front seats to restore the Beaver's full seating capacity as originally certified. There are other detail modifications available from Kenmore, from brakes for the amphibian's wheels to a water-rudder retraction kit.

It may not look like much, but this ex-U-6A, one of 980 Beavers ordered by the U.S. Army and Air Force, is the preferred basis from which zero-timed bush planes with pricetags inching toward the half-million mark are being constructed.
GREGG MUNRO, KENMORE AIR HARBOR

Or, if a Beaver owner yearns to restore the airplane right down to its factory cockpit placards, Kenmore can supply replicas of the following oft-ignored instructions: "This aeroplane must be operated as a normal category aeroplane in compliance with the operating limitations specified in approved flight and maintenance manuals," and, of course, the maximum weights placard, which lists those weights for wheel/ski, floats, amphib land and amphib water operations, and then, for good measure, adds "ACROBATICS AND SPINS NOT APPROVED." Speaking of maximum operating weights, one of Kenmore pilot Gerry Bruder's personal operating credos for the Beaver is that "if a Beaver floats after loading, it will fly."[2]

"Every airplane has a place," Rader says. We are surrounded by Kenmore's ten charter piston Beavers and two Turbo Beavers, including the last piston (1676 N900KA) and Turbo (1692 N9744T) Beavers built. As well, there are a number of Turbo Otters that Rader, anticipating another ex-Indian Air Force machine being converted at that moment in Kenmore's shop soon becoming available, counted as "four-and-a-half" of those. They include the eleventh Otter built. (Rader feels the Otter's only real weakness is its geared 600-hp P&W Wasp engine, which is replaced with a P&WC PT6A-27 which is not that much more powerful at

Kenmore Beaver N17598 at Big Goat Lake, Misty Fjords, Alaska. Summer 1985.

C. MARIN FAURE

662 horsepower for takeoff but has a much lower installed weight.) As for the Beaver, "it's easy to work on, inexpensive to operate, and the amount of work that it will do for you—nothing else can do it." Kenmore has rebuilt more than 130 of them. More than that, Rader claims to have kits for one or more Kenmore modifications on one-third of all the Beavers built.

Their prize project as the Beaver's forty-ninth birthday approached was a total rebuild of a military Beaver for an American entertainer that would involve three-thousand man-hours of work with the meter running toward US$400,000. Converting a military machine involves, among other changes, removing its "ejection doors," doors whose hinge pins can be pulled for quick exits. This one will have a rebuilt instrument panel structure that will support a complete avionics (radar, navigation, radio and intercom systems) suite. The entire skin will be replaced, leaving only the original battery compartment cover. Other than those minor changes, it will get the complete Kenmore treatment. That means Kenmore will completely rebuild the airframe, overhaul its engine, install modifications—everything but the instruments and propellers.

It seems that any Beaver operator, from the U.S. Army to the Australians, is tempted sooner or later to do something fairly extraordinary with the aircraft. For a couple of Kenmore customers, the bright idea was to fly Beavers across the North Atlantic. The Beaver's range varies from a little more than 200 miles fully loaded to about a thousand miles with the pilot and little else. The new owners of Beavers N130WA, Freebird Wilderness Tours, and N930AJ, an outfit called Beavair (heh-heh), crossed the Atlantic in 1988 and 1990, respectively. The first trip involved flying below 200-foot ceilings for 600 miles. The Beavair Beaver took 70 hours to fly from Seattle to Switzerland. In fact, this trip is becoming somewhat routine: N130WA has crossed the Atlantic three times.

That's not all. Like every charter operator, Kenmore sometimes carries bulky or potentially hazardous cargo. "Many Beavers have logged military service time before arriving at Kenmore Air Harbor, but never as dive bombers. . . ." Not that we know of, anyway. "In the '70s we transported unarmed torpedoes to a joint U.S.–Canadian test range facility [at Nanoose Bay] in the Strait of Georgia off Vancouver Island."[3]

In one of the open sheds at Kenmore's base is a collection of dirty white Beaver tails with blue registrations on them: VH-AAY, VH-IMF, VH-IDU. These are the remnants of the biggest-ever fleet of top-dresser Beavers, some of the nearly fifty used by Aerial Agricultural Aviation in Australia. There are seats, ailerons, cowling panels, wingtips, oil tanks—Kenmore's insurance against the day when a Beaver might alight on Lake Washington, its pilot looking for a part for an airplane twice his age, and not be able to find it. It won't happen during this century, at least.

The story of Bill Alder and the Sealand cabin extension for the Beaver is best rendered, not in print, but as a country-and-western lyric. Campbell River is a small city at the north end of the highway that runs up the east coast of Vancouver Island. There is probably no other city of its size that has benefited as much from the Beaver. Campbell River and Bill Alder were a good match: he had maintained Beaver CF-JPX in Dawson Creek, and there remained in 1979 a disproportionate number of Beaver floatplanes in the city that once thought of itself as the Floatplane Capital of the World. Not that Alder knew that. Campbell River was just where Alder and the pickup truck in which he was carrying all his possessions ended up. He was on the run from a divorce. Trucks have been big players in his life. He noticed right away how many Beavers there were in Campbell River, found out how far it was to Vancouver, where they had to be flown for routine maintenance, got himself a black van, filled it with tools, and went to work. Call this "The Ballad of Beaver Bill."

At one time Beavers brought celebrities north to fish for salmon the size of small sharks and stay at Painter's Lodge, where on certain weekends the celebrities on hand could outshine Las Vegas. Many of the floatplanes that brought them there are still tied up at the wharf along a salt-marsh spit at the mouth of the river for which the community is named. Almost all of them are Beavers. A dozen were there one recent Sunday afternoon.

Alder has made another observation about the Beaver that has affected his business. It is as follows: he remembers attending an auction twelve years ago at which Beavers "on floats, zero-time engines, fly away" went for an average of $40,000, "some as low as $35,000." In 1995, he says, Kenmore sold two Beavers for US$750,000 apiece.[4] There had to be something more he could do with the Beaver than overhaul it. By the early '80s he was out of the van and into a big shed on the river spit, with a partner and a new name, Sealand Aviation Ltd.

Once again, opportunity practically hit him between the eyes. Alder believes the first real cabin extension for the Beaver was by Bob Wipplinger's Whip Aire of Minneapolis. (These claims are always subject to dispute.) Whip Aire supplies premium-quality floats for Beavers, Otters and Twin Otters.

"We had a customer at Weldwood [a forest-products company] with the cabin extension. I phoned Wipplinger. I asked for a kit to install one here. He said, 'Nope. Not interested. If they want a cabin extension, bring the plane to Minnesota.'

"I went to Transport Canada. I said to them, 'All the good modifications done to this airplane are done by Americans. I'm going to do it.'

"They said, 'Who's going to engineer it?'

"So then I got Dick Hiscocks. The Transport Canada people tried to talk him out of it. There was not a hitch in the engineering. I thought, 'This is going to be a kit that works very very well. We'll ship them all over the world.' And it is. There's hardly a hole you have to drill."

A Beaver with the Sealand cabin has two more-or-less rectangular windows behind the passenger door. It was one thing to rearrange the space inside the fuselage of the Beaver, and it was something else entirely to cut a much bigger hole in its side. A customer of Alder's, Tim La Porte of Iliamna (Alaska) Air, mentioned one day that what he needed on his plane was "a big door." They drew some highly-imaginative lines on the side of La Porte's Beaver. La Porte was serious, so Alder arranged to use that airplane as the prototype. Neither had any idea what the airplane would be subjected to over the coming months.

"And that's when we started to get educated. We started with a Designated Type Representative. He represents Transport Canada. George Edwards. He was very good, very professional, helped a lot. We had to do stress analysis and a physical load test on it. We installed strain gauges all over the airplane—this was really heavy duty for us. We wired it all to a computer and put loads on the airplane with a scale and a hydraulic jack."

Of course Alder wanted to ship the Sealand conversion kit to the U.S. That meant having it certified there as well. It took seven weeks with a Seattle engineering firm, George Edwards, and FAA officials at Renton who "fell over backwards for us," Alder says, by processing the data collected over nearly two months in three days flat. As things worked out, Alder delivered La Porte's airplane two months late. But his Alaskan customer doesn't complain.

"For a couple of years he used to phone every month to gloat, 'Nobody else in Alaska has this door.' He loaded a four-wheel Honda ATV once. 'Rolls right in, close the door.'"

Unlike Al Beaulieu's Pacific Aircraft Salvage, or Kenmore, or even Bill Alder, Harbour Air Seaplanes is not trying to reinvent the Beaver. They are running an airline—the fastest-growing airline along the British Columbia coast—and, like all airlines, they do things by the book.

Harbour has done so well since it was founded by Greg McDougall and two partners in 1981 that the all-floatplane company recently made the leap from a mixed charter-scheduled operation to a high-intensity shuttle service, harbour-to-harbour, between Vancouver and Victoria.[5] The company acquired some of its first scheduled runs in 1993 with its purchase of the assets of Trans Provincial Airways of Prince Rupert, including TPA's three single-engine Otters (two of them turbos), two Twin Otters and four Beavers. With a number of leased Twin Otters, a baker's dozen Cessnas and no fewer than sixteen Beavers, Harbour Air has become the largest floatplane operator in the world. One of the ex-TPA Beavers, CF-OCJ (number 39, one of the Ontario government order) has been flown by father-and-son pilots, Dick and Rob Nichols. Dick says OCJ is in better shape now than it was twenty-five years ago.

Certainly CF-OCZ's condition has improved recently. It spent the winter of 1995–96 as Harbour's hangar queen, missing its flight surfaces and stripped down to the welded-tube truss that surrounds the cockpit area. This is a part of the world where salt water can do real damage. In a long and varied life since it was manufactured as the one-hundredth Beaver, OCZ has been a water-bomber with Ontario's Department of Lands and Forests, lived the life of Riley shuttling holidayers to and from the resort at Hilton Head, South Carolina (as N254BD), and returned to the

Harbour Air Seaplanes of Vancouver has become the world's largest floatplane operator with Beavers as the backbone of its fleet. C-FOCY, the 74th production unit, was acquired from Burrard Air in 1984. Harbour Air plans to add more Beavers to the 14 in its fleet in 1996.
MIKE REYNO VIA HARBOUR AIR

arduous routine of commercial flying along the North Pacific coast with Harbour Air. It has Kenmore rear windows and battery relocation, but is otherwise original. The four-year overhaul it was undergoing over the winter months is Harbour Air's normal routine, and the airline uses certified parts from either de Havilland, which it authenticates, or from Viking. Harbour Air can fabricate parts and has secured limited supplemental type approvals from Transport Canada for such useful modifications the airline has engineered as a strobe light and removal of the original fire extinguisher, which wasn't as durable as the aircraft itself. The company prefers to maintain its fleet by the letter of the law.

Outside Viking Air's main hangar at Victoria International Airport is a fenced-off yard littered with rectangular chunks of what looks like lead. There are also open structures that look like frames of some kind, built of welded square-section steel, some of them rusty, some painted a bright blue.

At first glance, Viking Air's facility is not all that different from Al Beaulieu's: both are World War II-era hangars. This too is an aviation backwater. Over in the next compound is an Antonov-2 Colt biplane transport—the Russian Otter, you might call it—and a two-seat Hawker Sea Fury carrier fighter. During the war Victoria was a training base for bomber pilots; nearby Patricia Bay is home to at least half-a-dozen drowned Handley-Page Hampden "flying suitcases," as the twin-engine aircraft with their short, slab-sided fuselages were nicknamed. Most of them suffered engine failure at the worst possible time, on takeoff.

Appearances aside, there is a world of difference between this place and Al Beaulieu's hangar at Vancouver's South Airport. In fact, Beaulieu and Viking are at opposite ends of this industry. Beaulieu is the lone artist, a one-man cottage industry that survives by the wits of its colourful chief cook and bottle washer. To hear him tell it, Beaulieu was constantly one stress calculation away from being closed down by Transport Canada, although he is doing much better with the authorities now that he has computerized his parts inventory. One accusation his critics make against Beaulieu is that he makes a lot of his own parts instead of buying parts supplied by Viking Air. But that is changing. In any small industry, how competitors see each other changes very slowly.

Only the most obvious of many differences between Beaulieu's hangar and Viking's operation is that Viking occupies three hangars, comprising a total of 120,000 square feet, and employs seventy-two people, twenty of them licensed airframe mechanics. That "junk" in Viking's fenced forecourt is the tooling, dies and jigs that were used to build the 1,692 Beavers (1,631 Wasp Junior Beavers, the single Alvis Leonides Mk.II, since converted to Wasp Junior power, and 60 Turbo Beavers).

There have been a number of attempts to improve on the Beaver's wing, often by modifying the outer panels to reduce stall speed at the tips, enabling the aircraft to fly slower but under control.
JOHN KIMBERLEY VIA STEVE TODD

Essentially, this is the hard metal core of the Downsview of the first ten postwar years picked up and moved 2,500 miles due west. If you wanted to reopen the Beaver production line after thirty years, this is the stuff you would need. Inside the main manufacturing hangar, in the mezzanine office area at one end, several large card-file cabinets along the windowed wall overlooking the shop floor contain all the Beaver and Otter engineering drawings, on microfiche. A microfiche reader sits on top.

Dave Curtis, who joined the company's predecessor, McKinnon Enterprises, to complete its purchase of the Beaver and Otter tooling and parts business, chuckles at the memory of this move after the deal was closed in 1983. "A huge moving van, a big semi-trailer, would arrive, and we'd say, 'Hooray, another shipment from Downsview.' We'd look inside this huge van, and there'd be, like, three or four of these lumps of lead in there. They were that heavy."

Curtis is not about to reopen the Beaver production line. But he is keeping Beavers flying by manufacturing, stocking and selling certified parts. (Viking also makes parts for Bell Helicopter and Boeing.) And he is building a better Beaver. It took Viking ten years to engineer, build, test and obtain type approval for the Six-Thousand-Pound High-Gross Turbo Beaver and a 5,600-pound piston Beaver. These are Beavers for the next fifty years.

The next of these uprated Turbos was in its jig being cleaned up after being stripped down to the basic airframe. (The first one, the former c-flpf, was bought by a Swedish missionary organization to be used in a longtime Beaver role: saving souls, this time in Bangladesh.) This one, the second Viking turbo conversion, was another ex-U.S. Army piston Beaver, thought to have been based at Fort Rucker. A Sealand cabin extension with its top-hinged Alaska door had already been installed. Viking holds a licence from Bill Alder and this was about the thirtieth they had installed. The front fuselage ended at the sixteenth station, just behind the pilot's seat (stations on an aircraft are reference points along the fuselage, often coinciding with formers or bulkheads). A thirty-two-inch plug would be added ahead of it, and the new engine-bearing structure would be hung from that. The pt6a-20 or -27 goes on the front, driving a three-bladed Hartzell propeller with a polished chrome spinner at the pointed end.

Viking's development of the Turbo Beaver in adding almost half-a-ton to its factory gross weight makes its facility a home away from home for dhc-built Turbos as well. "Maybe twenty"—one-third of the Downsview Turbos—"haven't been through here," Viking technical sales manager Michael La Fleur estimates.

There are at least two companies that have addressed the part of the Beaver airframe that was considered impossible to improve: Dick Hiscocks's wing. Lightly loaded, a standard piston Beaver will fly under control at 50 mph. Loaded, it will do as little as 60 in level flight. If buying a complete new wing from Advanced Wing Technologies or installing what the international AOG Air Support organization refers to as its DHC-2 STOL Kit can make one of the alltime STOL performers even better, why not? If doing so seems like "overkill," as Beaver pilot and *West Coast Aviator* editor Jack Schofield says, it is at least arguable that such a wing could make the Beaver a little more stall-proof and therefore even safer at low speeds.

Just mentioning the new Beaver wings is guaranteed to start an argument. Mike Quinn, whose Whistler Air Beaver has the Sealand cabin conversion which can move his aircraft's centre-of-balance aft, might be expected to support a wing that would give him and his sightseeing passengers greater lift in the air. But no. Quinn feels that any lake a Beaver can't get into with its factory wings should be out of bounds anyway. The Beaver's first pilot, Russ Bannock, is more emphatic: he feels pilots who become accustomed to the wing modifications could be dangerous to themselves and their passengers. Bannock says he can do anything in his Beaver any other pilot can do in one with a modified wing, and he is probably right.

Viking Air's Curtis has a point of view. He notes that during testing of the standard Beaver wing for his six-thousand-pound high-gross kit for the Turbo Beaver, his engineers put eighteen-thousand pounds on the wing. "It didn't fail."[6]

"We had to reinvent the entire airplane; resubstantiate the airplane. We incorporated the changes from the original Turbo Beaver wing"—which added airflow fences and fuel tankage to the piston Beaver's wing—"and we had to meet a certain time-to-climb requirement."

As with any small industry—or large one, for that matter—each operator or rebuilder has an opinion about the others. Each has a unique style. Some get along better with the regulatory authorities at Transport Canada than others do. Some are regarded as being outside the mainstream. Beaulieu is one of those. The government, Beaulieu used to say, "would like to see this airplane go down. Put 'em all in museums." An immensely charming, if world-weary character, Beaulieu is only now beginning to see things as the inspectors do. Greg McDougall of Harbour Air Seaplanes feels he can't afford not to. Kenmore answers to an American federal air transport authority that makes some Canadian bureaucrats look like pussycats. Some rebuilders make improvements to the Beaver; some consider the very idea of improvements to be heresy.

Their feeling is that, aside from basic structural or avionics improvements, the Beaver should stay exactly as it is. This belief is common enough to be an unspoken tribute to its designers. Even Downsview's improvements, such as the Turbo Beaver, were in some pilots' opinions, mistakes. At least—and this is an important qualification—in the environment to which its qualities ideally suit the Beaver:

the Pacific Coast. There, argues Gary Richards of Tofino on Vancouver Island's outer coast, a turboprop engine built to cruise at 13,000 feet for three hours at a stretch is beside the point when the flying consists of low-level island-hopping jaunts. Along an oft-fogbound coast, if you have to fly, the safe procedure is usually to fly underneath the soup. The number of Turbo Beavers built at Downsview seems to reflect that point of view. It may be that the gathering of Beavers in that part of the world has happened because, as Richards puts it, "aviation's just passed us by, in effect. The reason the Beaver's so outstanding is nobody's replaced it." Not even with a better Beaver.

For the most part, the differences among rebuilders separate them more than the great airplane in whose service they are united. This is, of course, only human nature.

But the work the Beaver rebuilding community does as a group is what makes the airplane unique in aviation history. As time passes, more rather than fewer of them have been made airworthy. Moreover, although a restored Beaver is a legitimate and appreciating collector's item, very few Beavers are destined for the genteel pensioning-off of a rich man's hangar. Karl Springer's Beaver is not a showpiece. It is working for a living in Alaska. Like almost all the other Beavers, wherever they may be. And all of these people who have devoted their working lives to an airplane are keeping them flying.

That is why it was such a big deal when Al Beaulieu showed up for a second time at Viking Air one spring day not so long ago. Beaulieu and Dave Curtis had visited each other's hangars once apiece before, checking each other out. Curtis got the feeling at Beaulieu's that he was not really welcome; he sensed that Beaulieu felt he had to hide his trade secrets from him. And of course Beaulieu had to at least see the new central depot in his line of work, Downsview's Pacific Coast satellite. These visits were mainly to satisfy mutual curiosity.

But not this time. This time Beaulieu was there to buy parts. He walked out, Curtis remembers with undisguised glee, with an armload of genuine de Havilland DHC-2 parts. If only the rest of the Beaver community could have seen him. Now they'll have to find some new way to misunderstand the artist among Beaver rebuilders.

Paul Stenner flies C-GUOY over the Gulf
Islands in the Strait of Georgia between
British Columbia's Lower Mainland
and the southern end of Vancouver Island.
A 767 pilot, Stenner flies his Beaver for
pleasure. GRAHAM OSBORNE

Chapter Fourteen

Under the weather

Paul Stenner's somewhat muffled voice comes from high up in his Beaver's cockpit. "Mags off," he calls out moments before he opens the door and climbs down. It is a long way up there, and a long way back down—a lot of trouble, in other words, to make sure C-GUOY's engine won't start when he pulls the propeller through. The Beaver's floats are set on the concrete floor of his hangar, so it would be difficult for the airplane to go anywhere anyway. But checking those few switches is good procedure. Besides, if the engine *did* start when he pulls the starboard prop blade down, it could do serious damage to him.

Stenner doesn't really have to pull the prop through either. He does so to get oil circulating into the uppermost cylinders of a gleaming Wasp Junior engine that is so clean the label of the Los Angeles shop that overhauled it can be read easily from a few feet below. Oil is subject to the law of gravity, and it tends to collect in the lower cylinders between flights. Moving the pistons within the cylinders by pulling the propeller around redistributes the oil to incur less wear when the engine is started.

Stenner is tall for a pilot at six-five. That's tall for anyone, but on a pilot the height seems worse than useless until he begins to prepare the Beaver for startup. Once he is back on the floor, every inch comes into play as he reaches up on tiptoes to grab one blade of Uniform Oscar Yankee's propeller to pull it through counterclockwise—"nine times," he gasps at full extension, barely able to breathe, "for nine cylinders."

He sounds somewhat apologetic as he confesses that he doesn't always pull it through all nine times. Sometimes he just does six. In five or six flights in Beavers myself, I'd never seen it done at all. Then again, those Beavers had been working all day. On water, most pilots would roll the engine over using the starter, with the magnetos switched off, and then prime it.

It is fortunate for Stenner that the men who called the shots at de Havilland when the Beaver was designed were almost as tall as he is and maybe heavier. The first impression you get of a Beaver close-up is that it is one big machine.

"Believe me," writes English pilot-writer Bob Grimstead, "it is not until you are standing with a bucket of icy water in one hand and a wet sponge in the other, looking twelve feet up at a grubby Beaver, that you start to appreciate what a big aeroplane it is. Well over thirty feet long with a forty-eight-foot span and stressed to 3.5g [able to support three-and-a-half times its weight in the air], it is a tribute to de Havilland engineering skill that at 3,600 pounds including floats the great lump nevertheless weighs much less than a Jaguar xj 220 [sports car]."[1]

A New Zealander's first impression of the Beaver was amazement that the wings were out of reach overhead; the tailplane, seen from the pilot's seat "appears almost to belong to another, following aircraft." Just getting to the cockpit door involves a major climb—and that was with the Beaver on wheels.[2] On floats, as Stenner's c-GUOY is, with the fuselage level, the Beaver is a foot-and-a-half further up. "I'm a big guy who needs a big aeroplane," Stenner says.

We don't have to stand underneath c-GUOY with sponges in hand because Stenner, an Air Canada 767 pilot, always washes it after flying from his saltwater base north of Victoria and houses it in this fabric-walled hangar along with several vehicles, including two-and-a-half Oldsmobile Toronados, one-and-a-half of which are, he notes, "the only American cars I've ever owned." The front half of one Toronado, neatly chopped off behind the front bench seat, is attached to long rails extending thirty-odd feet ahead to a wheeled hydraulic lift. This must be the most luxurious floatplane beaching gear on the Saanich Peninsula (although there are several Toronados being used this way in the Pacific Northwest). Stenner uses it to lift his Beaver by the float spreader bars, move it around on dry land, and launch it. (The second four-wheeled Toronado belongs to a friend.) A bumper sticker on the vehicle announces, "I ♥ aircraft noise." The Toronado was an early General Motors front-wheel-drive model with a big V8, which makes it ideal as a floatplane tractor.

C-GUOY is an almost-original ex-U.S. Air Force L-20A, built in 1957, passed to the army and redesignated a U-6A, the 1,101st Beaver off the line.[3] Stenner was one of many eager Beaver buyers who converged on the home of British Army Air Corps aviation at Middle Wallop during the summer of 1985, before the beautifully-maintained U.K. Beavers went on the block, but got nothing more than a delightful dinner in the officers mess with the CO, a colonel. At Stenner's suggestion, the British Beaver stationed at the Suffolk, Alberta, artillery and tank range was left in Canada to be sold, but it was disposed of by sealed bid. Stenner was disappointed again when he lost another Beaver at auction. By May 1981 UOY was at work with Landa Aviation in Hay River, Northwest Territories, where Stenner found it with the help of Viking Air president Dave Curtis. He bought it in October 1986 and had it overhauled at Viking.

The "ejection doors" have thankfully been removed, along with such additional military-spec equipment as the four cockpit skylights and ambulance litter fittings. Stenner still has the bench seat, which can be hung from the cabin rear bulkhead but is not installed right now. This example still has four of the heavier military seats, with their heavy-duty seatbelts and deep pans to accommodate parachutes. It also has the original porthole rear window, two-bladed prop and wingtip fuel tanks. UOY has a recent zero-time engine and flawless white paint with a yellow speed line bordered with navy blue, and the Beaver name in script on the pilot's door and Mosquito outline trademark on the fin. The only noticeable modifications are Kenmore bubble windows in the cargo doors and small floatplane finlets on the horizontal stabilizers. The finlets have replaced the factory ventral fin for floatplanes, which interfered with Stenner's Toronado beaching gear. Six aerials, five on the cabin roof and one emerging from each side of the vertical stabilizer, testify to a fairly complete avionics package that includes two VHF and one marine VHF/FM radios, an automatic direction finder and Loran C navigation equipment that give this Beaver limited Instrument Flight Rules (low-visibility) capability. One deliberate holdover from the Beaver's wheeled tail-dragger service life is a banged-up tailcone.

Stenner and his wife, Heidi, use UOY to fly into isolated destinations along the convoluted north British Columbia-Alaska coast. Both are tall, and they find that, with the second-row and bench seats removed, they can comfortably stretch out for the night on the cabin floor. Stenner owns the aircraft with Bill Eller, who uses it much more often in his logging business; the airline pilot flies it purely for pleasure. His affection for this realization of a long-held dream is obvious from the way he runs his hands over those flight surfaces he can reach from the hangar floor on his pre-flight walkaround after he pulls the prop through. He pats it here and there, gently moves the elevators up and down and the water-rudders at the aft ends of the floats left and right.

Once he has it out on the tarmac, Stenner climbs in and begins his startup procedure. The fly-away process would be simplified if he began the lengthy procedure of warming up the big Wasp Junior after launching UOY. But he does it on dry land to save the propeller some wear from the spray it would whip up. The Beaver's forward doors are narrow and lean backward and up in their openings; climbing inside requires a fluid hip swing and quick knee-bend to get under the dual-control wheels. This upward lambada seems second-nature to the pilot but has me bumping into everything along the way.

Starting a Beaver involves a series of carefully orchestrated moves and reactions that is so much second-nature to Stenner that, although his purpose is to brief me, his movements are too fluid and coordinated to describe as a series of separate steps. It helps that he has replaced the original inertial starter with a self-starter that eliminates some of the blackjack dealer's sleight-of-hand that goes into firing up other Beavers.

"Fuel on . . . ," he intones. "We give her a little wobble" with the hand fuel-pump, "we give her six good pumps with the primer. . ." which is located in the doorsill at Stenner's left foot.

I hear a faint squeak and what sounds like a slight hissing sound of compressed air being released—actually fuel being squirted into the cylinders. (On those Beavers with the geared inertial starter, a half-horsepower electric motor spins a small flywheel up to high rpm. The energy is used to rotate the engine crankshaft.) Stenner, having pumped up the fuel pressure with the wobble pump and primed the engine, indicates that we are now ready to start.

But first he interrupts this routine to open his door, look back and front, and yell, "All clear?"

He flips the master switch up and holds the toggle switch up to engage the starter for a few seconds. Then, with the throttle cracked, prop at low (fine) pitch and mixture at full rich on the three-slotted power lever console at the top middle of the instrument panel coaming just below the windshield . . .

"If you get it right the engine will catch . . . and, to the accompaniment of a swirling cloud of oily smoke stage right, the hiccupping bass thumping will grow into the irregular loping lumpy grumble of a healthy Pratt & Whitney R-985," writes Englishman Grimstead, obviously intrigued by this arcane North American ritual. "Except that this engine didn't throw any smoke." And neither does Uniform Oscar Yankee's.[5] This R-985's looks go more than skin deep. The engine that looked so shiny and clean outside is just the same inside its chrome pushrod housings and blue-grey crankcase enamel.

The engine instruments spring to life as it starts with no hesitation. We sit for five or six minutes. It does not occur to me to time this wait until Stenner explains

Nature photographer Gary Fiegehen
captures the Beaver in its element.

GARY FIEGEHEN

that warming up a Wasp Junior until the cylinder heads are 140°C (with oil temperature over 40°C for takeoff) can take twice that long. By the time Stenner runs it up to 1,400 rpm, checks the mags and carb heat and moves the prop governor lever to high pitch, the Beaver is lurching back and forth on its Toronado beaching gear.

Early in this lengthy warmup procedure, long before Stenner launches UOY, it is obvious that this is the smoothest-running Wasp Junior and most vibration-free Beaver I have ever been in. This airplane is Exhibit A, proof positive, for anyone who believes a Beaver is not noisy. This is especially impressive considering that Stenner had noted to me that his exhaust pipe, which exits on the co-pilot's side just behind the door, will be coming due for replacement some time soon. This engine is so smooth and quiet he is considering replacing the three-foot-long pipe with a short stack. That would cost him his cabin heat, but would play the R-985's music to his ears a tad louder. For just a moment Stenner reminds me of certain pals of mine who drove cars with throaty, chromed Walker Trombones under the passenger-side doors.

He closes the throttle to idle, flips the mag switches off, and makes sure the engine dies. The engine oil temperature is up to 42°C. "So it takes a while," he says.

We're ready to go. Stenner pulls a tide-chart booklet from his door-liner map pocket, takes a quick look, nods and puts it back. In a floatplane, that's as important as the latest weather forecast.

Stenner launches the Beaver with the Toronado dolly. As soon as we leave the ramp, he lowers the water rudders on the floats by means of a cable attached to a handle at his left foot. Next he tops up the front tank of the three under the floor at the fuel dock. With the front two underfloor tanks able to hold twenty-nine gallons apiece and the rearmost twenty-one, plus his wingtip tanks with eighteen each, we could carry 115 gallons, good for a little over five hours with a decent reserve. The Beaver is no econobox, but we are going to be flying for a total of perhaps forty-five minutes, with two takeoffs and landings and a touch-and-go for Stenner to demonstrate UOY's performance on floats. Only the front tank needle bobs on the three-tank fuel gauge low on the panel. That's all we'll need.

UOY has twin control wheels at the ends of a Y-shaped column so it can be flown from either seat. The instrument panel, in a pale grey krinkle finish, is divided roughly into four parts. The power quadrant at the top centre curves over the top toward the windshield with the big throttle, propeller pitch and fuel mixture levers with their generous knobs protruding upward. (The prop pitch lever has a square knob, so the all-important propeller-driven airplane's equivalent of a gearshift lever can be discerned by feel alone if the pilot is absorbed, for example, in switching fuel tanks with the low-mounted selector after he or she has let one run dry.) The six engine instruments are arranged in two vertical rows beneath, making those vital levers and instruments equally available to pilot or co-pilot.

Directly in front of the pilot are the flight instruments: compass, airspeed, artificial horizon, altitude, climb and turn-and-slip indicators. At the top of this left-hand panel, aligned with the pilot's line of sight, is an old-fashioned mechanical flap-position indicator with a small pointer that moves along a slot reading, from left-to-right, *full flap, landing, take-off, climb* and flaps up or *cruise* at the right end. Below this panel are switches for magnetos, generator, fuel pumps and the fuel tank selector. On the right side are the radios, Mode C transponder with altitude readout capability, and navigation equipment. A standby compass is mounted to the central windshield post.

At the base of the panel, where it meets the floor, the oil filler spout with its yellow top is a reminder of what this airplane was designed for. It invites the arctic bush pilot to pour the warmed-over oil he drained last night back into the engine, and do so *in*side the cockpit, out of the biting wind, on another sub-zero morning. It gives me the shivers just to look at it.

Stenner restarts the engine. The instruments on the middle panel between us return to life.

He knows these waters. Once, as a young pilot, he and a pal ditched a Harvard trainer not far from here. The engine stopped. How long did it float? Maybe thirty seconds. Did they recover it? No. A Harvard wasn't worth the expense in those days. "We bought another Harvard," he says. It cost $2,000.

Does Stenner mention this as a kind of warning that things can go wrong? Or is it to let me know that this not-quite-old pilot was once a bold pilot? It doesn't really matter, because as we begin to taxi, the hearty, upbeat guy I have joined in the cockpit of his airplane undergoes an almost instantaneous personality transformation. His eyes narrow and his lips purse behind his sponge-covered microphone. He becomes crisp and all business. The change is startling, but I decide that's okay. I don't mind in the least.

I imagine he would run through the checklist out loud with or without me there. "H-T-M-P-F-S-C and G," he says, and he runs through the entire list:

"H—hood, doors, harness, hydraulics . . . no need to worry about hydraulics. . . ." Not for any landing gear, anyway.

"T—trim, set." He reaches up to the roof, where the small elevator trim wheel is. "And the temperatures are all in the green.

"M—the manifold pressure checked.

"P—primer locked," he glances outside at the left wing's leading edge—"pitot head is clear out there, and I have checked the pressures. . . ."

And so on. Stenner reaches in front of me and dials in SHWNGN, or Shawnigan Lake on the Loran C (long-range offshore radio aid to navigation). It directs us almost due west from our base not far from Victoria's airport, on the west side of the Saanich Peninsula. I glance at the compass on the windshield post.

We identify ourselves to Victoria tower and they notify us of air traffic in the vicinity, none of which we will see. Stenner reaches up for the left lever of the three on top of the instrument panel and pushes it forward to thirty-two inches manifold pressure (maximum is 36.5) and 2,300 rpm. Despite using a reduced power takeoff, the Beaver leaps ahead.

As with the startup, Stenner's takeoff in the Beaver is the smoothest I've ever experienced. My previous takeoffs in Beavers involved bringing the nose up to get the front of the floats out of the water, and a subsequent nose-down movement to build up speed and get up on the step, the lowest part of a float's keel. Once on the step, it is usually a matter of seconds before a Beaver is airborne. This nose-up movement to get the floats unstuck created the cartoonlike impression of the aircraft gathering itself up to leap into the air that stayed with me the first time I left the water in one.

Stenner lightly moves the wheel back, but does so with such a touch that he leaves no impression of the nose rising at all. It feels like a smooth, steady takeoff. We leave the surface of Patricia Bay in what I estimate is an easy two hundred yards. We lift off at about 50 mph. And that's it. We're off.

We fly south along Finlayson Arm, climbing all the way. This is a good time for Stenner to perform one of his demonstrations of how the Beaver's lift enhancement devices work. Here, he says, is what happens when he allows the flaps, set at about fifteen degrees, to return to *full up*. He selects Flap Up on the selector lever between the seats, and after a few short pumps, the flaps disappear from view. We begin to descend. The change is abrupt. "Just a touch of flap," Stenner reports, and the plane rises. Neat.

I look around. What a view. This part of the world is known as Canada's Mediterranean. The mountain ridges that form Vancouver Island's outer-coast backbone put Victoria in their rain shadow, and warmth from currents and prevailing winds originating further south along the Pacific coast make Victoria and the Gulf Islands in the Strait of Georgia seem more a part of Oregon or California than Canada. This explains the intense greens and blues below us. This would be part of the United States had the border along the forty-ninth parallel not been deflected south to clear the bottom of Vancouver Island, putting Victoria, then the most populous city in the region and still consciously very British, barely within the Empire's confines. This was a pleasant early May day, but the high, billowing cumulonimbus clouds warn us of updrafts and other unseen air currents that we will, for the most part, be flying beneath.

We continue to climb. "We're going over the top of the Malahat," Stenner announces over the intercom. That's about 1,400 feet, so we were at about 1,800 ourselves. The Malahat is Vancouver Island's southeastern spine, a series of low coastal mountains that embrace picturesque alpine lakes such as the one we are headed for, Shawnigan Lake.

So effortless is this steady climb that Stenner feels compelled to call my attention to it. He's right: I hadn't noticed. True, Stenner has the Beaver on climb power, doing two-thousand rpm at thirty inches manifold pressure. "I seldom use it," he says of this engine work rate. We are climbing at a "respectable" six hundred feet per minute.

Soon we see Sooke Lake on our left, cross a ridge, and suddenly we are over our objective. Stenner reaches down with his right hand for the flap position lever and touches it. He leaves it at the Down position. Leaving the flap selector set at Up, he feels, can cause the hydraulic pressure to bleed off when the flaps are down. With the selector in the Down position, the flaps are ready to extend any time the hydraulic pressure handle is pumped. Such as when the engine quits. Or now, on approach to landing.

"B-U-M-G," Stenner announces, mentally reviewing his in-range check. Brakes, undercarriage, mixture, gas.

"And then, on final, C-U-P." Carb head, undercarriage—"no undercarriage," he says—and propeller pitch full fine.

On the approach and landing at Shawnigan Lake, I find myself totally absorbed in watching Stenner's right hand as it moves back and forth between the big throttle lever, to which he makes minute adjustments by handling it at its base, then moving quickly to the hydraulic pump between the seats, and then to the flap position lever. He would modulate the throttle a fraction of an inch at the lower (back) end of its

C-GUOY at the pilot's hideaway some-where along the British Columbia coast.
PAUL STENNER

slot, let go, put his hand down and pump a few times between the seats, then repeat the process. We bank left to perhaps as much as forty degrees—I'm looking out, not at the turn-and-bank indicator—after the downwind leg.

We set down not far from a small dock. The slight chop on the lake gives Stenner a good visual fix on the water's surface just before we touch down. I can't discern the moment when that happens; I only know for sure when Stenner chops the power, sets the prop at low pitch, drops the water rudders and selects Flaps Up. The engine idles at 240 rpm. We coast toward a dock. Sailing a floatplane, powerless and without brakes, to a dock without doing damage to one or the other is an art that is mastered only with much experience. We kiss the tire bumpers with the left float and Stenner scrambles out his door, down the float-strut footholds, and is quickly on the dock with a rope in his hand. To dock a Beaver or any other float-plane, it helps to be something of an athlete.

We have coffee overlooking the lake at a 1950s diner that was known as the Boat House when Stenner was a regular twenty years ago in his float-equipped Luscombe. It is now called the Galley. This is my fourth cup of coffee so far this morning, and I'd have had almost anything else to drink had I known that some tur-bulence was in my immediate future.

When we leave Shawnigan Lake, the takeoff run is about the same as before, the climbout a little more dramatic, and we head northeast toward the largest of the Gulf Islands, Saltspring. This island was home to escapees from slavery late in the nineteenth century, and the careful cultivation Saltspring has undergone since then is reflected in a precise patchwork of sheep pasture and wild thickets. As we approach the island, we can see the other islands in the strait, ocean-going ships and their wakes and, coming up fast, Saltspring's Mount Erskine. We bank around its peak and descend at an impressive rate to the body of water it overlooks, St. Mary's Lake. Stenner will say later that we did actually *touch* and go, but, to be honest, I never felt it. I'm willing to take his word for it. We were certainly low enough. I just didn't feel it.

Our climbout is impressive once again, this time dramatized by Mount Erskine as we climb near its slope. We pass by just below the peak. In the Beaver, we are part of the landscape, not far up in some alien medium. And we are reminded of that fact when a friend's voice is heard on the VHF radio—someone who knows the traffic fre-quency—asking us, with some mirth in his voice, to stop making so much noise.

Any time Stenner passes to the southwest of Saltspring Island, he flies along the shoreline to spot beached logs he can come back for in his boat. There are plenty today. The passage opens up as we approach the intersection of Satellite Channel, which separates the southwest beaches of Saltspring from Vancouver Island and the

Saanich Peninsula. Here we would be in relatively still air. Stenner decides it is time for the most important demonstration of all: how slow can we go and still hang in there?

Pretty slow. We get down to an indicated 60 mph in careful stages. We are lightly loaded, of course. A pilot, one passenger, neither of us overweight. Only one tank, and that maybe half full.

We are trimmed slightly nose-up, slight forward pressure on the wheel, medium power setting with some flap, climb flap indicated on that quaint slot in front of Stenner. No shaking, though. Nothing alarming about it. The airplane doesn't seem to be working especially hard. It's not hanging on its prop. I can't see the blades. We could go slower.

We are headed for home now. As we cross the expanse of Satellite Channel on our way to Saanich Inlet and Patricia Bay, an angry column of cloud and water stands in our path. My eyes are drawn upwards. At the top of this steel-grey funnel, clouds seem to roil upward like fresh smoke even as they release what looks like a solid discharge of dark fluids in front of us.

"This is a virga," Stenner says. I've written a book about meteorology, but I have never heard that term before.

"It is associated with cumulus buildup. It can produce downdrafts and micro bursts. You can experience downdrafts going in different directions on different sides. It can generate strong winds that radiate outward from its crown. In a jet airliner on approach for landing, you can find yourself in a headwind as you approach it. A headwind produces a higher indicated airspeed, which is fine," he explains.

"Coming out the other side, though, you find yourself with a strong tailwind. Tailwinds reduce your airspeed. Reduced airspeed reduces lift. You lose altitude. It can be very sudden . . . and fatal."

But we are not at that height, several thousand feet. We are not even at one thousand feet. Two-fifty, maybe. Never have I been airborne yet so happy to be close to Mother Earth's embrace. Coastal bush pilots will tell you that the Beaver's reputation for safety in bad weather comes from its ability to fly below the worst of it, and slow enough to see in conditions of bad visibility. This, it occurs to me, is not one of Stenner's planned demonstrations, but it is exactly why so many Beavers are enjoying second or third careers in this part of the world. Rain pounds the windshield and aluminum roof of our suddenly quite small airplane. We bounce a little. I regret the extra cup of coffee. But it is nothing particularly alarming. We fly right through it.

And we come out the other side, none the worse for wear. It reminds me of going through a carwash. Just what we need to get the salt water off the Beaver. All Paul Stenner will have to rinse on shore will be the floats.

Chapter Fifteen

FHB's last flight

George Neal is a winner of Canada's highest aviation award, the McKee Trophy (1989) and became a member of the Canadian Aviation Hall of Fame in 1995. The citations list his achievements as a test pilot—he certified the Beaver for operation on floats and piloted the de Havilland DHC-3 Otter's first flight—and recognize his efforts on behalf of this country's aviation history.

An airframe and engine mechanic as well as a pilot, Neal restored a prewar Hawker Hind combat aircraft for the National Aviation Museum. And he personally delivered the museum's most significant Canadian artifact—CF-FHB, the prototype Beaver.

George Neal describes his delivery flight to Ottawa, which turned out to be a bittersweet reacquaintance with an old friend and anything but a routine hop.

The owner, Norcanair of Prince Albert, flew FHB down to Sault Ste. Marie in late July 1980. Their chief engineer was with it. The museum had asked me to fly it down to Ottawa. I thought that putting it into the museum was a fitting retirement for the number one Beaver airplane because I did so much test-flying work with it at the beginning. I was happy that I was asked to do it, so I looked forward to the flight.

On my pre-flight inspection the airplane looked to be in reasonable shape considering the hard use it had been subjected to for so many years. It looked good. The paintwork was very good. Of course, that may not have meant very much—a Beaver always looks good to me.

The prop was a little short here and there. I could see some rework on the contours. That's normal for an airplane on floats. The water is hard on them.

I wasn't especially worried because the Norcanair chief engineer went with me. Now, we had a load in the airplane and he's no lightweight. The load was the wheeled undercarriage, which is fairly heavy, lashed down in the cabin. FHB was on floats. And of course it was a hot summer's day.

Well, I suspected everything wasn't just according to Hoyle when I took off out of Sault Ste. Marie: I went, and I went, and I went, and I could hardly get it up on the step. Normally a Beaver is off the water in sixteen to seventeen seconds with a five-mile-an-hour headwind. I kept going and going. After about thirty seconds I knew she was a tired old lady. It took about forty seconds to get it airborne and that is quite a change from the usual Beaver. Forty-five seconds doesn't seem long to the average person, but to me it seemed like a hell of a long time....

Few prototype aircraft ever enter commercial service after being wrung out in flight testing, but CF-FHB, bought on sight by bush flying legend Russ Baker and absorbed into the Pacific Western Airlines fleet, laboured on for 32 years. PWA was built on Beavers and Boeing 737s. ERNEST KRAHULEC

Getting FHB "up on the step" means having it plane on the point on the float where its keel ends abruptly, usually about halfway along the bottom of the float. Once the accelerating airplane is up on the step, most of the float's undersurface is out of the water, resistance is minimized, and the machine is level and about to take off.

FHB was developing barely enough power to get to that stage. FHB's performance handicap was emphasized by the difference between it and CF-OBS, the second Beaver built and first off the production line, which took off ahead of FHB after a more typical run.

For the former test pilot, the experience of flying the same type of airplane that had leapt into the air from a careering dolly in 1948, possibly saving his life, now able to perform a routine takeoff only with difficulty after thirty-two years of hard use, was disillusioning.

And then we did some air-to-air pictures with CF-OBS. It was being flown by Wally Warner. I climbed—I barely could get to 3,500 feet—and for a Beaver that is unbelievable. I couldn't go to 5,000 feet. There was no way the airplane could get there.

I just had to accept the fact that this was the airplane's last flight before an engine overhaul. You have to take these things into consideration. Since it was going to the museum, it would be foolish to put a newly overhauled engine in.

CF-OBS was delivered to the Ontario Department of Lands and Forests in April 1948, thus becoming the first of its type delivered to a customer.

Wally had no trouble catching me for the photo shoot. It was a lovely summer's day, quite warm, with a light wind. Just perfect. We finished with the photography and flew two hours to Trout Lake, North Bay, where we refuelled. It was quite turbulent because of the hot weather and the thermals rising around us.

Anyway, I got to Ottawa July 29, 1980. And the worst conditions prevailed. That is, glassy water on the river. I landed on the river, beside the Rockcliffe airfield. Late in the afternoon. Well, worse than that, it was evening. And the sun was in my eyes on my approach to land.

The trouble with glassy water is you can't tell where the surface is, because it's like a mirror. Getting down under those circumstances is not a trick. It's a straight instrument landing. I don't do any guessing where the surface is. You get down, you pick an area where there are trees along the river bank, and you watch the shoreline on either side of you, to get some idea of your height. You get down to where your wings are just below the tree level. I use that as a guide, just below the tree level.

Then I set up my airspeed. I have only 15 degrees of flap. I set my airspeed at 65 mph, and enough power to give me about 250-to-300-feet-per-minute rate of descent.

Then you don't do anything until you feel it touch. And I fly it just like that on instruments, until I feel it touch. And it just goes shhhhht!—like that, and you're on. And I chop the power. That's it. Fifteen degrees of flap and just a little bit of power gives you a nose-up attitude and avoids the possibility of the tips of the floats touching first and digging in the water. So you touch down just slightly aft of the step. It just greases on. All my glassy water landings—with the Beaver—same thing.

So, anyway, I landed in there, and I taxied it in. Fred Buller was there, waiting with the director of the museum at the time. And I thought I was finished.

Oh, no-o-o. The director, he wanted to go for a flight. He really wanted to go up. So I said o-kay.

Well, fortunately, I'm low on fuel. Fortunately in terms of getting off the water again. Here we are with glassy water, which means no wind, so I start the long run, and I think to myself, Oh God, this is no Beaver. And I finally get airborne, do a circuit and another glassy-water landing, and taxi it in. . . .

But, oh, what a letdown. Mind you, put a new engine and a new prop on it, and it'd just leap out. But it was rather disappointing to return it and have it be so sad. Knowing it was not to fly again.

—GEORGE NEAL, JUNE 16, 1995.

CF-FHB, at Beaver Lodge Lake, Saskatchewan, in February 1980, near the end of its service life with North Canada Air (Norcanair) of Prince Albert, Saskatchewan. VIA CHRIS BULLER

Appendix

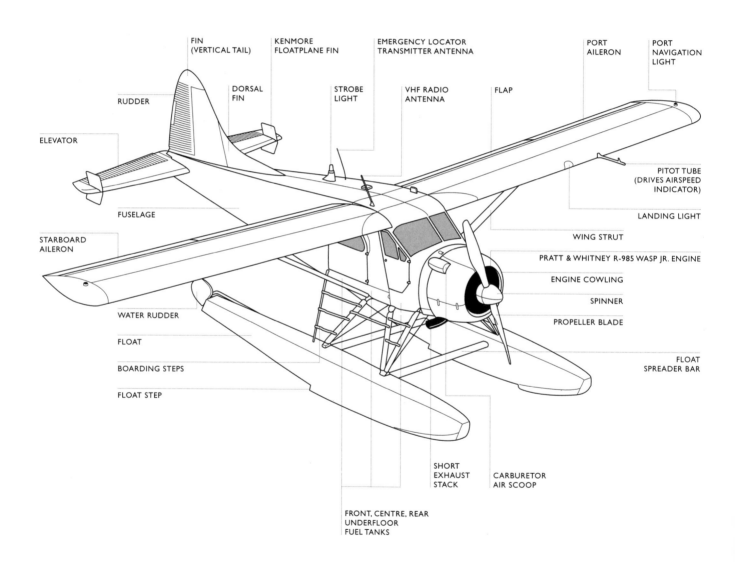

FIN
(VERTICAL TAIL)

KENMORE
FLOATPLANE FIN

EMERGENCY LOCATOR
TRANSMITTER ANTENNA

PORT
AILERON

PORT
NAVIGATION
LIGHT

RUDDER

DORSAL
FIN

STROBE
LIGHT

VHF RADIO
ANTENNA

FLAP

ELEVATOR

PITOT TUBE
(DRIVES AIRSPEED
INDICATOR)

FUSELAGE

LANDING LIGHT

STARBOARD
AILERON

WING STRUT

PRATT & WHITNEY R-985 WASP JR. ENGINE

ENGINE COWLING

SPINNER

PROPELLER BLADE

WATER RUDDER

FLOAT

BOARDING STEPS

FLOAT STEP

FLOAT
SPREADER BAR

SHORT
EXHAUST
STACK

CARBURETOR
AIR SCOOP

FRONT, CENTRE, REAR
UNDERFLOOR
FUEL TANKS

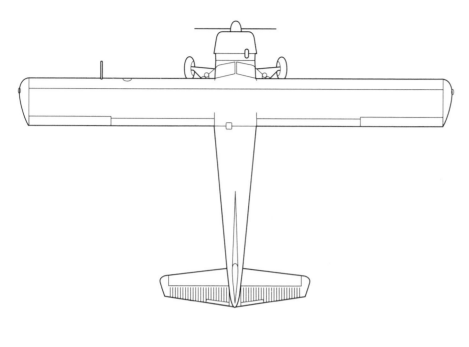

Beaver specifications

Beaver Mk. I
1,631 built

LANDPLANE

ENGINE
One 450-hp Pratt & Whitney
R-985 AN-6B or AN-14B Wasp Jr.

DIMENSIONS
Wing span: 48 ft (14.6 m)
Length: 30 ft 4 in (9.2 m)
Wing area: 250 sq ft (23.2 sq m)

OVERALL HEIGHT
Wheels: 9 ft (2.7 m)
Skis: 9 ft 6 in (2.9 m)

WEIGHTS
Landplane
Basic weight: 3,000 lb (1,360 kg)
Disposable load: 2,100 lb (953 kg)
Gross weight: 5,100 lb (2,313 kg)
Ski-wheels
Basic weight: 3,223 lb (1,465 kg)
Disposable load: 1,867 lb (847 kg)
Gross weight: 5,100 lb (2,313 kg)

PERFORMANCE
Maximum speed: 160 mph (257 km/hr)
Cruise: 130 mph (209 km/hr) at
    5,000 ft (1,524 m)
Initial rate of climb: 1,020 ft/min (311 m/min)
Service ceiling: 18,000 ft (5,486 m)

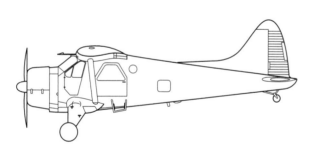

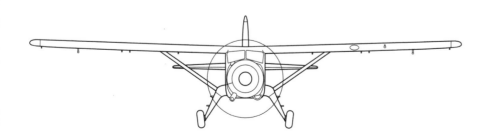

Beaver Mk.I

SEAPLANE/AMPHIBIAN

DIMENSIONS

Wing span, wing area and loaded weight
    as for Beaver I landplane
Overall height
Floats: 10 ft 5 in (3.2 m)
Amphibian: 14 ft 9 in (4.5 m)

WEIGHTS

Seaplane
Basic weight: 3,316 lb (1,504 kg)
Disposable load: 1,774 lb (805 kg)
Gross weight: 5,090 lb (2,309 kg)
Amphibian
Basic weight: 3,670 lb (1,664 kg)
Disposable load: land 1,430 lb (649 kg)
    water 1,330 lb (604 kg)
Gross weight: 5,100 lb (2,313 kg) as landplane;
    5,000 lb (2,268 kg) from water

PERFORMANCE

Seaplane
Maximum speed: 147 mph (236 km/hr) at
    5,000 ft (1,525 m)
Cruise: 127 mph (203 km/hr) at 5,000 ft (1,525 m)
Initial rate of climb: 920 ft/min (280 m/min)
Service ceiling: 15,750 ft (4,802 m)

Beaver Mk.II

One built, converted to Wasp Jr.

ENGINE

One 550-hp Alvis Leonides 502/4

DIMENSIONS

Wing span, wing area and loaded weight
    as for Beaver I landplane
Length: 30 ft 3 in (9.23 m)
Height: 10 ft 7 in (3.2 m)

WEIGHTS

Empty: 2,575 lb (1,169 kg)

PERFORMANCE

Landplane
Maximum speed: 170 mph (273 km/hr)
Cruise: 157 mph (252 km/hr)
Initial rate of climb: 1,185 ft/min (361 m/min)
Service ceiling: 20,500 ft (6,250 m)

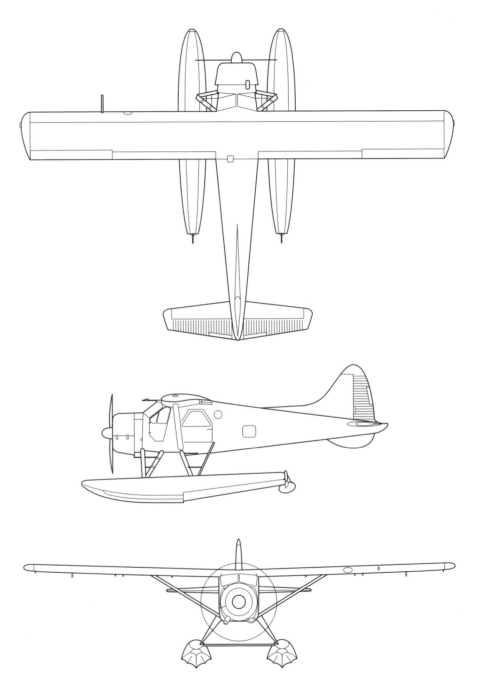

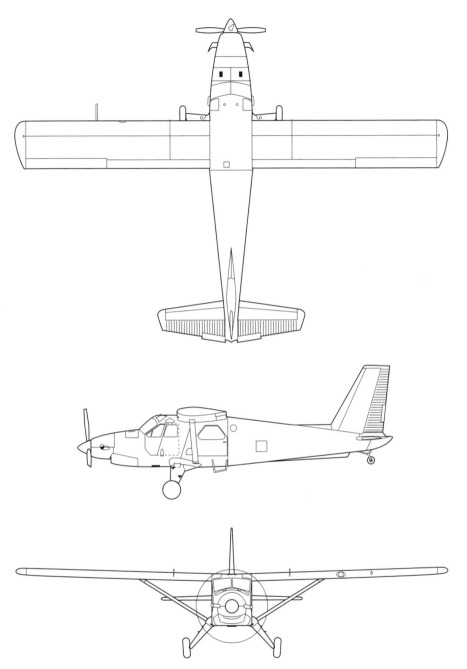

Turbo-Beaver Mk.III

60 built

ENGINE
One 550-hp Pratt & Whitney PT6A-6

DIMENSIONS
Wing span, wing area and loaded weight as for
    Beaver I and II
Length: 35 ft 3 in (10.74 m)
Height: 10 ft 3 in (3.12 m)

WEIGHTS
Empty: 3,255 lb (1,476 kg)

PERFORMANCE
Landplane
Maximum speed: 172 mph (278 km/hr)
Cruise: 155 mph (248 km/hr) at 10,000 ft (3,048 m)
Initial rate of climb: 1,460 ft/min (455 m/min)
Service ceiling: 23,000 ft (7,010 m)

Viking Turbo-Beaver

ENGINE
One Pratt & Whitney Canada PT6A-27.
PT6A-20 also available.

DIMENSIONS
Wing span, wing area, length and height as for
    Beaver III

WEIGHTS
Landplane
Basic equipped weight: 2,760 lb (1,252 kg)
Loaded (gross) weight: 6,000 lb (2,727 kg) for
    both landing and takeoff
Seaplane
Gross weight for takeoff: 6,000 lb, landing
    5,800 lb (2,630 kg)

PERFORMANCE
Landplane (based on PT6A-27 engine)
Cruise TAS at 10,000 ft (3,049 m): 163 mph
    (262 km/hr)
Rate of climb at sea level: 1,220 fpm (6.2 m/sec)
Service ceiling: 23,900 ft (7,290 m)
Seaplane (based on PT6A-27 engine)
Cruise TAS at 10,000 ft (3,049 m): 151 mph
    (243 km/hr)
Rate of climb at sea level: 1,140 fpm (5.8 m/sec)
Service ceiling: 21,700 ft (6,610 m)

Endnotes

Chapter 1: The Beaver takes off

1. Dick Hiscocks, dinner speech to the Canadian Aeronautics and Space Institute, Vancouver Bran ch, April 1993, p. 9 of speech notes.
2. Hiscocks, *ibid.*
3. Not everyone involved remembers the Beaver's wheeled landing gear as a last-minute item. Bill Burlison, under whose direction the Beaver prototype was constructed in the DHC experimental shop, says that was not the case. But the prototype underwent its first flight without the fairing at the top of each undercarriage leg that subsequently covered the rubber doughnuts at its hinge. This at least suggests that no such fairing had yet been fabricated.
4. See William M. Leary, ed. *Aviation's Golden Age: Portraits from the 1920s and 1930s.* Esp. "Daniel and Harry Guggenheim and the Philanthropy of Flight," by Richard Hallion, p. 31 *et seq*, on the safe aircraft competition of 1929.
5. Dick Hiscocks interview with the author, May 3, 1995.
6. "Comments on First Flight of DHC 2 Beaver at Downsview, Ontario on August 16th, 1947," by Russ Bannock. Prepared during March 1995. Augmented by interview with author June 10, 1995.
7. "Of Canadian Design and Build, New Bush Plane Tested." Copy of clipping of unbylined article in Toronto *Globe and Mail* in possession of Betty Buller. Text refers to first flight "yesterday," which would make date of publication August 17, 1947.

Chapter 2: First to fight: Jaki Jakimiuk and the PZL fighters

1. "The Era of the Gulls: The Chronicles of the Pulawski Fighter Line," by the editors, *Air Enthusiast* 28, July–October 1985.
2. The above article notes that the Luftwaffe Quartermaster-General's office acknowledged the loss of 285 aircraft in the Polish campaign, "and as the Polish Army possessed few anti-aircraft guns it may be assumed that the claims for the Polish fighter force, which consisted almost entirely of the P-11C, were in no way exaggerated," *op. cit.*, footnote, p. 35.
3. *Air International* lists Pulawski's death as March 31, 1931. Witold Liss's *Aircraft Profile* Number 75 has it ten days earlier, March 21, as does *Air Enthusiast* 28. He died in the crash of a light amphibian of his own design, due, Liss says, to a control malfunction.
4. *Air Enthusiast, op. cit.*, footnote p. 37.
5. In this case, the 585-hp Bristol Jupiter VIIF, a French Gnome-Rhone-built predecessor to the more powerful Mercury.
6. Fred W. Hotson, *The de Havilland Canada Story*, p. 64. "He was an engineer's engineer, totally European by culture and upbringing, proud and serious, and exuding confidence based on experience."
7. "Fighter A to Z," *Air International*, April 1991, p. 210.
8. *Ibid.*, p. 211.
9. *Air Enthusiast* 28, *op. cit.*
10. "First Encounter," by Jerzy B. Cynk. *Air Enthusiast* 48, December 1992–February 1993.
11. Dick Hiscocks believes the denial of visas may have been based on Ottawa's reluctance to grant access to top-secret information to "foreign nationals"—a reluctance, he says, that "often flew in the face of common sense."
12. Hotson, *op. cit.*, p. 64. Hotson quotes Polish engineer and refugee W.Z. Stepniewski: "I believe that de Havilland's guarantee was largely due to the confidence they held in Jakimiuk and his professional reputation."
13. The most frequently heard claim for the Beaver is that it was the first all-metal bush plane. That claim is based upon a fine distinction. It was the first all-metal aircraft *designed* as a bush plane. Many

all-metal Junkers models, from the F13 to, most notably, the W33 (first across the Atlantic westbound) were used around the world as bush planes. Aside from the structural advantages of all-metal construction, bush pilots liked being able to load their airplanes without worrying about punching holes in a doped-fabric skin. The legendary Russ Baker built Central British Columbia Airways with W34s on floats. See D.M. Bain, *Canadian Pacific Airlines: Its History and Aircraft*, p. 60. For an aircraft that made its first flight in 1926, the W34's record of remaining in service until 1947 might not be unique, but it is enormously impressive.

14. Hotson, *op. cit.*, p. 65.

Chapter 3: Downsview goes to war

1. Hotson, *The de Havilland Canada Story*, p. 59.
2. *Ibid.*, p. 53.
3. Dick Hiscocks, dinner speech to the Vancouver branch, Canadian Aeronautics and Space Institute, April 1993, p. 2. Fred Hotson feels Hiscocks's experience was unusual. Wing assembly was normally accomplished under the supervision of "senior men who knew how to assemble them without much reference to drawings," Hotson says. That may have been the problem.
4. "I soon found another reason for the honour—the assembly loft was high in the hangar under a corrugated metal roof, and in the notorious Toronto summer temperatures it was an oven...We melted in that loft for thirteen hours a day." Hiscocks, *ibid.*
5. Hotson, *op. cit.*
6. De Havilland, one of the handful of combined airframe and aero-engine manufacturers in the world, had developed a series of efficient in-line and air-cooled engines of four and six cylinders, which, in keeping with the moth theme of its airplanes, had names with a gypsy bent to them: Gipsy Minor and Major, and Gipsy Six. (De Havilland used the English spelling, i.e., gipsy rather than the North American gypsy.)
7. Interview with Dick Hiscocks, February 16, 1994.
8. The only Canadian-designed fighter of this period was the Gregor FDB-1, a biplane—but a biplane of all-metal construction with retractable landing gear and a teardrop-shaped cockpit canopy to protect the pilot from the weather at Canadian Car and Foundry's plant in Fort William, where it first flew December 17, 1938. It was a quintessentially-Canadian aviation creation: designed by a talented immigrant, conceptually-backward and yet advanced in detail, and built in a quantity of one. See Larry Milberry, *Aviation in Canada*, pp. 110–112.
9. Hotson, *op. cit.*, p. 60. The company's engineering capability before Jakimiuk appeared can be appreciated from the pride the company

took in what anywhere else would have been considered minor modifications of the Tiger Moth to create the DH.82C: full sliding canopies to keep student-pilots and their instructors from freezing over the winter prairies, the addition of wheel brakes and fully-castoring tailwheels (instead of tailskids, which had a braking effect on the grass fields common in the U.K. early in the war) to make them operable on concrete or frozen airfields, and the substitution of American-built Menasco Pirate engines for the Tiger Moth's similar Hatfield-built Gipsy Major. The Menasco was heavier and less powerful than the Gipsy, but incorporated a generator, which enabled ten of 136 built to be used as wireless radio trainers (p. 61).

10. "The DH.87 originated in 1934 as an experimental aeroplane," writes A.J. Jackson in *De Havilland Aircraft Since 1915*, p. 325, "to explore the suitability of the side-by-side cabin biplane....Up to that time the pilot of de Havilland light cabin types always sat away from the passengers so that his attention might not be distracted, but the Hornet Moth ended this practice and for the first time permitted sociability...." Any passenger of Garratt's was his captive for the duration of the flight.
11. Alice Gibson Sutherland, *Canada's Aviation Pioneers: Fifty Years of McKee Trophy Winners*, p. 200.
12. Frank H. Ellis, *Canada's Flying Heritage*, p. 370, citation for 1951 McKee Trophy. Ellis calls him a student at the Curtiss school but does not list him among its 1915 graduates. The school existed until the end of 1916, graduating fifty-four aviators, all of whom served with the Royal Flying Corps or Royal Naval Air Service in World War I.
13. *Ibid.*, p. 144.
14. Sutherland, *op. cit.*, p. 200.
15. Milberry, *op. cit.*, p. 195.
16. Editors of *Janes All The World's Aircraft. Aircraft of the RAF: A Pictorial Record 1918–1978*, p. 62.
17. Hotson, *op. cit.*, pp. 61–62.
18. *Ibid.*
19. Dick Hiscocks begs to point out that an American, Eugene Vidal, pioneered the moulded plywood technology adopted for the Anson V and produced prototype fuselages for Cockshutt Plow, which produced a large number of them. The National Research Council, where Hiscocks worked throughout the war, proceeded independently on moulded plywood for aircraft at the request of the British, who were worried about a possible shortage of aluminum. "Our task at NRC was to update wooden technology and produce reliable design data. We saw the merits of the Vidal process and built a Harvard trainer fuselage and a tailless glider using that process." Hiscocks has written about the NRC's moulded

plywood effort in the Winter 1988 issue of the *Canadian Aviation Historical Society Journal.*

20. Hotson, *op. cit.*, p. 62.

21. *Ibid.*, p. 63.

22. Hotson quotes "the shop poet laureate" on the suspended Ansons, p. 63:

> *The ships come pouring off the line*
> *At such a dizzying pace,*
> *And then go soaring for a time*
> *Until they take their place*
> *Beside the incompletes,*
> *That hang from up above,*
> *Awaiting wings and other things*
> *That all good airmen love.*
> *For without motors, wings and tails,*
> *They cannot turn and dive;*
> *Let's hope that they can hit the trail*
> *By Nineteen Forty-Five.*

23. Hiscocks interview with author, *op. cit.*, May 3, 1995.

24. Hotson, *op. cit.*, pp. 64–65.

25. *Ibid.*, p. 66.

26. *Ibid.*, p. 66.

Chapter 4: One thousand Mosquitoes

1. Firsts in aviation are seldom absolute, and speed claims for combat aircraft are particularly contentious. But the only possible contender for the same distinction is the Vought F4U Corsair, which flew for the first time almost six months before the Mosquito. But the Corsair had a far more protracted developmental road ahead of it, Marine examples going into combat only in early 1943.

   By then Mosquitoes had recorded their first photo-reconnaissance missions (September 20, 1941), first night-interception victories (May 1942), and their first precision-bombing sorties a few weeks after that. Despite its intensive operational use, the Mosquito remained a military secret for a further year, until 105 Squadron's daring daylight raid at rooftop level on the Gestapo headquarters at Oslo on September 25, 1942, was publicized. The purpose of the raid was to interrupt a meeting chaired by Vidkun Quisling, the Norwegian traitor, and kill as many Gestapo officers as possible.

2. Hiscocks interviews with the author, February 16, 1994, January 13, 1995. "I remember one time there was some catastrophe on the factory floor. I was there, and of course Phil soon appeared. And he said, 'Hiscocks, why do I always find you where there's a problem?'

   "And I said, 'That's what you pay me for.'"

3. Edward Bishop, *The Wooden Wonder: The Story of the de Havilland Mosquito.* The memorable day was January 30, 1943, the tenth anniversary of the Nazi ascension to power in Germany.

4. Hotson, *op. cit.*, chart, p. 237 showing Manpower, 1928–1982. Much of my information on the 1941–43 development of the company comes from pp. 68–89 of *The de Havilland Canada Story.*

5. McIntyre was an exceptionally bright man who grew up in Toronto, graduated from the University of Toronto in 1936, and attended Cambridge on a Massey Fellowship. Hired away from the U of T when Massey-Harris went to full wartime manufacturing, he was smart enough to resist Harry Povey's advice that his wing jigs should be wood, as Hatfield's were. McIntyre thought wooden jigs practically medieval and built his from metal. Promised for mid-May, the first set of Mosquito wings was delivered ahead of schedule, on May 9, and Massey-Harris deliveries continued that way.

6. Jigs are production tools in or on which complex parts are fabricated or joined. They are meant to assure uniformity from assembly to assembly. Metal jigs can be built with more precision and last longer than wooden ones, allowing more uniform assemblies over a longer series of repetitions. Wood vs. metal jigs was a major issue in the debate over British vs. North American production methods that persisted at DHC well into the assembly of the Beaver prototype.

7. William Green, *War Planes of the Second World War: Fighters*, Vol. 1, pp. 115–116.

8. Garratt quoted in Hotson, *op. cit.*, p. 73.

9. Dick Hiscocks's experience working at Hatfield qualifies his opinion on DHC's troubles producing Mosquitoes. Moreover, he worked at arm's length from Downsview during World War II on his assignment with the NRC in Ottawa, developing the all-wood Anson V. So he has no personal axe to grind on behalf of the wartime DHC.

   Dick Hiscocks comments in notes written for the author, June 24, 1995:

   I would make several points in defence of the Canadian company's tardiness in producing Mossies.

   a) The U.K. company had little experience with mass production and drawings were never complete or up-to-date (witness my anecdote about drawings for the Globe and Mail *Rapide a few years earlier). The staff at Hatfield were experienced craftsmen-woodworkers and required a minimum of guidance. If parts did not fit, a few strokes of a plane provided the necessary adjustment.*

   b) The Mossie prototype was built by hand at Salisbury Hall and I can just see the early production in the U.K. proceeding by word-of-mouth whilst the drawings slowly filtered down, with constant amendments. Interchangeability was honoured more often in the breach than the observance.

c) This can be contrasted with the situation in Canada where 99 per cent of the staff had no such background of experience. Ottawa contributed to the confusion in full measure by ignoring the urgings of Phil Garratt and others to build up parts and materials in advance. This was compounded by putting a large contingent of automotive production people in charge of the programs, with the naive idea that automotive production methods would prevail.

10. Hotson's account gives no date for the order-in-council that deposed Phil Garratt for the duration of the war. It appears in K.M. Molson and H.A. Taylor, *Canadian Aircraft Since 1909*, p. 254.

11. Fred Hotson knows de Havilland old-timers who, despite the fear Stewardson's sudden presence invoked in the plant, found him a reasonable man under his rough exterior. The same John Slaughter who made the first tailplane sets for DHC Mosquitoes when Boeing of Canada was late supplying them is quoted by Hotson as saying Stewardson was "just what we needed in the shop at the time." Slaughter became the new works manager's assistant. Hotson, Don Murray and George Neal left in early 1944 to instruct at the Air Observer Schools. Hotson, *op. cit.*, p. 76.

Chapter 5: Fred Buller joins DHC

1. Hotson, *The de Havilland Canada Story*, p. 76.

2. Fred Buller died on his and Betty's fiftieth wedding anniversary, June 7, 1994, after a long bout with Alzheimer's.

3. To illustrate his point about Fred Buller's boundless energy, Hiscocks tells the story of the two of them being dispatched to the snowy wilds of Labrador to examine the remains of a crashed RCAF DHC-3 Otter, probably during the late 1950s or early '60s.

   Fred hit the ground running, but Dick remembers immediately disappearing into twelve feet of snow. Once they were on snowshoes, he and Fred looked over the crash site, as Dick puts it, to "try and see what let go first and why."

   They put in a long day outdoors, then were ferried back to Goose Bay, where the Otter had been stationed.

   "I fell on an army cot," Hiscocks remembers, "dead to the world. And Fred lit up a cigarette and started systematically analyzing every possibility. I was ready to scream, but Fred just had this enormous energy."

4. It is tempting to infer from the range of his mind that Fred Buller could have succeeded in almost any field of science, so prolific was his problem-solving imagination and so acute his taste in selecting original solutions that had a simple and refined elegance.

   For recreation, he gobbled up whole disciplines: anatomy, from his doctor father's texts; the Latin names of trees and shrubs; a map of the night sky available in his mind's eye for quick reference, with the names of the constellations memorized. He mastered the poetry of Keats and Shelley, which he could recite at length. He entertained children by reciting "Jabberwocky" from Lewis Carroll's *Through the Looking-Glass*, from memory.

   Fred maintained a well-equipped woodworking shop, where be built furniture that featured contrasting woods worked into edge mouldings in inlaid patterns. Wood was the outlet for Fred's perfectionism. There was always some imperfection, in his eyes, to pieces that to others seemed flawless. Christopher Buller feels that although his father loved the textures and smells of wood, the time he spent working with it often frustrated him. One backhanded tribute to Fred's craftsmanship in wood is that neither Chris nor Betty can locate more than a few of his pieces—so many of them were snapped up at times when Fred was perfectly happy to see them go.

   At thirty-nine, Christopher is a leading cardiologist in Vancouver. He started out as a musician, a trombone player, who injured his lip and faced the end of his musical career after earning a four-year honours degree in music from the University of Toronto. As for Fred's musical tastes, Christopher finds it characteristic that his father loved the more structured composers—Mozart, and especially Bach—and was a fan of the latter composer's most rigorous interpreters, Glenn Gould and the harpsichordist Wanda Landowska. Fred's inclination toward precision showed up in his close-up photography of flowers and other still lifes.

   "Even in small things," says Betty Buller, he was precise. "He always wanted to know what people's hobbies were. He thought that was how you could get to know people."

   It was certainly how you got to know Fred Buller. "Of course," Betty added, "few people had as many hobbies as Fred did."

5. Not that Fred Buller gave up boats entirely, as anyone who knew him at the Royal Canadian Yacht Club in Toronto during the 1950s and '60s is aware. Buller designed the 14-foot Buller sailing/racing hull and often tested his sails with wool tufts attached to show the airflow over their surfaces, as airplane wings are often tested. He was a very competitive racer, virtually unbeatable in his chosen dinghy classes. The cockpit of a boat of his own design was one of the few places where he felt fully in control of his destiny.

   Fred liked to take his racing dinghy out into Toronto's waterfront during, of all times, snowstorms. For him, the behaviour of the snow as it was carried by air currents around the vertical airfoil of the sail or over the decks was like having a wind tunnel free of charge. He wanted to know how closely he could align the sail's leading edge with the wind—at what point it would start rippling, as an airplane's wing does, invisibly, at its stalling point.

6. The P.Eng designation is recognition of having qualified for

membership in a provincial engineering society. Although it is not technically essential to hold a degree in engineering to qualify, it is difficult to do so without it. Fred Buller took great pride in the fact that the principles and mechanisms developed for the Beaver were used on the subsequent DHC civil STOL aircraft.

7. John Condit, *Wings Over the West*, pp. 11–12. Despite his shortcomings as a mechanic, Baker could fix a plane in a pinch. He actually rebuilt a crashed DH Fox Moth belonging to B.C. airline pioneer Ginger Coote over the winter of 1936–37 at Gun Lake, B.C. He chartered the repaired aircraft from Coote the following summer, writing in his *Who's Who* entry for 1937 that he had "established own flying business in British Columbia."

8. *Ibid.*, p. 10.

9. Ernest Krahulec interview with the author, February 14, 1995. Fred was working for the company's overhaul facility on 98th Street in downtown Edmonton by 1940, and graduated to Aircraft Repair, at the airport, two years later.

10. Krahulec is right. "The landing gear mechanism was entirely Fred's," says Dick Hiscocks. "It worked like a charm. No maintenance. You replaced the rubber blocks after five years. It was so simple."

11. Buller was still in Edmonton on June 28, 1943, the day he had a patent application notarized for a "Hydraulic Means for Transmitting Movements and Cylinders for the Same." This was a proposal for an external sleeve enclosing a motion-transmission system, operated by hydraulic means, that would avoid loss of the hydraulic fluid. Two pencil sketches accompanied the application, which was not the only one he filed during the war.

By April 1944 Fred Buller was at Central Aircraft. On June 7, 1944, he and Betty married. He moved to de Havilland in mid-September of that year.

Just before he left Central Aircraft for DHC, September 1, 1944, he filed a Record of Principle, notarized in London, Ontario, for "a principle of so mounting a cylinder head in a sleeve-valve engine that it is readily capable of movement in relation to the cylinder, sleeve, and piston, while the engine is in operation, thus giving a variable compression ratio."

Even while doing repetitive, by-the-numbers inspection and fault-rectification work at Central Aircraft, Buller was thinking up new efficiencies for the internal combustion engine.

12. Fred Hotson feels the MacDonald questionnaire has been overrated as a factor in the Beaver's design process, citing personal conversations with Punch Dickins, who, Hotson says, declined credit for many of the features attributed to his influence. (Punch Dickins was dying during the summer of 1995, when the research for this book was being done.) One quality both bush pilots and engineers agreed upon was the desirability of a reserve of power when operating on floats, and Hiscocks and Buller were on record as wanting more power long before the questionnaire went out. Hotson telephone conversation with the author, June 15, 1995.

Chapter 6: Halfway to greatness

1. In perhaps the most famous example of an immediate design decision based upon German data, George Schairer of the Boeing Airplane Co. had that company's B-47 redesigned with swept wings when he saw how favourable such an arrangement could be in delaying the effects of air compressibility—the fluid effects of air through which an object is moving near the speed of sound—then known as the sound barrier. The B-47 became a prototype for Boeing's subsequent line of jet transports. Boeing passed its data on to North American Aviation of Inglewood, California, which redesigned the wing of its P-86 Sabre, the most important fighter of the 1950s. Schairer interview with the author, April 24, 1990.

2. Hiscocks was fortunate to draw Reimar Horten as his interviewee. He learned more about wing design from the elder Horten brother than he could have from better-known German designers. Reimar was the scientist; his brother Walter was a Luftwaffe fighter pilot in France and the administrator of their successively more ambitious flying-wing projects.

By the end of the war, the Hortens were testing a twin-jet flying-wing bomber designed to an ambitious Luftwaffe "1,000–1,000–1,000" requirement. This was the Ho IX, capable of flying 1,000 km with a 1,000-kg load at 1,000 km/hr. Several other Horten flying wing types were being manufactured. Two Horten flying wings are in the National Air & Space Museum collection in Washington, D.C.

The Hortens were far ahead of their time. They pioneered the construction of aircraft with composite materials, and had figured out by 1939 how to make tailless aircraft stable in all flight axes and spinproof.

During the war, the Horten brothers experimented with flying-wing-configured gliders while drawing up plans for a six-jet-powered flying-wing transport, the design of which they refined for the British. Nothing came of it.

"I was interrogated by the British after the collapse, along with other designers," Reimar recalls in his memoir *Nurflügel*, or *Flying Wing*, published in 1993 in Linz, Austria, by Herbert Weishaupt, and written with Peter Selinger. "We talked about our work, but did not reveal our findings."

Around 1947, Reimar recalls in the book, "[John] Northrop published details of a new aircraft similar to the H V at that time. [He is apparently referring to the N-9M, like the H V a pusher-propeller-

driven machine, which first flew two days after Christmas 1942.]
The machine had negative dihedral wingtips, in an apparent (but
useless) attempt to combat the skid-roll moment [the tendency of
most tailless aircraft to lose longitudinal stability, drop a wing and
eventually go into a spin]. I tried to contact Mr. Northrop and offer
my assistance, but without success. Later, the Northrop factory
wasted a large amount of money on several unsuccessful heavy
bombers [the XB-35/YB-49 series] similar to the H VIII or H XVIII.
They could certainly have benefited from my knowledge of high
aspect ratio flying wings!"

The inherent instability problems associated with flying wings
produced by other designers have only recently been solved by using
powerful computers connected to flying surfaces with all-electric
fly-by-wire technology to make hundreds of control-input decisions
per second. The Northrop B-2 Stealth bomber works that way.

Although the Hortens may not have revealed their test data, as
Reimar claims, he certainly offered Dick Hiscocks some good
advice about not designing his wing for a higher speed than the
Beaver was designed to fly.

3. Christopher Buller feels that Dick Hiscocks "is as close to my father
[in the way he looks for answers to problems] as anyone I've ever
met. I can see how when it came down to basics both would agree
on the elegance of a solution—if one of them *had* a solution."

What differences there were between the two often had to do
with administrative issues—the kinds of issues that can make close
colleagues seem constantly at odds to their co-workers. Contrary to
widespread belief at Downsview, Fred and Dick got along well,
despite their differing backgrounds and professional approaches
to their work. They capitalized on their differences by working as
a team.

Where Fred (and Phil Garratt), on the one hand, and Dick
Hiscocks, on the other, did differ was on the need for job defini-
tions in the rapidly expanding DHC of the 1950s. Their differences
were usually due to what Dick calls "the complete absence of a formal chain of command and line responsibility. Various departments
would request action from any one of a half-dozen people, so that
projects were often well underway before Fred or myself were aware
of them—and on many occasions were badly off the rails.

"He raised heck with me once," Hiscocks told the author. "A
fairly young man in the organization hadn't got a promotion. Fred
said he should be ranked with the junior engineers; I said he didn't
have a degree. Fred and I had had that out years ago; you had to
have some formality. There were scales. And the guy wasn't listed.

"Fred said, 'That guy is one of the most useful fellows in the
department.'"

So, as much to end the argument as anything else, Hiscocks said,
"I agree. Let's go sell it to the directors," fully anticipating the idea
would not fly. But in the DHC of the 1950s, it did fly.

"Fred was right. George Luesby was one of the stalwarts in engineering."

4. Redesigning the Beaver "wasn't easy," Hiscocks told the author
during our first conversation. "The design was well along at the
time. The nuts-and-bolts process descended upon myself and Fred
Buller. A lot of thinking, even into detail parts, had been done. So it
was expensive to change. So there were compromises." Hiscocks,
February 16, 1994.

5. Herschel Smith, *A History of Aircraft Piston Engines*, p. 170. At the
time the Gipsy Queen was on the testbed, the English de Havilland
company was at the forefront of jet engine design with the Goblin
engines that powered the DH-100 Vampire fighter and its successors.
At the time de Havilland was perhaps the most technically
advanced combined airframe-and-engine company in the world,
producing both the first 500-mph fighter, the Vampire, and by 1950
turning out the DH-106 Comet, the first jet airliner to achieve production. A new piston engine that was not reaching its projected
output might not have had top priority in 1946, although de
Havilland continued designing small to medium-sized airliners (the
DH-114 Heron series), equipped with as many as four of the unsu-
percharged Gipsy Queen 30s, which, by the mid-1950s in their 30-4
form, actually did develop a claimed 340 horsepower.

6. Jakimiuk had done his preliminary design with a recognized airfoil
developed by the Royal Aircraft Factory, Farnborough (where Sir
Geoffrey de Havilland was a designer) before World War I.

7. Even Bob Noorduyn, a visitor to Downsview during the Beaver gestation, advised against drooped ailerons. "It looks good," he said,
"but money, money, money"—making them work would be expensive. Dick Hiscocks, dinner speech to Vancouver branch, Canadian
Aeronautics and Space Institute, April 1993, p. 7.

Ernest Krahulec, Fred Buller's chief mechanic at Aircraft Repair,
worked on the Norseman, and feels that this aircraft's drooped
aileron system "worked very well. It was the teleflex cable control
that in very cold weather became stiff or froze up altogether."
Winterizing the system made it reliable. The Beaver's drooped
aileron actuation system was designed with rods.

8. At his first meeting with the author, in an effort to make the point
that Fred Buller was brilliant at finding simple solutions to
intractable problems, Russ Bannock suddenly got up from his
chair, went to his bookcase, pulled out a battered copy of the
Beaver operator's manual for his personal airplane, and turned
quickly to the page showing the aircraft's aileron droop mecha-

nism. Rendered as a simple line drawing, it is a thing of beauty.

9. Hiscocks: "I thought, in the euphoria of the first flight, all would be forgotten. And it was. But the drawings were never changed, and I get calls to this day from people saying, 'I've repaired XYZ and I see the drawings say Prototype Only. How do I get this approved?'"

10. Hiscocks quote combined from two conversations to make it clear that, while wanting to fit drooped ailerons was one thing, making them work was another. And it was Fred Buller who accomplished that. Interviews, as above, February 16, 1994, January 13, 1995.

Credit for certain design features on an aircraft are often better attributed to a team than to an individual, although the circumstances under which Buller and Hiscocks worked made them more individually responsible than many accounts of the Beaver's design process would suggest.

"No one person can really be said to have designed the Beaver," writes Robert S. Grant in an undated issue of *Air Progress* on file at the Downsview plant. That is literally true: two persons would be more like it. In fact, most of those present at DHC during the Beaver's gestation would credit Fred Buller. So much so that Phil Garratt's son John, who had a dinner-table seat for most of that period of the company's history, was surprised and gratified to learn that Hiscocks had personally devised the Beaver's airfoil, or wing profile—a job that only a qualified aerodynamicist could have done in any event.

Chapter 7: Phil Garratt's half-ton flying pickup truck becomes the Beaver

1. Photocopy of Inter Office Memo dated September 12, 1946, from R.D. Hiscocks of engineering to Mr. W.J. Jakimiuk.
2. Hotson, *The de Havilland Canada Story*, p. 94.
3. Sales figures for the Chipmunk from Hotson, *op. cit.*, p. 99.
4. Hatfield loved the Chipmunk at first sight. In a telegram from the English company dated January 21, 1947, and signed simply DE HAVILLAND, DHC's parent raved:

SIR GEOFFREY [DE HAVILLAND] AND MR. [ALAN] BUTLER BOTH FLEW CHIPMUNK TODAY 20TH AND DELIGHTED WITH IT AND THINK IT ONE OF THE NICEST AEROPLANES THEY HAVE EVER FLOWN SIR GEOFFREY SAYS IT HAS MORE THAN COME UP TO EXPECTATIONS STOP THERE ARE NO CRITICISMS STOP WE PROPOSE NOW INVITING FLIGHT AND AEROPLANE TO FLY IT

This was lavish praise from the gods in DHC's cosmos. Sir Geoffrey de Havilland, of course, designed some of England's first military aircraft for the Royal Aircraft Factory during World War I, and was the founder of the de Havilland Aircraft Co., registered

September 25, 1920, "with a working capital of £1,875 and perhaps an unwarranted degree of optimism," as he later put it in his autobiography, *Sky Fever*.

Alan S. Butler happened into the de Havilland story shortly thereafter, when the company's landlord at Stag Lane, a London suburb, insisted that the company buy the premises or leave. In waltzed Butler, a motor and aviation nut who wanted the company to build him an airplane with a Rolls-Royce Vulture engine.

"On one of his visits to review progress," writes Peter King in *Knights of the Air*, "he asked, 'Can you people do with some more capital? I'm keen to invest in an aircraft company, especially one interested in civil aeroplanes.' After de Havilland had explained their financial position, Butler offered to advance £10,000 'if that will help.' A few years later he became...chairman."

5. Text of Sandy MacDonald's letter to the Canadian bush flying community:

November 20th, 1946
Dear Sir,

We are considering the production of a five-place, single-engined, all-metal, high wing, monoplane, primarily designed for North country operation and offering somewhat higher payload, range, speed and power than our present Fox Moth. We propose to install a Gipsy Queen 51 (295 h.p.) or 71 (350 h.p.) engine in this aircraft.

With a view to determining as closely as possible the specific requirements of Northern operators with actual experience in this specialized field, we are enclosing a questionnaire, tentative specifications and a perspective drawing, and would be greatly obliged if you would permit us to benefit by your experience by filling in the questionnaire and returning it to us in the enclosed, stamped, self-addressed, envelope.

We can assure you that your opinions and suggestions will be given careful consideration by our Engineering Department.
Yours very truly,
The de Havilland Aircraft Company of Canada, Limited
A.F. MacDonald,
Sales Manager.

One reaction to this letter, forty-two years later, came from pilot-author Gerry Bruder of Seattle, in his article "de Havilland Beaver: A Classic Workhorse still pays its way," in the April 1988 *AOPA Pilot* magazine. Bruder quoted the letter, then asked, "Did Cessna, Piper or Beech ever ask for *your* input in a new design?"

6. Like everyone at Downsview, Bannock was a busy man at the time, and he had his secretary update his logbook whenever the two could get together. The March estimate is based upon a very unusual happening. It was at least unusual, perhaps unique, for managing director Phil Garratt to have someone else fly his yellow Hornet Moth

when he was in it, but Bannock's records and memory recall a flight that month to Montreal that included the fortuitous visit by the two to the office of Jim Young, president of Pratt & Whitney of Canada. Whoever was at the controls, the only available account of the crucial meeting is Bannock's.

7. And, as the author's historically-minded young Lake Union Air pilot pointed out the weekend in 1988 when Wayne Gretzky was traded (see foreword), at the rate Beavers are being restored to service after being rebuilt from wrecks or abandoned hulks, the P&W Wasp will likely be the first aero engine still being used commercially in original installations a hundred years after it was designed.

8. Russ Bannock interview with the author, January 5, 1995.

9. Dick Hiscocks's recollection.

10. Fred Buller was still alive and vital when he gave his account of the Beaver engine decision to Fred Hotson, probably during the 1970s, during the lengthy research process that led to *The de Havilland Canada Story*.

11. Hotson, *op. cit.*, p. 104.

12. Both Hiscocks and Bannock recall a meeting in Garratt's office, with all the key engineers present, to discuss the details of the engine change. Buller's agreement was in all likelihood good enough for Phil Garratt, but the details would still have had to be assessed.

13. Krahulec, a Beaver loyalist, energetically disputes assertions, including that of the author in a previously-published magazine article, that the Beaver is a noisy vibrator of an airplane. The entire powerplant installation was thoughtful and innovative, he says, paying tribute to Jim Houston, who was responsible for the engine and its surroundings. Yes, the radial was awfully close to the firewall, but it was joined to the engine-bearers by dynafocal mounts in one of the first such installations in a small plane. The rubber mounts were shaped so that they converged on the engine's crankshaft, cancelling out vibrations caused by cylinders firing around its circumference. The cowling that encloses the engine around its sides was secure but easy to remove, Krahulec says, and the long exhaust pipe Russ Bannock insisted upon (see next chapter) damped out much of the engine noise. As for prop tips going supersonic, many Beavers are now equipped with smaller-diameter three-bladed propellers, slowing tip speeds.

14. Hotson, *op. cit.*, p. 105.

15. Hiscocks dinner speech to Vancouver branch, Canadian Aeronautics and Space Institute, April 1993, p. 9.

Chapter 8: But will it fly? Testing the Beaver

1. "Comments on First Flight of DHC 2 Beaver at Downsview, Ontario on August 16th, 1947," by Russ Bannock. Prepared March 1995.

Augmented by interview with author June 10, 1995.

2. Dick Hiscocks, dinner speech to the Canadian Aeronautics and Space Institute, Vancouver Branch, April 1993, p. 10.

3. See Ted Barris, *Behind the Glory*, which makes the case that BCATP instructor pilots should be officially recognized for the vital and hazardous contributions they made to the war effort, contributions often discounted by those who made it overseas. Bannock has pointed out that his last command, 418 Squadron, was successful at its difficult night-intruder task because its pilots, most of them former instructors, were experienced in such a wide variety of aircraft.

4. Don McCafferty, *Air Aces: The Lives and Times of Twelve Canadian Fighter Pilots*.

5. Peter Pigott, *Flying Canucks: Famous Canadian Aviators*.

6. Tom Coughlin, *The Dangerous Sky: Canadian Airmen in World War II*, esp. pp. 32–36. My summary of Russ Bannock's wartime service is based upon Coughlin's account.

7. McCafferty, *op. cit.*, p. 137.

8. Russ Bannock, interview with the author, January 5, 1995. Hiscocks says Jakimiuk was joking—that the chief design engineer understood the need for a quieter powerplant.

9. George Neal got to do his own first flight for DHC when he took the prototype DHC-3 Otter, CF-DYK (DYK for Dick Hiscocks), into the air four days before Christmas 1951. This first flight was achieved less than a year after the design go-ahead was issued.

Doug Hunter told Neal at the end of his extended first flight in the Otter—it had been planned only for him to do a short circuit of the airfield—that he had seen a lot of test flights, "but that was the most complete flight test I've ever seen."

As with the Beaver test flights, Neal says today, "All I had was my stopwatch and knee [writing] pad, and the standard instruments."

10. The company, which by 1947 had been reduced from its wartime peak of 7,000 workers to a minimum of 500 and was now up to 2,000, was extraordinarily productive. With the Beaver in flight-test, Fred Buller was supervising the overhaul of Consolidated Canso flying-boats for the air-sea rescue role. DHC was also, at different times in the immediate postwar period, overhauling or modifying Lancaster bombers, Canadair North Star airliners, B-25 Mitchell bombers, DC-3s and Noorduyn Norsemans.

In addition, Bannock and Neal had been demonstrating the de Havilland DH.104 Dove, an all-metal, twin-engine replacement for the prewar Rapide. The first and fifteenth production-line Doves were shipped to Downsview, where the latter became the only Dove ever to fly with floats. About five hundred were built, but only a dozen or so were sold in Canada and the United States. And, of course, the Chipmunk was being made ready for production.

11. Dick Hiscocks, who worked closely with the test pilots to iron out snags during the Beaver test-flight program, sums up the relative styles of Bannock and Neal this way:

"To Russ, an airplane is a vehicle designed to do certain things, and he'll make it do those things. George becomes part of the airplane when he flies it. He feels he has to learn to fly the airplane. Their approaches were entirely different. And both good men."

12. Neal's hobby since his retirement from DHC has been building and flying full-scale replicas of between-the-wars combat aircraft. His most recent project was a Hawker Hart two-seat fighter from the early 1930s. His current project—as of this writing, he is seventy-seven—is a secret, but he hopes to fly it himself, with other vintage aircraft, at the Farnborough Air Show during this decade.

13. "I know how airplanes are built," Neal told the author. "I knew how you must do this and you mustn't do that—how fragile they can be. I had experience finding problems the pilots couldn't find. I still am a stickler for doing things right."

In our conversation, Neal felt that an explanation of flight-test procedures was necessary to counteract whatever I might have seen in movies. On a test-flight program for a new aircraft, "You don't just go up there and throw it around and do this and do that. You go up and do a systematic check on controls, displacements [how far the control surfaces move to achieve a change of attitude], forces—everything that Engineering wants to know. And in that way you work up to it and you find out whether there's any bad control characteristics or whether you run out of control or it's unstable. You do it to a program, so you know where you're at. You're always short of money, so you try and do it fast."

As for the glamour part of being a test pilot, Neal appears to have enjoyed that too, from the limited evidence available. Charlie Smith, of the DHC Retirees Association, has a snapshot of a handsome young George Neal being kissed simultaneously by two very attractive women at a party. Neal, by the way, says he has never seen *Test Pilot*. He does remember the photo though.

14. The first DHC Dash-8 twin-engine commuter airliner, which flew June 20, 1983, was registered C-GDNK after Douglas N. Kendall, then retiring as DHC chairman after thirteen years of leadership.

15. Phil Garratt was rewarded for his unwavering enthusiasm for the Beaver when, before the entire DHC workforce on November 10, 1956, he was presented with the thousandth Beaver off the line, registered CF-PCG. Asked what colour he wanted his new Beaver painted, P.C. borrowed Henry Ford's line about the colours Fords would be finished in. "You can paint it any colour you like, as long as it is yellow." It was finished in a bright canary yellow.

Chapter 9: Russ Bannock takes the brass fishing

1. See "Speech to U.S. Army Otter and Caribou Association, Dallas, Texas, 17 August 1990," by Lt.-Gen. (ret) Robert R. Williams, pp. 152–156; and "A Caribou Accident at Fort Bragg, North Carolina, or, How the U.S. Army Lost All Their Large Aircraft," by John Thompson, pp. 157–160. Both are reprinted in *De Havilland, You STOL My Heart Away*.

"Where did the Beaver come from and why is it important to the Otter and Caribou story?" Williams asked his audience in Dallas.

"It came from de Havilland of Canada, and, like the Otter and the Caribou, was developed without being contaminated by U.S. military advice and control. It is important because it initiated a great relationship between the U.S. Army and de Havilland. . . ."

2. This one-ton payload airplane, known as the King Beaver during its preliminary design phase, was at first to inspire much greater hopes at DHC than the Beaver. It became, of course, the DHC-3 Otter, which first flew in George Neal's hands December 21, 1951. The RCAF had not bought the Beaver, so its participation in early research to define the aircraft's specifications and performance was one hopeful sign that the King Beaver would be a winner. One reminder of attitudes about the two aircraft is the fact that Phil Garratt won the first of his two McKee Trophies in 1951, not for the Beaver, but for the Otter.

The Otter was a very ambitious project. Fred Hotson explains that it was designed "to have the same takeoff performance as the Beaver with twice the payload. The cabin volume was to be increased two-and-a-half times. This was a formidable challenge, considering that there was only 33.3 per cent more power to do all these wonderful things."

Not until the Beaver had won the USAF and U.S. Army competitions for a STOL utility aircraft in early 1951 did the extent of the Beaver's market potential become apparent. Bannock believes Beaver production only reached twenty-five a month because the sale to the U.S. military "awakened the rest of the world." Interview with the author, January 5, 1995.

3. Fred Hotson, *The Bremen*, esp. Ch. 11. A classic of its kind by a former president of the Canadian Aviation Historical Society, *The Bremen* gives rare and valuable insights into Balchen's personality and outlines Floyd Bennett's confession to Balchen that he and Byrd had not overflown the North Pole.

4. Anthony Fokker and Bruce Gould, *Flying Dutchman: The Life of Anthony Fokker*. Originally published in 1931, shortly after the wave of late-1920s ocean crossings by air, many of them made in Fokker's aircraft, this still-readable autobiography had gone through three

printings before it appeared in paperback seven years later.

Fokker, witlessly accused of incompetence and cowardice in Commander Richard Byrd's 1927 autobiography, *Skyward* (which itself went through nineteen printings before my May 1937 edition appeared), strikes back by awarding Bernt Balchen credit for saving the lives of Byrd and his crew in the ditching that ended Byrd's trans-Atlantic flight. Fokker is candid about why Byrd minimized Balchen's contributions to his flights across the Atlantic and over the South Pole. Even at that, Fokker did not know that Byrd's favourite pilot, Floyd Bennett, had made a near-deathbed confession to Balchen that he and Byrd had not even flown near the North Pole during the 1926 flight that led to Byrd's first New York ticker-tape parade and his Congressional Medal of Honor.

5. Rear Admiral Richard Evelyn Byrd, *Skyward*. The dedication, "To those who have stuck by me through thick and thin: among the front rank of whom are Edsel Ford, Floyd Bennett and my always splendid shopmates," shows Byrd's primary loyalty to those blindly loyal to him, among them his brave but near-useless sidekick, Lt. George Noville.

6. See Col. Bernt Balchen, Maj. Corey Ford and Maj. Oliver La Farge, *War Below Zero: The Battle for Greenland*.

7. The accounts of Bannock's expedition with the U.S. Air Force brass to the Alaska grayling stream and, later in the chapter, with the army artillery officers to the Fort Bragg drop zone, are taken from interviews with Bannock during 1995 and Bannock's own account in "Selling Aircraft to the U.S. Armed Forces" in *De Havilland, You STOL My Heart Away*, esp. pp. 122–124.

8. See Edward H. Phillips, *Beechcraft: Staggerwing to Starship*, esp. pp. 46–47.

9. The Noorduyn Norseman, which first flew in 1935, was not only still in production in 1951, but two years later Bob Noorduyn reassumed control of the company from Canadian Car and Foundry and extended its production run to 1959. The last Norseman took to the air on December 17 of that year. An estimated 905 Norsemans were built. See D.M. Bain, *Canadian Pacific Air Lines: Its History and Aircraft*, pp. 64–65.

Chapter 10: Fort Rucker, Alabama, to Wanganui, New Zealand

1. The first USAF order for Beavers was for six test aircraft, designated YL-20s, which were taken from the production line and amounted to civil Beavers in military markings (mostly overall white). Beavers destined for U.S. military use had four windows in the cockpit roof, increased instrumentation and more sophisticated avionics, and seating changes. Most army Beavers were painted in olive drab camouflage. With the redesignation of U.S. military aircraft in 1962, Beavers, for the most part now assigned to the army, became known as U-6As. The original six test Beavers were sold to Iran. Information from Alan W. Hall, "Aircraft in Detail: DHC-2 Beaver" in *Scale Aircraft Modelling*, April 7, 1987.

2. The first great period of heavier-than-air army aviation came before the advent of air forces as separate entities. During the early part of the First War, military aviation was directed toward the ground forces' objectives of scouting the enemy, artillery spotting or, rarely, of performing direct attacks on opposing troops. Air-to-air combat evolved as the means of protecting scout planes performing these tasks. Before long, achieving air supremacy became important as an end in itself. As the roles of combat aircraft became more specialized, the less-glamorous but essential tasks of battlefield patrol and local reconnaissance, casualty evacuation and communication fell to general aviation types, usually light aircraft barely able to carry the bulky radios of World War II. General Dwight Eisenhower overflew the beaches of Normandy in a field-converted two-seater P-51B Mustang fighter, there being no obvious Allied observation type in which the life of the supreme commander could reasonably be risked—even in an environment that had been largely cleared of the Luftwaffe. The Beaver reinstated army aviation by bringing much greater capabilities to the utility role.

3. A later use for these bomb shackles Down Under was to carry ten-foot fence posts in bundles like firewood and drop them along remote fence lines on huge sheep ranches in the Australian Outback or the mountainous Southern Alps on New Zealand's South Island. No more eloquent compliment to the strength of the Beaver's wing could be imagined.

4. See Note 1, chapter 9.

5. This extraordinary regimental airlift is claimed in DHC's *DHC-2 Beaver* sales brochure without further documentation. The author is so far unable to more fully describe the incident.

As for its performance in mountainous regions, the fact that the Chilean, Peruvian and Colombian air forces were among the early customers for the Beaver speaks for itself. In addition to Colombia, Japan, New Zealand, Australia and Great Britain equipped their International Geophysical Year Antarctic expeditions with Beavers.

6. Generals Matthew Ridgeway and Mark Clark flew Beavers in Korea, as did President Dwight Eisenhower during his 1952 visit.

7. Author interview with Colonel K. Randall Mattocks, June 13, 1995.

8. By the late 1950s, the RCAF had completed its transition from World War II-era fighters, such as the P-51 Mustang and de Havilland

Vampire, to the F-86 Sabre. The Avro Arrow was nearing completion, only to be scrapped in 1959, and a few years later the first Mach 2 CF-104 Starfighters would appear in the RCAF. Meanwhile, the transport role was shifting from such stopgap wartime leftovers as the Lancaster and Mitchell bombers and Douglas C-47 Dakota, to the noisy North Star, to the Yukon, a version of the Bristol Britannia turboprop, a genuine intercontinental machine. In 1953 the RCAF had been one of the first jet-transport air arms when it began operating the de Havilland Comet.

When the army began expressing an interest in the DHC design that became the Caribou, the RCAF staff realized what a large and important gap was being left in its capabilities, a gap the army felt had to be addressed. So the RCAF invoked an old rule about the maximum size of aircraft the army could operate, and claimed the Caribou, and its battlefield tactical role, for itself. This sequence of events mirrored those in Great Britain and the United States. As DHC's product line increased in size from the Otter to the DHC-5 Buffalo, the USAF decided the army was infringing upon its role, claimed the bigger battlefield transports, which were turned over January 1, 1967, and left army aviation largely to helicopters.

9. *Air Pictorial*, July 1974, special issue on naval aviation, pp. 268–271.
10. Military serials and construction numbers courtesy of Eric Munk, Zwolle, The Netherlands.
11. The number 46 for the British Army Air Corps order comes from Hotson, *The de Havilland Canada Story*, p. 125.
12. Hotson, *op. cit.*, p. 124.
13. NZ6001, as the Antarctic Beaver has been memorialized, was photographed with that serial and its original paint scheme at Wigram in 1956, the photo appearing in *Aeroplane Monthly*, January 1976, p. 22, with an extended caption including information on the rescue of NZ6001's crew.
14. ZK-CKH as NZ6001 appears in John King, *Vintage Aeroplanes in New Zealand*, p. 85. Chapter 6, entitled "Made in Canada," forwarded by the Royal New Zealand Air Force Museum, Wigram, N.Z.
15. RNZAF Museum diorama of ex-Fieldair Holdings ZK-CMU as NZ6001 photographed at the museum by Peter R. Arnold. Colour photo appeared in "Wigram Pictorial," *Air Enthusiast* 58, summer 1995, p. 60 with extended caption.
16. King, *op. cit.*, p. 87.
17. Hatfield's missile division was eventually passed over to the Canadian affiliate, sold and eventually became Spar Aerospace, the country's leading aerospace engineering firm, makers of the celebrated Canadarm materials-handling device aboard the National Air and Space Administration's space shuttle.
18. From Janic Geelen, *The Top Dressers*, NZ Aviation Press, 1983.

19. Author interview with David Salter, April 30, 1996.
20. Project DHC-2 Beaver negative list, courtesy Steve Todd, Campbell River, B.C.

Chapter 11: The Turbo Beaver

1. See Kenneth H. Sullivan and Larry Milberry, *Power: The Pratt & Whitney Canada Story*, esp. p. 138. The authors list aircraft handling and performance, specific fuel consumption, propeller handling, propeller drag (when feathered), air starting, accessory loading and noise/vibration levels.

   "MacNeil," the authors write, "carried out a series of in-flight propeller reversing tests in 1963." An aircraft that is able to reverse the pitch of its propellers does so as an air-braking process to help reduce the length of its runout after landing. Propeller-reversing is not normally done in flight, for obvious reasons, although because it can happen, testing is done to see what will happen.

   "He described this as 'quite interesting' and went on: 'This aircraft is rather unstable in this configuration, and suffers from elevator buffet. As reverse power is applied the buffeting increases.... At this point [220 shaft horsepower, *or about half the power the PT-6 was capable of generating*] a decision was made to stop further application of reverse power because elevator buffet was becoming too severe to manage, and the possibilities of flutter were becoming a concern.'"

   In other words, MacNeil was becoming worried about flying his tail off. Italicized insert this author's.
2. This information is combined from the Sullivan-Milberry account, pp. 146–7, and Hotson, *op. cit.*, pp. 139–142.
3. "Bob Fowler's contributions were in the interpretation of human reactions to steep descent and the coordination needed for landings in this configuration," is Hotson's dry summary on p. 142 of *The DHC Story* of the emotions Fowler must have felt in performing barely-controlled crashes.
4. The PT-6 was offering 500 shaft horsepower (shp) in its early forms, and, like any engine in its early stages of development, had considerable growth potential.
5. John Condit, *Wings Over the West*, p. 62.
6. Performance figures and dimensions are given first in the form in which they were originally determined.
7. "de Havilland Beaver: A classic workhorse still pays its way," *AOPA Pilot*, April 1988. Kenmore engineered and certified many of the first Beaver modifications and operates nine piston Beavers, two Turbos, and four Otters converted to turbine power. For a profile of Kenmore, see Chapter 13.
8. Much of the information on water-bombing is from "Canada's flying firemen," by Colin J. Ashford, *Aeroplane Monthly*, June/July 1976.

9. Bruce West, *The Firebirds*, Ontario Ministry of Natural Resources, 1974, pp. 222–227.

10. In 1996 Viking was quoting prices of US$735,000 for the landplane Viking Turbo Beaver, $795,000 with floats, and $895,000 for the amphibian.

Chapter 12: Adventure stories from the moody Pacific Coast

1. Author interview with Maurie Mercer, January 26, 1995.

    The weight an aircraft is cleared to carry is a conservative calculation, intended to allow a generous margin of safety. This figure often changes after structural and flight testing. As the aircraft is developed in testing and use, it is normal for its certified operating weight to increase. The Beaver's "original loaded weight was 4,500 lb (2,043 kg), which rapidly and progressively increased to 5,100 lb (2,313 kg)," write K.M. Molson and H.A Taylor in *Canadian Aircraft Since 1909*, p. 267. The latter figure has been the airplane's loaded weight for most of its 50-year life. More recently, Beavers cleared to gross weights of 6,000 pounds have appeared. Throughout this history of weight growth, the Beaver's wing has been strengthened only by the use of steel strut-attachment hardware.

    Bush pilots who say they were flying the Beaver at higher weights than the Beaver is or was certified to fly, did so as a result of experience. While technically they may have been operating outside the letter of the regulations and were liable to be penalized, subsequent legal weight growth of the Beaver suggests they may have been well within its structural limits.

2. This story, among many items of Beaver lore from Campbell River, is from Steve Todd of Project DHC-2 Beaver. The Beaver has been an interest of Todd's for twenty years. Between them, he and his wife, Valerie, have worked for five airlines based in Campbell River that operated Beavers. Todd says he once started six of them one after another so he could listen to the music of a half-dozen Wasp Juniors, all at once.

3. Author interview with Larry Langford, March 24, 1994.

4. Author interview with Frank Roberts, March 22, 1994.

5. Author interview with Tom Baxter, undated.

6. Author interview with Bill Pennings, February 24, 1994.

7. Steve Todd told the story; Lee Frankham confirmed it in an interview with the author, March 28, 1994.

8. Maurie Mercer knew Doucette, and told me the story of his Beaver continuing to fly with a broken wing spar. Doucette was killed in October 1961 flying a floatplane Cessna 185. He was fifty-eight.

9. Author visit to Whistler Air base, Whistler, B.C., September 16, 1995.

10. Story adapted from an account written by Jack Schofield and submitted to the author in early 1994. It was too long for inclusion in the author's article "The Beaver Then and Now," published in the *Georgia Straight*, April 29–May 6, 1994.

Chapter 13: Beavers better than new

1. Dick Hiscocks is not all that impressed with 24,000 hours, either. He knows of 37,000-hour Beavers.

2. Quoted with permission from Gerry Bruder, "de Havilland Beaver: A classic workhorse still pays its way," Aircraft Owners and Pilots Association *Pilot* magazine, April 1988.

3. Kenmore Air Harbor's Land and Seaplane Catalog contains these and many other fascinating tidbits, and is surely a bargain for Beaver enthusiasts at US$4. Kenmore Air Harbor, 6321 N.E. 175th St., Seattle, WA 98155, U.S.A.

4. This figure went unconfirmed at Kenmore. The chief engineer doesn't make sales.

5. Harbour Air Seaplanes' success made it the subject of a major article by Jack Meadows in the April 1996 *Air International* magazine.

6. Viking's engineering advisor on the Six-thousand-pound Turbo Beaver project was the late Willy Kraus, who worked on aircraft-manufacturing projects from the World War II Messerschmitt Bf 109 to the DHC Dash-7. "Transport Canada," Curtis notes, "just bought whatever he had to say."

Chapter 14: Under the weather

1. "de Havilland Beaver floatplane," by Bob Grimstead in the British *Pilot* magazine, June 1992. Copy provided by Steve Todd, Project DHC-2, Campbell River, B.C. A Jaguar XJ-220 is a limited-production sports car that is lighter than most models from that company. Grimstead flew the only float-equipped Beaver in the U.K. at the time, G-DHC-B.

2. John King, *Vintage Aeroplanes in New Zealand*, op. cit., p. 83.

3. The above information about UOY's previous identities comes from *American Civil Air Registers: DHC-2 Beaver*, courtesy Steve Todd. The constructor's number comes from the airplane's identity plate, of course.

4. For any floatplane operational procedure, *Flying a Floatplane* by Marin Faure is a good resource. Faure concentrates on the Beaver as the ultimate floatplane. Illustrations throughout the book show Beavers and the photographs are of Kenmore Air Harbor DHC-2s.

5. Grimstead, *op. cit.* Stenner's movements in starting UOY were so deft I was unable to record the procedure firsthand. I have happily resorted to Grimstead's account, which seems accurate to me and, rare among such reports, highly readable.

Bibliography

On the DHC-2 Beaver and de Havilland Canada

Ellis, Bert, ed. *De Havilland, You STOL My Heart Away.* Toronto, De Havilland Inc., 1993. Recollections of De Havilland Canada employees, 1927 to date. Includes two articles by Dick Hiscocks, "The Ubiquitous Beaver," pp. 76–87, and "Whither STOL?" pp. 269–276. See also Russ Bannock's account of "Selling Aircraft to the U.S. Armed Forces," pp. 122–124.

Hotson, Fred W. *The de Havilland Canada Story.* Toronto, CANAV Books, 1983. Contains the best available account of the Beaver's design, development and sales.

Molson, K.M. *Canada's National Aviation Museum: Its History and Collections.* Ottawa, National Aviation Museum, 1988. Esp. p. 54, CF-FHB's acquisition, and pp. 136–137, profile.

Molson, K.M., and Taylor, H.A. *Canadian Aircraft Since 1908.* London, Putnam, 1982 ed. Beaver pp. 266–272. Includes entire DHC line of aircraft to the Dash-8.

Whitesitt, Larry L. *Flight of the Red Beaver: A Yukon Adventure.* Spokane, Lawton Publishing Co., 1990. Second ed. Personal bush flying memoir with Beaver flight characteristics described and accounts of its use. Available only by mail through the author: Box 887, Veradale, WA 99037-0887, U.S.A., US$16.95.

On the English de Havilland Company, Hatfield

Bishop, Edward. *The Wooden Wonder: The Story of the de Havilland Mosquito.* Shrewsbury, Airlife Publishing Co., 1980 ed. Story of the aircraft whose Canadian building program transformed DHC into a company capable of designing and assembling its own aircraft.

de Havilland, Sir Geoffrey. *Sky Fever.* Shrewsbury, Airlife, 1979 ed. Autobiography of the founder of the most prolific of British aircraft manufacturers.

Jackson, A.J. *De Havilland Aircraft Since 1915.* London, Putnam, 1962 ed. Includes index of DHC designs to 1962 and the DHC-4 Caribou.

King, Peter. *Knights of the Air.* London, Constable & Co., 1989. On the pioneers of British aircraft manufacturing, including Geoffrey de Havilland, and the origins of their companies.

On the Ontario Provincial Air Service (Beaver launch customer) and its aircraft

Ashford, Colin J. "Canada's Flying Firemen," in *Aeroplane Monthly,* June/July 1986.

Dillon, J.C. *Early Days: A Record of the Early Days of the Provincial Air Service of Ontario, of the Men and the Ships They Flew.* Toronto, Ontario Department of Lands and Forests, 1964 ed. OPAS, its pilots and aircraft to acquisition of the Beaver.

West, Bruce. *The Firebirds: How bush flying won its wings.* Toronto, Ontario Ministry of Natural Resources, 1974.

On Pratt & Whitney Aircraft of Canada

Sullivan, Kenneth, and Larry Milberry. *Power: The Pratt & Whitney Canada Story.* Toronto, CANAV Books, 1989. Authoritative accounts of the development of powerplants for the Beaver and Turbo Beaver.

On W/C Russ Bannock's RCAF career

Transcript of an interview with Russ Bannock by Ted Barris for *Behind the Glory* (Toronto, Macmillan, 1992). The story of the British Commonwealth Air Training Plan in Canada, including Bannock's experiences as an instructor. Courtesy of Ted Barris.

Coughlin, Tom, with foreword by Douglas Bader. *The Dangerous Sky: Canadian Airmen in World War II.* Toronto, Ryerson Press, 1968. Esp pp. 32–36.

McCafferty, Dan. *Air Aces: The Lives and Times of Twelve Canadian Fighter Pilots.* Toronto, James Lorimer & Co., 1990.

Pigott, Peter. *Flying Canucks: Famous Canadian Aviators.* Toronto, Hounslow Press, 1994. Esp. p. 7.

On Beavers in Australia and New Zealand

Geelen, Janic. *The Top Dressers.* Auckland, NZ Aviation Press, 1983.

King, John. *Vintage Aeroplanes in New Zealand.* Auckland, Heinemann, 1986. Esp. Chapter 6, "Made in Canada," on Chipmunks and Beavers in New Zealand. Includes flying impressions.

On the Noorduyn Norseman

Grant, Robert S. "Canada's Thunder Chicken," *Air Enthusiast 29,* November 1985–February 1986: pp. 11–22.

Wenstedt, Joop. "The Flying Viking," *Aeroplane Monthly,* February 1987: pp. 87–90.

On the PZL P-11 series fighters

Cynk, Jerzy B. "First Encounter," *Air Enthusiast 48,* p. 68.

The editors. *Air International* "Fighter A to Z" March–April 1991. Tight, precise accounts of the design and characteristics of the PZL series with specifications.

Liss, Witold. *The PZL P-11.* Aircraft Profile Number 75, Garden City, N.J., Doubleday & Co. ed., 1968. The story of W. J. Jakimiuk's pioneer all-metal fighter.

The editors. "The Era of the Gulls," *Air Enthusiast 28,* p. 35, P-1 to P-24.

Other useful sources

Bain, D.M. *Canadian Pacific Airlines: Its History and Aircraft.* Calgary, Kishorn Publications, 1987. A good guide to bushplanes in use in western Canada at the time of the Beaver's introduction.

Condit, John; foreword by Pierre Berton. *Wings Over the West: Russ Baker and the rise of Pacific Western Airlines.* Madeira Park, Harbour Publishing, 1984. Ongoing story of CF-FHB, the Beaver prototype, flown by Baker and PWA from May 1948 to March 1966.

Ellis, Frank H. *Canada's Flying Heritage.* Toronto, University of Toronto Press, rev. ed. 1961.

Faure, Marin C. *Flying a Floatplane.* New York, TAB Books, 1990 ed. A guide to safety, water handling, and flying floatplanes, featuring the Beaver. Many fine photographs of Beavers by the author.

Horten, Reimar, and Selinger, Peter F. *Nurflügel: Die Geschischte der Horten-Flugzeuge 1933–1960.* Graz, H. Weishaupt Verlag, 1993. An account in German with partial translations into English of the pioneers of flying wing design credited by Dick Hiscocks with influencing his formulation of the Beaver's airfoil.

Milberry, Larry. *Aviation in Canada.* Toronto, CANAV Books, McGraw-Hill Ryerson Ltd., 1979. Esp. pp. 125–126.

Sutherland, Alice Gibson. *Canada's Aviation Pioneers: Fifty Years of McKee Trophy Winners.* Toronto, McGraw-Hill Ryerson Ltd., 1978. Profiles of Phil Garratt, "Punch" Dickins, Max Ward and other heroes of Canadian aviation.

Articles on the de Havilland DHC-2 Beaver

Bruder, Gerry. "de Havilland Beaver: A classic workhorse still pays its way," *AOPA Pilot* April 1988. AOPA stands for Aircraft Owners and Pilot's Association. The best article I've seen on flying the Beaver, written by a published author and staff pilot with Kenmore Air Harbor, Seattle, WA.

Grant, Robert S. "Beavers in the bush," *Air International* July 1981.

Grimstead, Bob. "de Havilland Beaver floatplane," *Pilot* magazine (U.K.) June 1992. Flying a Beaver floatplane.

Hall, Alan W. "The versatile DHC-2 Beaver," *Scale Aircraft Modelling,* April 7, 1987. Design process, users, markings.

"de Havilland Canada's Beaver bushplane/Among top 10 engineering achievements," photocopy from DHC archives, undated and unsigned, possibly from *Just Plane Facts.*

Hiscocks, R.D. "The Enduring Beaver," three-part series August-September-October 1991 in *Just Plane Facts,* DHC employee newsletter. Perceived market, design process, post-production mods.

Marriott, Terence. "Inside Story 10, DHC-2 Beaver," *Scale Aircraft Modelling,* May 8, 1991. Short history, many photos of ex-U.S. Army U-6A 0-82062 displayed at the Midland Air Museum, Baginton, England.

Ramsden, J.M. "Ah! Beaver," *Flight International,* December 27, 1986. Harbour Air flight from Vancouver to Saltspring Island.

Rossiter, Sean. "Leave It To Beavers," *Western Living* Canadian Classics column, May 1994. Design origins.

Rossiter, Sean. "The Beaver Then and Now," *Georgia Straight,* April 29–May 6, 1994. Beavers rebuilt and used commercially along the British Columbia coast.

Siuru, William Jr. "Leave It To Beaver," *Airpower* magazine, September 1981.

Other documents from De Havilland Canada archives, include 3-views, specs, photocopied sales catalogue.

Speeches and addresses

Hiscocks, R.D. Untitled dinner speech to the Canadian Aeronautics and Space Institute, Vancouver branch, April 1993; and a presentation to the Society of Automotive Engineers, Vancouver chapter, April 10, 1995; both on the design development of the DHC-2 Beaver in the context of Canadian aviation history to that point.

Index